5|14

THE SECRETS OF ITALY

THE
SECRETS
OF
ITALY

PEOPLE, PLACES, AND
HIDDEN HISTORIES

———

CORRADO AUGIAS

TRANSLATED FROM THE ITALIAN BY
ALTA L. PRICE

Rizzoli
ex libris

Published in the United States of America in 2014
By Rizzoli Ex Libris, an imprint of
Rizzoli International Publications, Inc.
300 Park Avenue South
New York, NY 10010
www.rizzoliusa.com

Originally published in Italy as *I Segreti d'Italia*
Copyright © 2012 RCS Libri S.p.A., Milano
Translation Copyright © 2014 Alta L. Price

2014 2015 2016 2017 / 10 9 8 7 6 5 4 3 2 1

Distributed in the U.S. trade by Random House, New York
Printed in U.S.A.

ISBN-13: 978–0-8478–4274–2
Library of Congress Catalog Control Number: 2013943447

CONTENTS

TRANSLATOR'S NOTE

The most recent in a long line of books centering on the specificity of place and the way history, culture, and literature intertwine, Corrado Augias's *The Secrets of Italy* is best read as a meandering stroll through time, in the company of some curious characters. Like his previous books on Rome, London, Paris, and New York, this is a series of essays highlighting unique episodes in Italian history. Because the scope has been broadened from one specific city to an entire country, introductory chapters on Italy as a whole lead into the discussions of individual places and people.

The author is a distinguished journalist, essayist, former parliamentary representative, and television host who aims to make history accessible and bring literature to life for the average twenty-first-century citizen. He has provided notes and sources for many of his references, and in addition to providing English publication information where available, I have added notes where more details would be helpful. Naturally, the original presumed a fair amount of knowledge most non-Italians would be unfamiliar with, so I strove to provide the necessary background without intruding on the author's work. Notes aside, it is our hope that the main text stand on its own, as a personal musing enriched by excerpts from the work of other writers.

A final word on terminology and perspective: because Italy is a relatively young country, many of the events discussed here did not technically take place in Italy—rather, they happened in the many territories that predated unification. Italy as we currently know it was only unified in 1861, and to this day many of its residents feel it remains a rather divided country in terms of political, linguistic, and cultural differences. Therefore, I have maintained the author's references to "the Italian peninsula" in pre-1861 passages so as to respect that historic distinction. The many chapters of this book skip around from North to South and East to West, drawing connections and highlighting the unique aspects of each area. Italy exists in the heart and mind as much as it does on the geographic map, and I hope this translation offers the reader new insight into its most intriguing corners.

—ALP

A PREFACE,
OF SORTS

I'd like to begin with an episode that perhaps still holds some significance. It's a distant memory but is seared into my mind with the clarity often granted to recollections of childhood events, especially those that took place at epic moments. The Villa Celimontana in Rome is a gorgeous place where not many people go. Unfairly, it is less famous than the Villa Borghese or the Janiculum, which is a shame because its lanes dotted with ancient Roman ruins, its woods, the hidden little obelisk, the palazzo that houses Italy's Geographic Society, and the hill overlooking the gigantic remains of the Baths of Caracalla all help make it one of the enchanted places that the city offers those who know how to find them. It's one of the many spots in Rome where neoclassic and romantic canons intertwine, becoming indistinguishable from one another.

As its name implies, the villa is located atop the Caelian, a hill once covered by vineyards that the prominent Mattei family transformed into a peaceful rural garden oasis in the sixteenth century. The main entrance is next to the basilica of Santa Maria in Domnica (also known as Santa Maria alla Navicella), one of the ancient early Christian basilicas that are so much more beautiful than the more lavish baroque ones that ended up becoming the city's stylistic hallmarks. I highly recommend it.

In June 1944 American troops had set up camp in the villa. It was solidly fenced off, looming atop a wall overlooking the Via della Navicella, so it was a natural choice for stationing troop quarters. Up sprouted tents, shacks, the ever-present flagpole waving the Stars and Stripes, bugle calls—everything that comes with a military encampment. That flag was also the first flag I ever saw at half-mast, and my mother explained why: "Their president has passed away," she said. So it must have been April 1945, since the 12th of that month marked the death of Franklin Delano Roosevelt, the man who had held the country together through endless war.

But the memory I wanted to share is a different, earlier one. It was a Sunday and the air was neither cool nor hot, so it was probably sometime around the fall of 1944 when, with the occupation over, the city began trying to come back to life. My mother held my hand as we walked home past the Villa Celimontana after visiting a friend. A festive group of American soldiers leaned out over the top of the wall, dressed in neat uniforms with crisp folds in their freshly ironed shirts. I was used to seeing Italian infantrymen with loosened or sagging greaves, in uniforms of uselessly heavy, coarse cloth. The Americans' freshly ironed shirts, robust khaki belts, and the scent of soap, tobacco, and brilliantine all struck me as the absolute paragon of elegance—indeed, of true wealth. It looked like they were having a great time up there. One by one they drew cigarettes from their packs and tossed them down to the street—one cigarette, another cigarette, then another—taking their sweet time between one toss and the next. A crowd of young Italian men stood at the foot of the wall; at each toss they dashed forward, pushing toward the spot the cigarette would land. It was part play, part brawl, part competition, and all tumult. My mother crossed the street, pulling me away; perhaps I turned to watch, and the scene quietly lay in some corner of my mind all these years.

Many years later, on yet another Sunday, I took my daughter to the zoo. In front of one of the cages a group of people, also festive, were tossing nuts to the monkeys inside. Their gestures echoed those of the soldiers and the distant memory surfaced. Not that I was at all comparing the poor young Romans of '44 to monkeys—rather, the memory emerged because the roles each played were based on similar behaviors: a mixture of complicity and sheer enjoyment, competition and play, on one side as much as on the other.

Then, after yet more years had passed, as I was working on a history of Rome I happened across a few magnificent lines from the sixth book of the *Aeneid*. Aeneas has encountered his father's shadow and tries in vain to embrace him. Anchises then explains his theory of the cycles that govern the universe, prophesies great descendants, and adds that other populations will rise to glory in the arts and sciences. The Romans, on the other hand, will rule the world thanks to the wisdom of law: *Tu regere imperio populos, Romane, memento (hae tibi erunt artes) pacique imponere morem, parcere subiectis et debellare superbos*; "Remember, Roman, it is for you to rule the nations with your power (that will be your skill), to crown peace with law, to spare the conquered, and subdue the proud."[1]

The Americans certainly spared us Italians following a senseless war that we'd thrust upon them in a moment of thoughtless insanity. But in my memories those carefree soldiers, bored by having to spend Sunday in the camp instead of out on the town in their freshly pressed shirts, cruising for girls, had perhaps unconsciously found a way to show, with just a few cigarettes, who had really won the war and who had lost, despite our ambiguous relationship as last-minute "Allies."

Parcere subiectis indeed—the conquered are to be spared, but that doesn't mean you can't have a little fun with them.

———————

"Secrets" is a weighty and complicated word. And the idea of "secrets of Italy" is even more so, given all the things that have happened in this country over the centuries. Entire libraries wouldn't suffice to cover it all. But in our case the word "secrets" should be stripped of some of its strength and brought down to size. Of Italian history's countless secrets we could choose just one, the secret of secrets, which might best be summed up in a deceptively simple question: Why did things turn out the way they did? Why has the Italian peninsula witnessed so many twists and turns, so many manias, misfortunes, and missed opportunities? And why, on the other hand, has this little patch of land—cast crookedly into the middle of the Mediterranean, along the dangerously ambiguous border between the Balkans, North Africa, and Europe—been populated more than so many others by so many geniuses? What is it that makes Italy such a special country, one that has caught foreigners' attention since time immemorial, at times inspiring admiration and at others sparking hostility and ridicule? In other words, why has the story of this nation been so eventful, so controversial? Italy's international status fluctuates much like the stock market: It can reach remarkable highs, but it can also plummet.

The first people responsible for such uncertainties are Italians themselves, who don't always have a clear idea of their potential. Who are the Italians, exactly? The emigrants who disembarked on faraway shores shouldering bundles of rags? Those who, for a pittance, accepted the most menial and dangerous jobs? Or the brilliant architects, the great fashion designers, the superb artists who garnered the admiration of the whole world? There is no other people—at least not in Europe—that has embodied such distant extremes. This is the real secret, the one that encompasses (almost) all the others. How might we try to describe it?

––––––––––

Italy is a country made up of cities. Be they large or small, glorious or obscure, they all deserve some attention, if for no other reason than for the charged past they preserve—some would even say an excess of past. If you rob France of Paris or Great Britain of London, not much remains. But if you rob Italy of Rome there's a lot left. Indeed, within the story of a whole nation lie a hundred stories of its hundred cities, stories not only in the metaphorical sense, but in the literal sense: the stories told through the characters and plotlines of literature.

Our voyage begins, for that very reason, with two exceptional books centered on lead characters that profoundly influenced the collective Italian consciousness. Are they pages of history? Technically speaking, no; but they might well be even more important, because the human archetypes they portray are ageless stand-ins for possible Italians; they can be found among present-day Italians, and it's not uncommon to run into them on the bus or read about them in the papers.

A lot has been written about Rome and Milan, Italy's two capitals, so it's hard to find a new angle, an aspect that hasn't been examined in great depth. Hard, but not impossible. Major cities are like huge warehouses filled with stories, and in such places even the walls talk. We'll hear about Rome from none other than Giacomo Leopardi, who was a guest of his mother's relatives in their vast, run-down residence during the restoration period, a tough time in which the papal government was recovering from the revolutions of the late eighteenth century and the great, irreverent, blasphemous poet Giuseppe Gioachino Belli earned his living as a papal censor. We'll hear about Milan, on the other hand, from a perspective that might seem marginal but isn't, through a freeze-frame taken right after 1945 as the Milanese, and Italians in general, proved capable of emerging from their mourning and from the ruins with a drive that forever changed the face of the country, not to mention its character. The sheer energy and vision of those years seem incredible when viewed from the midst of the opaque mediocrity, shortsightedness, and resignation that have characterized the early twenty-first century. But both the energy and the vision were very real. People might've been dressed in worn-out clothes, so threadbare it was scary, but they nevertheless worked together to rebuild it all: homes, factories, their culture, and the civil framework, aided by the miracle of a new constitution.

Then there's the large territory that was once called the Kingdom of the Two Sicilies, which became known as *il Mezzogiorno*, the South, after 1861. These pages harbor some real surprises for many readers. For example, various accounts and parliamentary surveys filed soon after unification expose how anxious officials and functionaries from

Piedmont who'd just arrived down South were wondering how much of a commitment it would be, how many resources it would take to improve living conditions in those impoverished regions. On the occasion of the 150th anniversary of Italian unification in 2011 a few books of "Southernist" bent, so to speak, wrote that the Piedmontese collected significant government funds from southern banks and transferred the money to the North, thereby condemning the South to perpetual underdevelopment. If that's true, it's certainly grave—but the situation is grave no matter how you look at it. Having a huge treasury and nevertheless keeping the population in the desperate conditions they were found in upon Garibaldi's arrival, with illiteracy rates verging on 87 percent, is certainly no less grave than the supposed transferral of those funds up to Turin.

Take a city like Parma, which fortune seems to have smiled upon given its geographic position, revenue streams, and high-quality local products. Despite all that, over the last few years a series of somewhat insane events has shaken its foundations. First came the Parmalat scandal, which undermined one of the city's largest, most successful companies.[2] Only a huge tide of uncontrolled madness could have so deeply crushed the company's "ingenuous" founder. Then came a municipal administration that fell far below all expectations, led by an unconscionably carefree fop, to say nothing of the widespread corruption and money tossed to the wind. This streak of insanity wasn't limited to a single person and a few cronies—it infected so much of the general population that they actually elected that mayor. In reaction another administration came in, one that might be innovative or maybe just eccentric, but either way it stands a fifty-fifty chance of either becoming a model for the future or turning out to be a devastating disillusion. And yet Parma's past is filled with people and events that made it one of the most fascinating little courts in Europe, a mythical place of the spirit, as Stendhal so clearly understood when he conjured up Fabrizio del Dongo, a leading man of world literature. Once again it's just such high-caliber texts that offer us one possible portrait of the idealized city.

The way in which the Republic of Venice—aptly known as *la Serenissima*, the "most serene"—fell into decline is a painful exemplar; in the pessimistic periods that current events sometimes foist on us it's tempting to view Venice as a stand-in for Italy as a whole, crippled by its inability to overcome caste-based selfishness, unable to see beyond the narrow horizon of short-term interest even during the deepest times of crisis. Venice was gambled away by Napoleon, ceded to Austria as part of the machinations he carried out to create the Cisalpine Republic. It's possible that, in retrospect, that swap had a degree of farsightedness, and could almost be seen as a preamble to the country's ultimate unification; to look on the bright side, that wasn't the worst aspect of the deal. The worst part was the way in which the handover, or betrayal, was carried out: the doge was scared witless; the city's nobles were spineless; the populace was powerless; and on top of it all came contradictory orders, complete inertia, and a retreat like so many others in Italian history, echoed on October 24, 1917, and again on September 8, 1943. The pages penned by Ippolito Nievo in his great novel *Le confessioni di un italiano* (literally "Confessions of an Italian") are quite eloquent, and offer a terribly precise account of the human side of such tragedy.[3]

Palermo is a different matter—every city in Italy has its own particular history, and Palermo's was shaped by a different sea, far from the shores of the upper Adriatic. I'm not talking about the Palermo of the mafia and the murderous attacks that fill the newspapers; our real interest lies in the ancient events that anticipated the city's present day, in the streak of folly that, once again, is concretely visible, beginning with the nobles who wandered amid luxurious yet decadent mansions and, like a bunch of spoiled children, squandered their family fortunes on gambling and women of all sorts—dancers, cabaret singers, demimondaines. Here the folly goes far beyond the individual level, and is best explained as a result of Sicilians' internal "crazy cord," a phenomenon many authors, from Pirandello to Sciascia, have written about.[4]

The city of Palermo is steeped in a dark religiosity with somber Spanish roots, a religiosity that can also be unbridled at times, its old traditions hung on to for so long that they've become a part of the people's collective identity, transformed into second nature. Ernst Bloch once wrote that there are places that have an excess of past, where there is not only a past that is over and done with, but also a still living, not yet discharged past—and therefore a "future in the past" as well.[5] He certainly wasn't writing with Palermo in mind, but his theory does apply to the Sicilian capital, since a real surplus of past is visible all over the city.

There are many events that prove how deeply intertwined the Italian peninsula's various cities have been throughout history. One curious example is that in 1248, when Frederick II, Holy Roman Emperor (a.k.a. *stupor mundi*, the "world wonder"), lost a decisive battle in Parma, the city's inhabitants took possession of the harem that followed him everywhere he went and divvied up its three hundred concubines. The emperor had gathered women from all across Europe at his main residence in Palermo, and they all ended up in Parma.[6]

The few lines I quoted from Virgil's *Aeneid* earlier on have to do with the methodology I follow in recounting the stories featured throughout this book. I often combine real history as it actually happened with the stories (and histories) of literature. Although the latter may be interwoven with fantasy, it also supplements reality, exposing its true power. Attilio Brilli, an expert on travel writing, maintains that the written word can become a tool for time travel as well: "[The printed page] can become the best passport for those of us who move about in a world without differences, flattened atop a great void. Visiting a place means going beyond appearances, beyond the obvious, to listen to the echoing remembrances that have accumulated there; reading, then, means seeing places through our own eyes as well as through the eyes of those who came long before us, with their preferences and their tastes, creating a fascinating play of reflected doubles and recompositions."[7] The work of poet and essayist Giacomo Leopardi fits this idea perfectly, as we shall see in the chapter on Rome. He traveled a lot despite his poor health, and was tossed about in unbelievably uncomfortable horse-drawn carriages on abominably rough roads for days on end. In his travels he's accompanied by a deep discontent for which he knew only one remedy. On July 23, 1827, he writes:

> After changing my place of residence many times and staying here or there for different periods of time, either months or years, I noticed that I was never happy, never centered within myself, never at home in any place, however excellent it might otherwise be, until I had memories to attach to that place, to the rooms where I lived, to the streets, to the houses I visited. The memories consisted only in my being able to say: I was here a long time ago. This is what I did, saw, heard so many months ago; a thing that would not be of any importance otherwise, but the recollection, being able to recall it, made it important and sweet.[8]

These recollections, the memories and fantasies he referred to as "fictions" and "illusions," were what held him back from the brink of despair. In 1828, when he was thirty years old, he recorded a related thought:

> For the sensitive and imaginative man who lives as I have lived for a long time, continually feeling and imagining, the world and objects are in a peculiar way double. He will see a tower, a landscape, with his eyes; he will hear the sound of a bell with his ears; and at the same time in his imagination he will see another tower, another landscape, he will hear another sound. In this second mode of perceiving objects resides all the beauty and pleasure of concrete things.[9]

In this sense, fantasies can help us better see reality; they're useful in transforming history into a story—not to confuse ideas further, but rather to clarify them.

———————————

In 2008 I came across a book, hot off the press, devoted to Italian travel writers (from the period between 1700 and 1861) with a superb preface by Luca Clerici. It includes some curious points of view, such as the adventures of Vincenzo Coronelli (1650–1718), a Franciscan friar, cartographer, encyclopedist, and overall bizarre character. One of the indomitable friar's ventures, from 1681 to 1683, was to construct two massive world maps for Louis XIV, the Sun King, and he moved to Paris expressly for the job. The first globe, measuring almost sixteen feet in diameter, depicts planet Earth with all the continents known at the time. The second depicts the heavens, with the constellations positioned exactly as they had been at the king's birth. The two ingenious artifacts weigh a total of about four tons, and are now in the collection of the Bibliothèque Nationale de France. Their restless designer made an interesting observation about travel, which serves, he wrote, to become acquainted with "the spirit of nations, their laws, the products they make, and their uses."[10] That's one way to use travel: as a means to open yourself up to other experiences or, as we now think of it, other cultures.

The poet Ippolito Pindemonte saw travel differently. In his satirical sermon *I Viaggi* ("Travel") he declares his absolute conviction that it's best to just stay put: *"Oh felice chi mai non pose il piede / fuor della terra, nel cui grembo nacque!"*—"How happy is he who never sets foot outside the land he was born in!" And then there's Carlo Silvestri, a nobleman from Rovigo, who wrote a book dedicated to the bishop of nearby Adria with the longwinded title *Istorica e geografica descrizione delle antiche paludi Adriane, ora chiamate Lagune di Venezia, e del corso di que' fiumi, che in varj tempi hanno contributto al loro interramento* ("Historical and Geographic Description of the Ancient Hatrian Marshes, Now Known as the Venetian Lagoon, and the Courses of Those Rivers Which, over Various Time Periods, Have Contributed to Their Infilling," and that's just the title—there's a subtitle, too). In it, he confesses that he's open to the idea of travel as long as it has a specific aim, and he criticizes those who "Sweat and fret and go to great lengths to hear all about . . . India, Japan, New Zealand, the Australian lands, and other not-quite-discovered places that might well be sheer fantasy—all the while gravely paying no attention to the events happening in their very own homeland; indeed, they remain so ignorant that they could scarcely say a thing about it, it would be like asking them about some unexplored land situated in the imaginary terrain of the Moon."

These words of the forgotten Silvestri give us another good idea of what travel is, they elucidate what a true voyage of discovery can be; as Proust once observed, it isn't a matter of seeking out new lands, but of gaining new eyes, a fresh perspective. Ultimately, the true voyage lies somewhere between fantasy and reality, and we can't necessarily assume that so-called reality is always the most important aspect. In Italy, as I said earlier, the past is of such importance (such weight, some would say) that you can't really ignore it if you want to gain some understanding of the place.

I've taken you through a rather long, somewhat circuitous introduction, so let us now return to the initial question of "secrets." This book explores a few places, people, archetypal figures, and moments—both real and fictional—culled from the chronicles of history as well as from literature. I certainly could've chosen others, or could have included two or three or a hundred times as many tales. Italian history harbors such (dramatic) richness that there are plenty of examples like the ones included here. Thousands of years, millions of protagonists, dozens of armies, hundreds of cities, entire civilizations born and wiped out from this narrow territory—to quote Petrarch, "let that fair land the Apennines divide / and sea and Alps surround . . . hear it ring out."[11] And so my choices were personal—that is, arbitrary. A series of impressions, memories, and readings from my youth suggested this selection. The only criterion that could be considered objective was my goal of finding some degree of geographic balance between North, Center, and South in such a long and narrow land.

It isn't enough to look at Italy as it is today; if we're to have any understanding of it we have to remember the many events of its past, the more fantastic side of things, and its "chimeras." This voyage will therefore take us not only through space, but also back through time.

ITALIANS AS SEEN
FROM THE OUTSIDE

George Gordon Byron arrived in Pisa in November 1821, where he stayed along the banks of the Arno in Palazzo Lanfranchi. Once there, he began frequenting the Shelleys and their circle of sophisticated eccentrics, which also included Teresa and Pietro Gamba, and they all whiled away the days with literary pursuits, long rides on horseback, and shooting practice at a nearby countryside property. In a December 1821 letter to publisher John Murray, Byron writes:

> I have got here into a famous old feudal palazzo, on the Arno, large enough for a garrison, with dungeons below and cells in the walls, and so full of *Ghosts*, that the learned Fletcher (my valet) has begged leave to change his room, and then refused to occupy his *new* room, because there were more ghosts there than in the other. It is quite true that there are most extraordinary noises (as in all old buildings), which have terrified the servants so as to incommode me extremely.[1]

Aside from the supposed ghosts lurking in Byron's palazzo, there's another ghost that's long haunted, and continues to haunt, Italians' consciences: the way that they, as a people, might be judged from the outside—the way foreigners might think of them and describe them. Italians had inhabited the peninsula for a long time, well before the Kingdom of Italy was officially established. In the interest of rigor, and perhaps to be a bit provocative, the early statesman Massimo d'Azeglio's famous prophecy could be turned on its head:[2] It was the Italians, not Italy, that already existed—therefore, the only thing left to be unified wasn't the Italian people, but rather the country of Italy.

Outside eyes looking in at the peninsula's varied populations have always understood that reality, and have managed to capture certain behavioral constants in the context of a geographic entity, infused with customs, that often appeared fractured and contradictory—fascinating in some respects, repulsive in others. This vast gap between very positive and very negative poles is practically unique in all of Europe. No other population has ever been the subject of such sharply contrasting judgments, also because no other population has ever judged itself in such contrasting ways.

In short, the way in which foreigners have viewed Italians is in large part a consequence of the way in which Italians have viewed themselves. This was the case long ago, and remains true to this day—a fact made clear when the judgments some "authoritative" foreign news publications issue on Italy from time to time are generally based on similar evaluations expressed in Italian newspapers.

Some years ago a group of students at Princeton University was asked to define the Italian temperament, and the vast majority chose three adjectives: *artistic, impulsive, passionate.* This social psychology survey dates back nearly three decades, but I don't think such judgments have changed much since, especially because similar sentiments were already surfacing not just thirty years ago, but two hundred years ago; in some cases the judgments were even harsher back then, in the sense that terms like *impulsivity* and *passion* were more closely associated with crime, betrayal, and corruption. I mentioned these perspectives in an earlier book of mine,[3] but I'm bringing them up again because their validity is also proven, for what it's worth, by my experiences living abroad; I've heard those adjectives, or similar ones, repeated countless times. Lucio Sponza, an economist from Venice who now teaches in England, has done extensive research into how Great Britain's ideas about Italy took shape, and what impact they've had.

Here's one possible summary of his findings: "On one side of the coin was 'Italy,' the country of beauty and culture; on the other side were the 'Italians,' an ingenious but corrupt, untrustworthy, and licentious race."[4] This judgment exposes an erroneous stereotype, as its internal contradiction makes clear: how is it possible that a people so "corrupt, untrustworthy, and licentious" managed to create such a strong tradition—not just of beauty, but of a harmonious, coherent, affable beauty? But the power of prejudice lies precisely in its ability to prevail irrespective of any coherent thought, obeying solely the need to sum up a series of disparate impressions into a single judgment, however brutal. Mario Praz, one of Italy's sharpest scholars of English literature, once wrote an essay that touches upon the way a few late-eighteenth-century English writers described Italians:

> The general Italian populace was viewed as filthy, lazy, criminal; the upper classes were considered poor, rude, and universally adulterous; both plebeians and aristocrats were thought superstitious and abject in the the face of tyrants. Venetians quickly came to blows at the slightest provocation, Neapolitans were naturally diabolical, and so on. Above all, Italians' religious devotion ir-ritated the English of that period.[5]

Travelers returning to England from their grand tour in Italy unanimously referred to the fact that the Italian peninsula was like an enormous museum fallen into ruin, populated by wretched, dissolute masses who noisily gathered in the streets—practically living outdoors thanks to the gentle climate—covered in rags or half naked, utterly unaware of its past glory. This vision, which inspired mixed reactions of both allure and horror, was applied with particular frequency to the Papal States and the South, described as the most destitute regions, inhabited by indolent, often ravenous ne'er-do-wells who were quick only when it came time to draw their daggers.

One of the most successful gothic genre novels of the time that used just such tropes was Ann Radcliffe's *The Italian, or the Confessional of the Black Penitents* (1797), whose title contains all the major plot elements. The action begins in 1764 in a convent near Naples, with the Inquisition as sinister backdrop. The plot centers on the mysterious Father Schedoni and two unhappy lovers, Elena Rosalba and Vincenzo di Vivaldi. It's filled with dark adventures, shady atmospherics, sins, betrayals, and crimes. Schedoni always wears black, and dons a wide-brimmed hat that nearly hides his "lambent lustre of eyes, which seemed to still retain somewhat of the fire and genius."[6] Thus, as early as the late eighteenth century, we've already found a hugely popular novel depicting the archetype of the treacherous Italian, which became widespread not only in literature but in newspaper accounts as well—a stereotype that the foreign policies of countless successive governments only reinforced over time.

An old note I once jotted down, unfortunately without any source citation, quotes an English critic from around the late nineteenth century, I believe: "Monasteries appeared as subtle and sadistic prisons, while in the churches each confessional box seemed to shade the progress of some wicked machination." Not least because of its boisterous, pagan religiosity (that's how the English have always seen it, at least), Italy became the favorite setting for stories filled with horrific events, conspiracies, imbroglios, merciless murders. To once again quote Praz: "These scandals, with their attendant dark and mysterious atmospheres, couldn't help but rehash the contemporary cultural agenda in 'black' novels modeled on Horace Walpole's *Castle of Otranto* (1765); Mrs. Radcliffe took that model and perfected it toward the end of the century, pilfering picturesque descriptions of the Italian landscape from recent travelers' reports, and turning to Elizabethan drama for tips on how to portray the quintessentially sinister, Machiavellian Italian."[7]

The great romantic poet Percy Bysshe Shelley, a man with most refined sensibilities, writes in one of his letters from Italy: "The men are hardly men; they look like a tribe of stupid and shrivelled slaves."[8] As for the women: "[T]he Italian women . . . are perhaps the most contemptible of all who exist under the moon—the most ignorant, the most disgusting, the most bigoted."[9] Those are pretty excessive judgments, even if you consider the fact that he had been marveling at the miserable conditions most Italians lived in at the time.

The Swiss writer Charles Victor de Bonstetten (1745–1832) took an interest in various aspects of European culture and published many works on the topic, including a book titled *L'homme du midi et l'homme du nord* ("Northerners and Southerners," 1824). One of its central ideas is that Northerners, forced by the harsh, inclement climate to spend most of their time indoors, are more inclined to be reflective, to have a calm balance, and, collectively speaking, organize harmonious social lives. Southerners, on the other hand, surrounded as they are by a paradisiacal climate and a benevolent, sunny, mild natural realm (it's no accident that a famous Neapolitan song says *"Chist' è 'o paese d'o sole,"* "This is the land of the sun"), have, over time, metamorphosed into "creatures light as flies, living day to day from the nectar of the many flowers that cover the land in which they live."

In Bonstetten's rather naive view, the "South" includes everything below the Alps, such that various Italians become one stereotypical Italian, a model that pays no heed to social class, geographic differences, or professional types. Ultimately, he participates in the widespread nineteenth-century prejudice that considers Italy solely in light of its climate, "landscape," and fascinating "ruins," all of which become the stereotype of an idealized past, when not reduced to being mere "picturesque backdrops" for a few watercolors. The Italians who live in such places exist only as anthropological specimens, and beyond that function they're considered an irritating reality, sometimes even an obstacle interrupting the contemplation of an otherwise extraordinary scene infused with nature and culture. From the hundreds of examples of how the Italian landscape was portrayed according to a "transfigured realism" in the arts, let's take the paintings of Jean-Baptiste-Camille Corot (1796–1875), in which a simultaneously lush yet harsh form of nature is depicted before a backdrop of imposing classical-era ruins. These are the city walls, arches, columns—the simulacra and the lonely towers Leopardi speaks of—now separated from all possible "glory." For more than a century, those were the only things foreign visitors to Italy were capable of taking in.

But then even Marcel Proust once wrote, heading home after a trip to Italy, that the real barbarian territory isn't a land that's never had any art, but the one that's chock-full of masterpieces yet doesn't know how to appreciate or preserve them.[10] These few lines echo, albeit from a different perspective, the same condemnation repeated countless times, in countless essays and works of literature.

In one of his *Promenades dans Rome* Marie-Henri Beyle, better known as Stendhal, includes a short note that gives a more detailed diagnosis, so to speak, in that it points to one possible cause of such inadequacy.[11] He writes of meeting two young Roman couples, accompanied by their families, riding home aboard a cart from a day trip to Monte Testaccio. They were all singing and gesticulating, and both men and women seemed absolutely out of their minds. According to Stendhal this wasn't because of any physical drunkenness, rather it was the result of some kind of "moral drunkenness."

It's a harsh judgment, issued by a writer who, by the way, really loved Italy: He appreciated its inhabitants' impassioned souls, and saw their behavior as the simple expression of a "romantic" vision—a vision he expanded upon to include the criminality and propensity for intrigue Italians seemed to embody. The scene of the two young couples in the throes of a disorderly joyousness causes him to make a pronouncement caustic as lye; his immediate reaction captures the most deplorable, primitive aspect of Italian character, a rather central cause of much of their misfortune. Stendhal calls it moral drunkenness, but in reality it could be an even more dangerous characteristic if you consider that, sooner or later, drunkenness passes; to the contrary, many observers of the same condition he denounced considered it a permanent condition. Many have dubbed it a "lightness of spirit," an apparent fatuousness, a predilection for the smooth surface of things, for the pleasurable aspects of life around which everything—religion, social life, pastimes—revolves. It's that talent for passing time (or of letting time pass, especially in politics) that Federico Fellini captured in his brilliant film *La dolce vita*, whose title is a nod to the sweet life Italians are so known for.

Over the course of history it's been these same characteristics that have often made Italians ferocious but not exactly courageous, ready more for a scuffle than for full-on war, adept at uprisings and turmoil but not real revolution, quick to take sudden and audacious action but unequipped with the stubborn tenacity that protracted conflict requires. To borrow Giacomo Leopardi's words, it's sheer "enjoyment, unaccompanied by any conscious effort."

In chapter 21 of his novel *Doctor Faustus,* Thomas Mann, donning the guise of the learned narrator, plays the same chords, giving a clearcut judgment of the differences between Italians and Germans. In H. T. Lowe-Porter's translation it sounds like this: "With profound consternation we read of the landing of American and Canadian troops on the southeast coast of Sicily. . . ." The narrator goes on, confirming that he also learned "with a mixture of terror and envy" that the Italians, following a succession of defeats and losses, finally relieved themselves of their "great man," and soon thereafter issued their unconditional surrender. He continues: "That is what the world demands of us too, but to consent to it our most desperate situation would still be much too holy and dear." After this preamble he concludes his reasoning, explaining why he believes Italians managed to pull off what the Germans would've found impossible:

Yes, we are an utterly different people; we deny and reject the foregone conclusion; we are a people of a mightily tragic soul, and our love belongs to fate—to any fate, if only it be one, even destruction kindling heaven with the crimson flames of the death of the gods![12]

This tragic aspect is exactly what's missing from the Italians' history—not because they haven't suffered true, major tragedies (they've certainly had their fair share), but rather because they didn't fully seize upon the spirit of such tragedies, or at least because their tragic circumstances never gave rise to any lasting memories.

That's not to say that the Germans' tragic bent is invariably a positive quality, nor is it to say that the Italians' knack for adapting to circumstances is only a defect, even if it means they're then viewed as weak, sentimental, or, conversely, downright cynical. It depends on your chosen point of view, whether you're given to an imperative sense of duty or to the sweetness of life.

This attitude has always struck, and sometimes seduced, foreign observers—but the arena in which it grows dangerous is war. The reputation gained at the World War I Battle of Caporetto, which still comes up today in discussions of Italians' comportment, wouldn't have lasted so long were it not based on the widespread assumption of Italians' cowardice.[13] The debacle of Caporetto could be contrasted with the World War II Battle of El Alamein, where Italian soldiers fought in the sandy trenches of North Africa, with little logistical preparation and minimal weaponry, yet still acted heroically. But the power of commonplace convictions is that they're both undemonstrable and insurmountable. German chancellor Helmut Schmidt once remarked that Italian tanks have four gears just like everyone else's, but one moves forward while the other three go in reverse. Winston Churchill, commenting on Mussolini's ill-fated Greco-Italian War, quipped that Europe's worst army had beat its second-worst army. During the Falklands War, anyone who asked the commander of the English naval and air campaign for his prediction of how the battle with the Argentines would go was told that if they were of Spanish extraction they'd fight back, if they were of Italian descent they'd retreat. The Battle of El Alamein proved the opposite, but what does it matter? On January 23, 2012, Jan Fleischhauer, an online op-ed writer for the German weekly *Der Spiegel*, wrote about the cruise ship disaster on the Italian island of Giglio: "Is it any surprise that the captain of the *Costa Concordia* was an Italian?" He then moved on to his real objective, the Eurozone's economic crisis: "The monetary crisis shows what can happen when, for political reasons, we choose to ignore differences in national populations' psychological makeup."

Many years ago in Strasbourg I heard Wolfgang Schäuble, at the time a Christian Democratic minister in Chancellor Helmut Kohl's administration, say with deep conviction (to paraphrase from memory): we Germans need Europe, we must be part of a supranational structure capable of holding back the demon that grips our people from time to time.

Italians have never portrayed themselves as a tragic people because they're aware of the fact that they're cast from a different mold. They don't have much of a taste for tragedy, and it's no accident that, aside from Vittorio Alfieri, known as the founder of Italian tragic drama, virtually no Italian authors have ever written tragedies.[14] Paradoxically, as Praz observed, Shakespeare and his fellow Elizabethans drew upon reports of both contemporary and historical happenings in Italy when writing their tragedies, albeit rereading and evaluating such events through their own perspectives. As the painter Mario Cavaradossi cries in the opera *Tosca*, "*L'ora è fuggita, io muoio disperato*" ("The time has passed and now I die, despairing"). But his cry is still sung, and Puccini's pathos-induced vibrato isn't enough to give his desperation the depth of true tragedy.

I would add—without any tinge of political acrimony, and solely in the interest of painting a complete picture, anthropologically speaking—that in no other nation worldwide has the head of government ever dared show his face in public with such heavy plastic surgery and makeup, further enhanced by hair replacements and almost high-heeled orthopedic shoes. I need hardly name names, and in any other country such a mask, most suitable for melodramatic theater or an opening-act comedian, would've won its wearer a ridiculous reputation; in Italy, it assured him a long-standing victory.

The few short months of the Italian Social Republic, Fascism's last gasp, also known as the Republic of Salò, were a concentrated dose of tragedy. Mussolini was reduced to the shadow of his former self, firmly in the hands of his Nazi puppet masters; his Black Brigades turned countless Italian villages into slaughterhouses, partisans were hanged by wire, apartments were transformed into torture chambers, and criminal gangs acted on their own authority, taking prisoners and raping and killing civilians without any fear of political or hierarchical oversight. An unspeakably dark atmosphere took over, and the vast number of prison-cell walls encrusted with dried blood was discovered only after Liberation. Seen in this framework, the Nazis' pressure on Mussolini to send his son-in-law, Galeazzo Ciano, to the firing squads was the very essence of tragedy. His daughter Edda begged him to spare the father of his grandchildren, and pathetically threatened to release her husband's diaries—as if those pages, which have since become rich material for historians, could've somehow changed the course of the carnage already well under way. This was a tragedy in the fullest sense of the word, a man torn between two choices, two laws: his love for his daughter versus his duty to the terrible regime that had allowed him to live just a bit longer. It was a prime example of what is widely known as the devil's alternative, where there's no good option—both are bad, no matter which you choose. The lesser of two evils is still evil.

Such tragedy demanded an equally tragic finale, an act capable of bringing some closure to a period that had so deeply scarred the country, in both human and political terms—a period that had exposed how little Italians actually valued freedom. Such an act might have proven that behind all the resounding parades, tin armor, and cardboard dag-gers there was something real—that having believed, having died for that Italy, wasn't just a proof of carelessness or stupidity.

But there was no such act. Crouched down in the back of a German truck, wearing the coat of a foreign army, collar raised high to hide his terrified eyes, his large head covered by a crooked helmet—that's how il Duce surrendered, confused and trembling. There was no "destruction kindling heaven with the crimson flames of . . . death." Instead, there was just fear and blundering, and two machine-gun rounds ringing out in front of the pilaster of the villa where Mussolini had been taken along with his companion, Claretta Petacci—a heroic woman indeed. Il Duce could have offered some interpretation of his ultimate tragedy, after all the tragedies he himself had caused, but he didn't have the heart; he was unforgivably absent, even for that miss-ing final act.

———————————

One of the characteristics that makes Italians so recognizable to for-eigners is their religiosity. According to one vein of historical thought, when all is said and done, Italians and the Catholic religion have done mutual harm to one another. The question of whether religion encour-aged the people's collective bad behavior or vice versa—whether the Italian people had a negative influence on the religious spirit—is both controversial and probably unanswerable. During the years I lived abroad (in the United States and France) I had experiences that would make me inclined to go with the second hypothesis, but such opinions are, by definition, debatable.

On the Boulevard des Invalides in Paris's seventh arrondissement there's a church dedicated to Saint Francis Xavier and run, as the name suggests, by the Jesuits. It isn't a particularly beautiful building, and cer-tainly can't hold a candle to Rome's more ostentatious Chiesa del Gesù or Chiesa di Sant'Ignazio. What's striking about it is that all masses are held in an impeccable Latin.

Even more striking is the fact that the assembled faithful are able to answer their celebrant with the same tone, also in Latin. It's an unusual church with conservative leanings, which also explains its unusually high attendance rates, especially compared with so many other churches that remain half empty even at Sunday mass. The concentrated seriousness of its priests and congregants inspires respect even among non-Catholics. French friends of mine pointed out that in France, Catholicism, although it's the country's prevalent religion, has to compete with various Protestant denominations, whereas in Italy, and especially in Rome, there is no such competition. Indeed, Italian Catholics' sense of religiosity often falls into indifference, becoming a bland association with the Church that often brings with it a deplorable degree of disinformation about the nature of faith and religious doctrine.

Now let's jump to New York. In a study titled *The Madonna of 115th Street,* Italian-American anthropologist Robert A. Orsi reports that, up until a few decades ago, during the liturgical feast of Our Lady of Mount Carmel (July 16) it was customary for a few women to be led up to the altar, licking the floor with their tongues as they approached. The practice was considered revolting, even among other Catholics.

On 115th Street in Manhattan there was—and still is—a church dedicated to Our Lady of Mount Carmel. For many years its congregation followed the kind of primitive religious observances many Italian immigrants, especially from the South, brought with them. These immigrants were humble and often illiterate, and most had faced tiring, sometimes humiliating red tape as soon as they stepped off the boat at Ellis Island. Many had arrived with the naive conviction that the streets of New York were paved with gold. In reality the most thankless jobs awaited them: building streets, digging subway tunnels, collecting garbage, constructing skyscrapers. In 1939 Pietro Di Donato's famous novel *Christ in Concrete* was released, the same year John Steinbeck's *Grapes of Wrath* came out. It was a time in which literature exposed the high price paid to build America.

These extremely poor immigrants had also brought a primitive, superstitious, entirely exterior religiosity along with them to the United States. Today that Little Italy is no more. But for many decades it had remained a theater of noisy processions, complete with statues of the Madonna and various saints (for instance the Neapolitans' San Gennaro, or Saint Januarius) carried atop community members' shoulders and covered in dollar bills as the procession passed shouting spectators, accompanied by the deafening notes of amateur musicians, hearty applause, invocations, tears. As evening descended the parades metamorphosed into dances and endless banquets at tables set up in the middle of the street, just as they had been in the villages these people had left behind.

This kind of religious observance greatly irritated other Catholics, not least the Irish and Polish, who shared the Italians' same faith but interpreted it in a much more reserved manner. Differences in doctrine led to discord and offense, as the Italians' entirely exterior approach to religious observance struck others as lacking in spiritual content, or too close to the kind of paganism that lived on in certain corners of southern Italy. Social differences were also a factor in such critiques, since the prevalently puritanical and antipapal culture of the United States viewed such effusive manifestations of religion as yet another example of Catholicism's ridiculousness.

We could look at a lot more examples, but they'd just be pointless repetitions. Let's instead try the opposite, and have a close look at the case of Italian statesman Camillo Benso, Count of Cavour. Although almost everything about him is already known, his personality is still somewhat more eccentric than one would expect given the context. Giuseppe Garibaldi, for example, is the ideal hero of the people, the Italian par excellence: impetuous, honest, a good general, a political naïf. Cavour was the opposite, as unsuited for military life as he was brilliant in politics: he came from a rich family yet wisely made the most of his initial fortune, multiplying it many times over; he was born the subject of a tiny kingdom (Piedmont-Sardinia) but managed to broaden his own intellectual horizons to include all of Europe; he studied the consequences the nascent industrial revolution would have on society; and governed the complex movement toward Italian unification, leading it to the best possible conclusion. The eminent British statesman John Bright, a formidable orator and contemporary of Cavour, wrote of him in his diary: "He has the appearance of an intelligent English gentleman farmer, rather than of a *fine* and subtle Italian."[15]

Now that's a curious compliment. Precisely because the Italian stereotype was so strong, all you needed to do to sing an Italian's praises was say he didn't seem Italian. Even the philosopher Henri Bergson was convinced Cavour was better than Bismarck—and he certainly was. Cavour was one of Europe's most farsighted, forward-looking politicians. Unfortunately he served an enfeebled dynasty and a country whose history was far too complex to fit into one shared narrative.

2

ITALIANS AS SEEN
FROM THE INSIDE

Unlike in the previous chapter, here I'm going to forgo choosing a
single person, event, or place to start with. Instead, I'd like to tell you
about a couple of fairly special books, two novels that helped establish Italians' self-image, providing what we might call a preview of one
possible anthropological take on Italy's people as a whole. Although
they were written many years ago the descendants of their protagonists still show up in the news today, so it could be said that, literary
criticisms aside, these novels introduced prototypical characters who
made a deep mark on the nation. But that shouldn't be so surpris-
ing—literature often has a way of collecting and condensing history
into its stories. Italo Calvino once wrote that "a classic is the term given
to any book which comes to represent the whole universe."[1] In our
case we're not talking about an entire universe—rather more modestly,
we're dealing with the Italian peninsula and the various sorts of human
beings who inhabit it. That's why rereading certain pages is a lot like
(and sometimes even better than) visiting a place or meeting a person.

The 1880s were a significant decade: in 1881 Giovanni Verga's
I Malavoglia (*The House by the Medlar Tree*) was published, followed
by Antonio Fogazzaro's *Malombra* later that same year; 1883 saw the

release of *Le avventure di Pinocchio* (*The Adventures of Pinocchio*) by
Carlo Lorenzini, a.k.a. Carlo Collodi.[2] Above all, two other titles rose
to fame during that same period, and those are the ones we'll look
at most closely: Edmondo De Amicis's *Cuore* (*The Heart of a Boy*)
and Gabriele D'Annunzio's *Il piacere* (*The Child of Pleasure*).[3] They
appeared just a few years apart, but in many respects came from different worlds: the former has a quintessentially Turinese tone, while the
latter is intensely Roman in character. These two cities are separated
not only by hundreds of miles, but also by deep differences in terms
of customs and lifestyles.

———————————

Edmondo De Amicis was born in 1846 in the Ligurian town of Oneglia.
When *Heart* was published he'd just turned thirty and was enjoying a
degree of fame as a polite and precise reporter. In September 1870 the
periodical *L'Italia militare* ("Military Italy") sent him to report on the
breach of Porta Pia, a watershed event during the Capture of Rome,
the final event of Italian unification. A few months later, bolstered by
reader support, he began collecting and publishing his many travel
writings, chronicling trips to Spain in 1872, Holland and London in
1874, and Morocco, Constantinople, and Paris in 1879. Nowadays we'd
say he started out as a "special envoy." He wrote a fluid, transparent
prose whose simplicity draws you in, sometimes focusing on effect but
primarily hinging on sentiment. He favored small events and observed
them in minute detail, remarking on what he saw with great subtlety
and from an intimate point of view. Conscious of the fact that he wasn't
an epic writer, he took refuge in the prose sketch and keen observation
of habits and customs.

His two sons, Furio and Ugo, brought him back to covering elementary school experiences after a few initial pieces, penned years
before, included pages wherein the tone and cadence of *Heart* were
already present.

Indeed, little me, poor me, I who live on brown bread and go about dressed in rags, unknown to the world and subject of compassion for the few who know me; I—if I so desire, if I study a lot, if I work hard—one day I'll make tens of thousands of people, the crème de la crème of this city, shut right up, as they do now, to hear my name and strain to catch a glimpse of me, whispering "There he is," and telling their little boys, all dressed in velvet, "Do as he does! . . ." I can stay up all night, I can. And if I don't have a lamp? Well then, I'll have my neighbor give me the stubs of his spent candles.[4]

The writer closely follows his two boys' progress, so school life is right before his eyes each day: his sons, his sons' friends, the teachers, the parents waiting in a crowd outside for their kids to exit. He steals a gesture here and there, an overheard phrase, the image of a boy consoling one of his poorer classmates, a teacher's nod. Thus *Heart* was born. On February 16, 1886, he writes to his publisher: "Enthusiasm has swept me off my feet. I can think of nothing else, and care for nothing but my book *Heart*; chapter follows chapter, half of the work is already done—written down between alternating tears and bursts of joy."[5] In an interview years later his son Ugo revealed that in the months his father was writing *Heart* the author smoked dozens of cigars a day and never left the house. He worked standing up, writing on a tall lectern in his apartment overlooking the Piazza san Martino.

By May it was done, after just six months of work. In a letter to his friend Orazio Barberis he confides: "At this very moment, midnight, I finished my children's book, and I cannot hold back from sharing the news with you, my dearest friend."

On October 15, 1886, just in time for the first day of school, the book appeared in shop windows, with a fire engine–red cover. The school featured in the book was based on the Moncenisio School on Via Cittadella, in Turin—and so it was to be a children's book, or rather a "chapter book for first-grade elementary school students," as the author specified in one of his letters. And yet the book that was released after those six months of intense work was something else entirely. In 1923 *Heart* celebrated its first million copies sold. By 1958 it had sold three million. After that everyone lost track, and there's no telling how many millions of copies there are in circulation today.

Where did its immense success come from?

Heart's plot strikes chords as elementary as the school in which the story takes place. The author puts himself in the shoes of a third-grade pupil, Enrico Bottini, as he keeps a diary of his school year, as the subtitle, "A Schoolboy's Journal," implies. The congenial Enrico so completely takes on the role of narrator that he's the book's least colorful character. Around him we find an entire class (an overcrowded class, but that's how it was back then) of fifty-four pupils, a dozen of whom we get to know quite well as the story develops. As the author introduces them one by one, the reader realizes that each character embodies not just a psychology, but a concrete function. As each makes his entry, De Amicis outlines his key characteristics: Coretti is the one who "wears chocolate-colored trousers and a catskin cap"; Garrone "is the biggest boy in the class . . . his head is large, his shoulders broad"; Votini is the boy "who is very well dressed, who always wears fine Florentine plush"; Nobis "seems very haughty," and so on.[6] Much like in ancient poetry, the repetition of these attributes helps orient the reader amid the crowd of students. But it also has a more rhetorical function, and shows us that we're dealing not so much with real flesh-and-blood boys as we are their stand-ins, the roles each one has to play, improbable as they may seem at times. Basically, from the first page onward *Heart* takes the tone of an "epic," or of an agitprop drama, if you will. As in Jesuit theater, the works of Bertolt Brecht, and Homer's *Odyssey*— to reference the loftiest, most remote example—repetition serves the purpose of proving to the reader that the characters are moved by forces beyond their own voluntary control, obedient solely to the function they're there to carry out.

Around and above this little brigade of students come the parents, schoolmasters, and schoolmistresses, two of whom were destined to become proverbial figures. One is "called 'the little nun,' because she always dresses in dark colors, with a black apron, and has a small white face, hair that is always smooth, very bright eyes, and a delicate voice, that seems to be forever murmuring prayers." The other is the even more famous young teacher "who wears a large red feather on her little bonnet."[7] These two semilegendary characters have been lost along with the mythic schools of yore, the desks carved up by pocketknives, the permanently inkless inkwells, and chalk screeching across slate blackboards.

The material might be simplistic, but the structure is highly articulated. There's Enrico's narration, which forces him to be present at all times. There are letters from his father, mother, and occasionally his sister, also included in his diary—a strategy that allows the author to step out of the schoolboy's perspective and provide an adult's point of view. Last, there are nine "monthly stories" set within the broader narrative. They include: "The Little Vidette of Lombardy," "The Little Florentine Writer," "The Sardinian Drummer Boy," and, most famous of all, "From the Appenines to the Andes" (the longest, too, at thirty-four pages), which brought me to tears twice—once as I read it, and again when I saw the film adaptation Flavio Calzavara produced in 1943.

Completely surrendering to the author's intentions, I lost myself in the story, absorbed in the fate of the poor little boy who'd gone halfway around the world to find his mother. One day he approaches a carriage to ask the coachman something. His mother is right there inside, just a step away, but the carriage drives off and they don't spot each other. It's an emotional stroke of genius. I even remember, if memory serves, hearing sobs rise up in the dark theater from the distressed, disillusioned audience as the carriage began rolling away.

All in all, it's a singular book with rich emotional content and a fairly innovative structure, when compared with standard late nineteenth-century literary canons.

De Amicis was a lot less naive than we naive readers might think—indeed, he knew exactly what he was going for. First, to push us to tears, something he certainly succeeded at in my case. Then, through intense sentiment, to attain the goal he forthrightly states in his preface: "Now read this book, boys; I hope you will be pleased with it, and that it may do you good."[8] Therefore, *Heart* is supposed to "do you good." The author was convinced that literature has a moral end, and remained convinced of it when he later became a socialist. In an 1895 interview with fellow writer Ugo Ojetti, he reaffirmed that belief: "Art, if it is really art, mustn't preach, but must instead serve a concrete purpose."

Part of the "good" that reading *Heart* was to do was also to spread the kind of work ethic so deeply rooted in the Anglo-Saxon mentality yet so ephemeral in Latin countries. Translated into the perspective of a late nineteenth-century Piedmontese, that meant solidarity between socioeconomic classes, a respect for the State (or love of country, if you will, complete with repeated references to the flag and the army), good faith, a clear conscience. Such values could seem superfluous, outdated, or even ambiguous—but the lack of such values was evident back when De Amicis was writing, and remains evident today.

Once the Kingdom of Italy was unified, for better or worse, the coexistence of its people had to be based on uniform codes of conduct. The page in which the Calabrian boy, Coraci, is welcomed by his third-grade classmates, all Piedmontese, is just one of the many examples from the book. Back then there was a huge gap to bridge, and the gap remains equally vast for Coraci's present-day counterparts, often named Mehmed, Murad, or Josip.

The backdrop behind the characters is the school itself, the teachers, the lessons, the simple fact of sharing a classroom for a few hours each day. De Amicis insists on the concept: "The school seems to make them all equals and friends," and later on, "Hurrah for brave comrades, and hurrah for school, which makes one family of you, of those who have and those who have not!"[9] He portrays school as the place where you learn not only reading, writing, and arithmetic, but also to live alongside others with a spirit of solidarity, if nothing else; it's the place where national identity is built. The only two characters who are irredeemable according to this progressive vision are, not surprisingly, Carlo Nobis, the vain young aristocrat, and the wicked, underprivileged Franti. Neither of them share the group's values—indeed, they reject them and, motivated by opposing logics, consider them unfitting to their status as outsiders with respect to the overarching bourgeois order of things. With the exclusion of those two extremes, the pedagogy presented in *Heart* harmoniously unites the entire socioeconomic field, the various trades and professions, and the nascent industrial society De Amicis had admired at the 1878 Universal Exposition in Paris.

This new society could only gain a foothold through a massive drive for collective education, to help spread an ingrained "sense of duty." In order for this to succeed major effort had to be made, and a large part of it fell to the schools. The scholastic system therefore became the front line upon which the nation's future depended. Given that perspective, the following scene is less a model of bourgeois urbanity than it is the embodiment of a precise moral message. Here is how Enrico Bottini describes the meeting between his father and his father's old teacher:

> "Are you," asked my father, raising his hat, "Vincenzo Crosetti, the schoolmaster?" The old man raised his hat also, and replied: "I am," in a voice that was somewhat tremulous, but full. "Well, then," said my father, taking one of his hands, "permit one of your old scholars to shake your hand and to inquire how you are. I have come from Turin to see you."[10]

But even this scene has its opposite, as recorded in the same period. In a report filed by senator and teacher Francesco Torraca for the years 1895–96 we read that "a majority of municipal administrators, and along with them the most well-to-do citizens, outright hate and oppose

public education—they view it as an equalizing force, which terrifies
them." He further notes that this is especially the case in southern
Italy, but is also a factor in the North. That sense of terror has survived
through the years, and remains fully intact today. When the right-wing
exponent Letizia Moratti became minister of public education in the
early twenty-first century, she was quick to remove the adjective "Public" from her department's title—she, too, was terrified by its egalitar-
ian sound, even if she was likely unaware that by doing so she dredged
up a reactionary old taboo.

───────────────

Heart immediately won a vast readership and met with a triumphal
welcome nationwide, with the exception of the Catholic community,
which was bothered by the fact that the author had utterly ignored
religion, and went so far as to omit any mention of the major religious
holidays that take place during the school year. In *Heart* there's no
Christmas, no Easter, no Feast of the Immaculate Conception. Each
episode is steeped in the civic, state-based religiosity that characterized
the liberal currents of the Risorgimento.[11] The ecclesiastical authorities were unwavering, and the book was flagged as a text "unsuitable
for children."

The debate was launched by an article published in *L'Unità cattolica* ("Catholic Unity"). The liberal and Protestant press then reacted.
In Turin a Waldensian pastor organized a well-attended conference in
defense of the book, focusing on the subject of "De Amicis's *Heart* and
the heart of the *L'Unità cattolica.*" De Amicis didn't attend, but they told
him about it and their support comforted him. A few days later he sent
the news to his publisher, writing: "I tell you this as a bit of consolation after the clerical attacks, which it seems to me, deep down, have
made you detest the fact that I didn't sanctify Christmas, Easter, and
the Resurrection in my book."

Its major success, both domestic and international, inevitably inspired plagiarisms and parodies. The poet Francesco Gaeta, skeptical

of *Heart*'s values, once told the philosopher Benedetto Croce about his idea for a sequel, a tale that amused him no end. Croce summed it up this way: "In Gaeta's playful continuation of the story Enrico—who had spent his youth surrounded by the incessant sweetness of moral, tender, sublime spectacles—hadn't developed sufficient defenses against actual reality and its demonic powers. In the end, between the seduction of the new and his own inexperience, he winds up in jail!" Another parody was inspired by the episode that, in *Heart*, is dated December 17 and titled "The School-Mistress":

> Signora Cromi, the oldest of the schoolmistresses, came to teach the school; she has two grown-up children, and she has taught several women to read and write, who now come to accompany their sons . . . She was sad to-day, because one of her sons is ill. No sooner had they caught sight of her, than they began to make an uproar. But she said, in a slow and tranquil tone, "Respect my white hair; I am not only a school-teacher, I am also a mother"; and then no one dared to speak again.[12]

In M. Nigra Garigliola's *Buon Cuore* (1906), schoolmistress Cromi becomes schoolmistress Dorati, and the new version sounds like this: "Signora Dorati, the oldest of the schoolmistresses, has one son in the loony bin, and her other son wants to become a priest. As she entered there was an infernal uproar; the good woman stepped to the lectern and, caressing the tumultuous class with her calm gaze, said: 'Would you prefer that schoolmaster Bonfanti come instead, the one who always threatens severe punishment, and has already maimed half of his students?' And then no one dared to speak again."

Then came Umberto Eco's essay "Elogio di Franti" ("In Praise of Franti"), first published in 1963. Eco imagines the notorious Franti "with the vivid memory of the gesture Coretti's father had given his son, his hands still warm, the affection of the King . . . by the dawn of the new century, a long ascent had prepared him to practice under

the pseudonym Gaetano Bresci."[13] Each era has recast *Heart* according
to its tastes. Even the author Alberto Arbasino reckoned with *Heart*
(in his 1964 book *Certi romanzi*, "Certain Novels"), underlining the
sadistic/penitential atmosphere that hangs over the entire book, much
as it does in all of Puccini's operas. But then he adds: "Edmondo [De
Amicis] and Giacomo [Puccini], and even Gabriele [D'Annunzio] remain 'minor masters,' unsurpassed in their ability to industrially trans-
form even the most disconcerting 'transgressions' into impeccably
functional products." Criticism, objections, and mockery, over a century after the book's debut, are yet another sign of its unquestionable
vitality. That said, Eco took all the necessary precautions, stipulating:
"But in order to laugh, and to give his laughter its full strength, anyone
who laughs must accept and believe in, even parenthetically, the thing
he's laughing at. He must also laugh from within it, if you can say such
a thing, otherwise his laughter is meaningless. . . . Anyone who laughs
must therefore be the 'son' of a given situation and completely accept
it, almost love it, and therefore, like a wicked child, be able to mock it."[14]

The truth is that it's easy to parody any work that exhibits—or,
in this case, flaunts—any conception of common values. Any positive
spin put on such supposed shared values brings with it the reasoning
behind its weaknesses, and any propaganda—from medieval tragedy
to Jesuit theater and "Socialist Realism"—can be made fun of, rendering its ethical and ideological assumptions void.

De Amicis drops precise references to the political and social
pecking order of various characters and episodes throughout his novel;
his aim is to prove that, despite class differences, bonds of friendship
and mutual respect can nevertheless be formed between these third-
grade students. As literary critic Alberto Asor Rosa quite fairly writes
(in *Storia d'Italia*, "History of Italy," vol. 4), this is the very same bond
the fate of a future Italy could have been based upon, had it risen to
become a bona fide "national pact."

In March 1908, a record number of people attended De Amicis's
funeral—second only to the funeral held for the composer Giuseppe

Verdi a few years before. But neither the author's popularity nor the undeniable success of *Heart* was enough to make that "national pact" come about; back then, as today, it remained a distant dream.

Gabriele D'Annunzio, a writer as driven as De Amicis, also completed *The Child of Pleasure* in only six months, as the manuscript proudly stated: "Francavilla al Mare, July–December, 1888."

It was Turin against Rome. These books embodied two extremes: one side offered an overtly pedagogical aim; the other offered an explosive, hedonistic sensuality. Conversely, the latter could be read as a languid yearning stoked by a selfish quest for what the title explicitly declares—*pleasure*. De Amicis offered a spare, functional prose; D'Annunzio, on the other hand, offered a lush, sensual, highly refined language.

In a newspaper article a few years later, in 1893, D'Annunzio reminisced about the atmosphere of Rome back in the early 1880s:

> It was a time in which the industriousness of wrecking crews and building crews was in full swing. Along with the clouds of dust came a kind of building frenzy, a sudden, spreading whirlwind . . . There it was, everywhere, like a vulgar contagion. Amid the incessant business disputes, the almost ferocious flurry of appetites and passions, and the unorganized and exclusive manner in which useful activities were done, all aesthetic sense was lost, all respect for the past was forgotten.[15]

That's what the capital of the Kingdom of Italy looked like to young D'Annunzio when he left his provincial hometown to live in the big city. The scene struck the writer with such intensity that he was enthralled by it. You might say the city made an impression in his very flesh, and with his writing he managed to give it back to the reader as a transfigured city, a combination of things he'd seen, things he'd imagined, and things that had never really happened outside of his own head. He wrote about the noble classes and the commoners, fashion and architecture, with scenes and figures taken partly from reality, or completely made up, but somehow linked to things he saw in the teeming city all around him. His is a dreamed-up realism, a painting with veiled contours, distorted by a perturbing ideal, yet nevertheless recognizable.

D'Annunzio arrived in Rome when he was just eighteen. He had recently finished high school in Prato, having earned top grades and sparked a few scandals during his time at the Liceo Cicognini. The city attracted him or, better yet, ensnared him. Looking around each day as he exited his modest lodging at 12 Via Borgognona, everything seemed worth writing about. He enrolled at the university's literature department, which was why his family had sent him to Rome in the first place, but rarely attended class. He made up for it by becoming a regular on the editorial teams of several journals, where his reputation had preceded him thanks to a collection of poems (*Primo vere*, 1879) published while he was still in high school. He showed up "all curls and smiles," and received a warm welcome. Fellow writer Edoardo Scarfoglio vividly remembered his arrival at the offices of the literary and satirical journal *Capitan Fracassa*: "I recall it perfectly—I was reclining on a bench . . . and yawning amid a bunch of people bantering. As soon as I saw this little man with curly hair and sweetly feminine eyes approaching, saying my name and introducing himself to me in an equally womanly tone, I started and jumped up, strangely struck. He had the same effect on everyone who saw him. We led him into the lounge, and everyone gathered around him. Never—even in that office, where any and everything new easily triggered intense admiration and curiosity—had a triumphant humorist received such a festive welcome."[16]

The luxurious abodes and villas, the city's surroundings, the carriages, the evenings out in high society, the people, everything drew him in—above all, he was captivated by the women, who sparked his imagination and sensuous temperament. In one of the poems collected in *Intermezzo di rime* (1884), which caused great scandal, he wrote with no hesitation whatsoever: "My barbarous, strong youth / killed itself in the arms of many women."[17]

———————

His first noteworthy affair in Rome was with Maria Hardouin di Gallese, whom he met in February 1883. In April he wrote to his friend Enrico Nencioni: "I go riding a lot, by myself, in search of an Amazon I rarely meet . . . I *love*, my dear Enrico, finally I love with full abandon, utterly losing myself." That love, complete with its sense of abandon, was fully requited. One May evening Maria gave in, and Gabriele rushed to make it known in one of the poems later included in *Intermezzo di rime*. The entire sequence of events, culminating in an intimate encounter on a lawn in Villa Borghese, is retold with brazen tactlessness. The composition, titled "Il peccato di maggio" ("Sin in May"), sounds more like a radio newscast than a short poem:

> Her head
> fell back, and suddenly she lost it. Her locks
> spread out, forming a bed where she, as if
> about to die, reclined. She stiffened,
> as if frozen by death. Fear
> filled me . . .
> But death
> didn't last. Life returned in a wave of pleasure.
> I bent my entire body over her mouth, as if drinking
> from a chalice; quivering at this conquest, I felt
> her breasts and nipples rise to the lascivious
> touch of my fingers, those fleshy flowers . . .[18]

And so on and so forth.

The consequences of that "Sin in May" forced the two into a hasty marriage.

In his own way D'Annunzio did love his wife—in his own way meaning he turned their marriage into a union of convenience, clearly separated from his activities as an artist and his liaisons with other women. One of these other women, Olga Ossani, was a key model for one of the characters in *The Child of Pleasure*. Ossani, a Neapolitan journalist who published under the pseudonym Febea, was a few years older than D'Annunzio (he was twenty-one when he met her), and was known for her beauty—in particular, for the fact that she had completely white hair by the time she was twenty, which sharply contrasted with her fresh, young body and lively gaze. Their love affair was intense and brief, and ended on March 25, 1885, just four months after it had begun. Ossani had a strong personality and clear ideas about what she wanted. Four months were enough for her to know that she'd never be able to put up with the subterfuge a clandestine affair would've required.

Whereas De Amicis drew on the world of school to turn experience into literature, D'Annunzio drew on women. The third affair we should examine is the one he had with Elvira Natalia Fraternali, whom he met on April 2, 1887, at a concert on Via Margutta. Elvira was a pianist and a sophisticate, and her intellect also made an impression on the poet. But their cultural interests weren't what set their relationship apart; rather, it was that they were a perfect match on a sensual level. Elvira, nicknamed Barbara and sometimes Barbarella, was certainly the woman D'Annunzio loved, or desired, more than any other among the many he had throughout his life. She might also have satisfied his predilections in ways no one else managed to, as seems to be the case judging from the incessant correspondence (over a thousand letters) the two exchanged. Born in 1862, she was a year older than Gabriele. Three years before she met the poet she'd married Ercole Leoni, a count of dubious lineage from Bologna, but the two soon separated after her husband gave her a rather unpleasant venereal disease.

As the affair between Leoni and D'Annunzio brought them public notoriety the count began to go crazy, perhaps more out of a wounded sense of pride than out of real jealousy. He then tried to get his wife back and even forced her, despite the public humiliation it cost him, to have conjugal relations with him. There are clear traces of this tie, split between opposing tensions and pressures, in *The Child of Pleasure*.

Between April and June 1887 the lovers met up on an almost daily basis. Their encounters took place in the studios of two of D'Annunzio's friends: the artist Guido Boggiani's place on Via san Nicola da Tolentino; and the composer Francesco Paolo Tosti's place on Via de' Prefetti. At least three of the author's works reflect the impact of this relationship. She shows up in his work as early as the first poem in his book *Elegie Romane*, "Il Vespro":

> When (my veins tremble with sweetness at the very thought)
> I left, as if inebriated, the beloved house;
> and strolled the streets still abuzz with the sound of the day's
> labors, the click and clack of carts, gruff shouts,
> I felt my whole soul rise up from that secret heart
> lustfully . . .
> His cheeks flush and large, the Triton blew not fire
> but water, which fanned out like foliage.
> A flickering of flashes, tinged purple atop,
> free up in the sky, the grand home of the Barberini
> looked to me like the perfect palace I'd have chosen for our
> lovemaking; and desire made me fantasize of superb loves yonder:
> radiant loves and admirable luxuries and deep leisure;
> a wider strength, a warmer life.[19]

Palazzo Barberini is mentioned here, and it's also where the first amorous encounter takes place between Andrea Sperelli and Elena Muti, the lead characters of *The Child of Pleasure*. Both Leoni and Ossani influenced the writer's construction of Elena. In a letter to Leoni, D'Annunzio wrote:

When I think back on the kisses I gave you all over your body—
on your small, perky breasts, on your stomach as perfect as a
sculpted virgin's, on the warm, living, soft rose between your
lips, and on your mouth, on your thighs as soft as velvet and as
flavorful as a succulent fruit, on your knees, which you denied
me in vain, laughing and twisting away, and on the back of your
knees, so fresh and delicate and childlike, and on your back, all
golden and dotted with gold beads, with the groove where my
wet tongue ran swiftly up and down, caressing you, and on your
loins, and on your marvelously beautiful hips, and on the nape
of your neck amid your hair, and on your long, beating eyelashes,
and on your throat—when I think back on that wave of sheer joy
that coursed through my veins even when I just looked at you
nude, I quiver and tremble and am set ablaze.[20]

In the novel, one of the first encounters between Andrea and Elena
has a similar tone:

"Afterwards, you remember on the sofa—I smothered you in
flowers—your face, your bosom, your shoulders, and you raised
yourself out of them every moment to offer me your lips, your
throat, your half closed lids. And between your skin and my lips I
felt the rose leaves soft and cool. I kissed your throat and a shiver
ran through you . . . nothing in this world could be so dear and
sweet. . . ."[21]

The lead character of *The Child of Pleasure* is Count Andrea Sperelli
Fieschi D'Ugenta, a highly sensitive poet and etcher; he's also possessed by a "sensual selfishness," and is aware of his own moral im-
potence. Abandoned by his lover, Elena Muti, at the height of their
passionate affair, Andrea tries in vain to forget her by pursuing other
women. Elena has left him to marry into wealth, in order to restore her
family's shaky finances. One of Andrea's many affairs forces him into

a duel, which leaves him wounded. During his convalescence in the countryside at Villa Schifanoja, he reflects on his own past and repudiates its squalor, dreaming of a redemption of sorts through a renewed dedication to his art practice.

At the villa he meets young Maria Ferres, a married woman and "nobly spiritual creature," and becomes her lover. Sperelli's full recovery and return to Rome lead him right back into his previous lifestyle. What's more, when he runs into Elena by chance one day he realizes not only that he loves her with the same fierce passion he used to, but that his feeling for her fuses with his new feelings toward Maria, such that the two women meld into one in his mind, creating a single, ambiguous tangle of desire. Andrea basically uses Maria as a substitute for Elena, who now rejects him. This strange relationship goes on for some time, coasting on an unstable equilibrium—but then, just as Maria's family falls into hardship and she needs her lover's support and understanding more than ever, in a moment of unchecked passion Andrea mistakenly utters Elena's name. Maria gets the turbid mind game Andrea is playing, and flees. It's the same day that everything in Maria's apartment is being auctioned off to repay her husband's gambling debts; he'd been caught cheating, and has lost all social standing. The novel comes to a close with a scene of utter desolation and abandonment, with porters carrying off the last few furnishings and tapestries, a transparent symbol of a much more deeply rooted failure.

Reduced to its core plot, *The Child of Pleasure* sounds like something straight out of a popular newspaper serial. Indeed, its "modernity" lies not in its storyline, but rather in the psychological tangles connecting the characters, as well as Andrea's introspective realizations. But the book's real power might lie elsewhere still—many other writers, from Dostoyevsky to Proust, had already dealt with their characters' psychological sides, or were about to. Its real strength just might be how well it evokes Rome and Roman society in that era. Between the lines of his story D'Annunzio hid some precise references to the period. We know that *The Child of Pleasure* begins at 3:25 P.M. on December 31, 1886 (a date revealed by the famous incipit of the Italian edition: *"L'anno moriva, assai dolcemente"*—"The year was dying, quite sweetly"); it ends just after sundown on Monday, June 20, 1887. From a strictly chronological point of view, the story itself (just like its composition) unfolds over a six-month period. But the psychological vicissitudes it covers are much more vast, since the relationship between Elena and Andrea is already over when the book begins, and the reader learns of it only through Andrea's reminiscences.

When Elena first appears, D'Annunzio describes only the way she's dressed. The sole physical feature he refers to is her eyes:

> She was standing in the middle of the room—a little undecided and ill at ease in spite of her rapid and lightly spoken words. A velvet coat with Empire sleeves, very full at the shoulders and buttoned closely at the wrists and with an immense collar of blue fox for sole trimming, covered her from head to foot, but without disguising the grace of her figure. She looked at Andrea with eyes in which a curious tremulous smile softened the flash and sparkle.[22]

Even when Andrea thinks back on the circumstances in which he met Elena, D'Annunzio only gives us a fleeting glimpse of her. Andrea re-members seeing her from behind as she ascended the grand staircase of Palazzo Roccagiovane:

> She ascended in front of him with a slow and rhythmic move-ment; her cloak, lined with fur as white as swan's-down, was un-clasped at the throat, and slipping back, revealed her shoulders, pale as polished ivory, the shoulder-blades disappearing into the lace of the corsage with an indescribably soft and fleeting curve as of wings. The neck rose slender and round, and the hair,

twisted into a great knot on the crown of her head, was held in place by jewelled pins.[23]

The third description of Elena is, once again, partial. We see her make a minor gesture, but it immediately lights up Andrea's senses:

> She made no reply, but she lifted the bunch of violets to her face, and inhaled the perfume. In so doing, the wide sleeve of her evening cloak slipped back over her arm beyond her elbow . . . [The sight of her lively flesh, emerging from amid the fur cloak like a bunch of white roses pushing through the snow] thrill[ed] the young man's senses almost beyond control . . . [due to the singularly provocative power the nude female form acquires when exposed from behind a thick, heavy garment.] His lips trembled, and he with difficulty restrained the burning words that rose to them.[24]

It isn't the first time such a "thick, heavy garment"—put more prosaically, a fur coat—inspires sensations of the sort in D'Annunzio. In a newspaper gossip column titled "Cronachetta delle pellicce" ("Little Column of the Fur Coats"), published in the December 1884 issue of *La Tribuna* under the pseudonym Happemouche, he writes:

> Nothing is more nobly voluptuous than a well-worn fur-seal coat. Their skins agreeably conform to all the curves and folds of the female body—not with the light adherence of silk or satin, but with a certain gravity that isn't without its own grace, the sweet kind of grace that animals with thick fur have as they furtively move about. There's always a kind of lightning, a kind of quick, brilliant flash that precedes or accompanies their movement, or gives their movement a strange beauty.

Only upon her fourth appearance is Elena finally shown to Andrea in her full radiance. The scene takes place in the grand rooms of the

French Embassy in Palazzo Farnese, around eleven at night. Andrea arrived early, anxiously consumed by the thought of once again seeing Elena, who hasn't come yet. He already fears she's decided not to show when:

> She advanced along the frescoed gallery where the crowd was thinnest, her long white train rippling like a wave over the floor behind her. All white and simple, she passed slowly along, turning from side to side in answer to the numerous greetings, with an air of manifest fatigue and a somewhat strained smile which drew down the corners of her mouth, while her eyes looked larger than ever under the low white brow, her extreme pallor imparting to her whole face a look so ethereal and delicate as to be almost ghostly . . . Her beauty at this moment was of ideal nobility, and shone with additional splendour among all these women heated with the dance, over-excited and restless in their manner.[25]

D'Annunzio was twenty-five when he wrote *The Child of Pleasure*, and it was his first novel. Yet the skillfully crafted crescendo with which he prepares the reader for Elena's entrance is enough to prove his natural narrative instincts. Elena is gradually given to the reader, in stages. When the time is ripe, D'Annunzio introduces her with this slow, grandiose, solemn advance, which allows her pale, intense beauty to shine in contrast to that of the other women, who are "heated with the dance, over-excited and restless in their manner."

Another majestic scene is the one in which the two lovers finally give themselves to one another. After an intense, prolonged preparation, the lightning-quick conclusion mimics what often happens in reality: "With a sudden movement she raised herself from the pillows, and taking Andrea's head between her two hands, she drew him to her, [breathed her desire into his face,] and their lips met in a long and passionate kiss. Afterwards she fell back again . . . and [offered herself to him]."[26]

In his later book titled *Libro segreto* ("Secret Book"), D'Annunzio smugly describes an episode involving a similarly literary "atmosphere." When he went to give one of the first printed copies to his fellow writer Jacob Moleschott, the old doctor's face lit up "with a broad smile." He then scanned the pages, sniffed them, and, great physiologist that he was, pronounced an instinctive judgment that in some way also sounded like a literary verdict: "It reeks of sperm."

In an off-the-cuff column written in the summer of 1887 (a year before the book was drafted), the author repeatedly returned to a character named Diambra, "Princess of Scurcola," to whom he devoted various episodes that seem like studies for his upcoming novel. One study exploring the female nude and feminine sensuality is undoubtedly a description of a striptease: "She begins with slow, languid, occasionally hesitant gestures, pausing with each move, as if to stop and listen. She takes off her fine silk stockings . . . then lets the ribbon holding her last bit of clothing, her thinnest, most precious camisole, slip off her shoulder . . . its snowy whiteness flows down over her breasts, along the arch of her lower back, and stops for a moment at her hips; then it suddenly falls to her feet, like a wisp of sea foam."

Behind the lead characters lies Rome, or rather the part of Rome centered around Piazza di Spagna and Via Sistina, between the Spanish Steps and Piazza Barberini, and from there outward, across Via dei Condotti and Via del Babuino to the many eighteenth-century churches (in the famous baroque style of the Counterreformation), piazzas large and small, fountains and papal shrines. D'Annunzio's Rome isn't the Rome of Chateaubriand, Stendhal, or Goethe; instead, it's the Rome of the newborn Kingdom of Italy, the one best suited to act as a backdrop for the time in which he experienced it: "The grand receptions, auctions, wolf hunts, streets, small shops, concerts, fencing academies, the silvery sheen of the court, and the feathers adorning the large hats of the 'ladies along the Tiber' all came together to form the massive chorus of this great ballet."

This is the Rome D'Annunzio brings us with his refined ability to paint a full picture: he offers up a series of scenes, some as sumptuous as rich oil paintings, others as transparent and liquid as watercolors. Later in the same column from July 1887 he writes: "Have you ever contemplated the city on a July afternoon from the shade of the holm oaks that stand like a rigid green wall in front of the Villa Medici? When has Rome ever seemed more solemn, more sacred? When has Rome ever inspired the heart with such a strong feeling of divinity? The boulevard is deserted. The vast, motionless trees protect the fountain and are reflected in the pool where the water, in their shade, is as dark and soft as velvet."

Even Benedetto Croce, who wrote D'Annunzio off as a "sensational dilettante" (a dilettante, but nevertheless an artist, he added), had to admit that he not only "saw things with extraordinary lucidity," but also "perfectly portrayed" what he saw.

———————————

Sometime before *The Child of Pleasure* came out, D'Annunzio had announced in the political and literary weekly *Fanfulla della Domenica* that he was working on a "novel about contemporary customs." In truth, the "customs" he describes weren't yet "contemporary"; but certain social circles soon adopted them after reading his narrative, turning them into a trend, and sometimes being caricatured in turn.

Scandal and controversy also played a part. Some of the story's apparent affirmations irritated people more than its sexual transgressions did. For example, the phrase with which Andrea comments on the tumultuous repercussions of the Italian soldiers massacred in Dogali in January 1887. Short, terrible words. Watching the scene from within his carriage as it moves past a riled crowd, Andrea murmurs: "And all this for four hundred brutes who had died the death of brutes!"[27]

As early as his first reading of the manuscript the publisher had intuited that the phrase might cause a stir given the political atmosphere of the time, and tried to convince D'Annunzio to tone it down a bit. The author refused, writing: "Dear sir, any and all advice is useless. That statement is uttered by Andrea Sperelli, not myself, and it fits well in the mouth of such a monster. I trust you will have understood that by studying Sperelli I aimed at studying the moral order of a monster. Why should critics go insane over it?"

Obviously, he was lying. A few years later he wrote to Georges Hérelle, the book's French translator, affirming: *"Dans Andrea Sperelli, il y a une part vivante de moi"* ("There is a living part of me in Andrea Sperelli"). None of his readers had ever doubted it.

———————————

I'll try to draw a conclusion, even if I shouldn't even really say—all literary considerations aside—why these two novels are essentially, as I mentioned earlier, two anthropologies, insofar as they faithfully portray two different ways of being Italian: two categories, two lifestyles, two different ways of perceiving oneself, one's relationships to others, and one's relation to the country and the "national pact" Asor Rosa spoke of.

De Amicis idealized the Piedmontese bourgeoisie by celebrating their values; D'Annunzio titillated the Roman bourgeoisie by seeking to spark a scandal, albeit with such skill that he made the most of inciting real irritation, transforming it into an even greater source of success. The former openly adheres to his own history, is moved by the characters he's created, and lives their same life; the latter feigns detachment to make ironic observations. But his detachment is only an affect, because in reality he, too, experiences his characters with an equal intensity. He steeps himself in their moods, mixing them in with his own.

Looking back at these two novels today, with the comfort of hindsight, we can clearly see what kinds of human archetypes followed, imitated, and surpassed the characters that populated those pages, carrying them through the past century and a half of Italian history.

Traits like heartfelt sentiment, political correctness, and middle-class diligence are all descendants of *Heart*. People who are satisfied with what they have, who carefully tend to their family so they can make it to the end of each month, who are basically good, if sometimes a bit dull, all come from that same place: a place of dimly lit apartments furnished as well as could be managed, short trips to the beach, new shoes for Christmas, a respect for institutions, a reverence for those in power, the compulsion to recycle as a contribution to a more decent coexistence.

The writer Guido Gozzano (in his book *L'amica di nonna Speranza*) described them thus:

> Stuffed birds and busts of Alfieri and Napoleon,
> framed flowers (good things in bad taste!)
> a dark hearth, boxes without candies,
> marble fruits protected under glass bell jars,
> the occasional plaything, little chests made of half-shells,
> objects emblazoned with words to the wise, *welcome, remember,*
>   coconut shells,
> little mosaics of Venetian scenes, somewhat faded watercolors,
> prints, trunks of things, albums painted with archaic anemones.[28]

It's all so nineteenth century. Nowadays, of course, the objects are different. Nobody (well, almost nobody) decorates his dresser with a snow globe of Venice. But the spirit remains the same, I mean the measure of things—the size of people's horizons, of their lives—is the same.

The other Italians are descendants of Count Andrea Sperelli. They're the ones who are unreliable, imaginative, uninvolved, the ones capable of spending money they don't have, who mysteriously always live beyond their means, who say "jail is for the poor," who have yachts and glitzy lights, who gamble, who have affairs, who like sex as a fleeting kind of mayhem—taken by force, bought, stolen. They're quick to laugh, have loose tongues, like to make bets, challenges, like to beat their adversaries by force or by slander; institutions exist to serve them, and they cozy up to the powerful, whoever it might be today. And then there are their slogans: "they're sad so we're happy"; "they want rules but we love freedom."

Back in the day it was easier to distinguish between the former and the latter, but over time everything's grown a bit more confusing. Nevertheless, these two key archetypes remain, and the second kind of Italians described above, although they're certainly in the minority, are almost always the ones who most recognizably shape the era.

I've told you about two novels, but really I should've talked about three in order to give you a full trilogy of 1880s Italy. In 1885 Antonio Fogazzaro published his second novel, *Daniele Cortis*. Fogazzaro was a Catholic from Vicenza, and was open to the cultural current that later became known as modernism. The motto of the day was *non expedit* ("it is not expedient," which were the words the Holy See used to discourage Italian Catholics from voting in parliamentary elections). After the Breach of Porta Pia, Pope Pius IX prohibited Catholics from participating in the newborn democracy, arguing that engaging in politics was "inopportune." Fogazzaro's novel also deals with that subject. Daniele Cortis, the main character, is a parliamentary representative from Friuli; he's conservative but openminded; he rails against corruption and would be happy to see a strong man lead the nation, someone in the vein of Bismarck; so he goes against the pope's orders because, like Cavour, he wants a free State and a free Church, safely separated from one another. What's really curious is that at one point Daniele seems to invent, so to speak, the name of what would later become Italy's majority political party for more than half a century: "In my mind, I'm picturing a bright, possible ideal that might best be called Christian Democracy."

In the book, passages about the young representative's political life are mixed in with ones about his love affair with his cousin Elena, who at nineteen was mismatched and married off to the Sicilian baron Carmine di Santa Giulia, an inveterate gambler and philanderer.

Elena is incredibly elegant and burns with love for Daniele just as he does for her, although the most they exchange is a kiss, perhaps two kisses. All the rest is just holding hands, caresses given by prudently well-covered limbs: "She released herself from the gallant hands that had been holding her, and moved toward the entryway. Once there she turned and, quickly gazing at him, silently poured her soul out before his eyes. Then she disappeared."

The book also depicts life in Montecitorio, Italy's chamber of deputies; Fogazzaro made the long journey to Rome in order to observe it up close, filling several journals with his notes. We see representatives from the provinces as they wander lost through the city or the parliament building's endless hallways, reacting with dismay upon discovering the feel of corruption in the air, overhearing conversations among certain groups of colleagues and trying to understand what it's all about, receiving threats in the form of anonymous letters.

In *Daniele Cortis*, Fogazzaro wrote the first true "parliamentary novel," which completes our picture of Italy in the years it began to take shape as a unified state. Considered from the viewpoint of literature as a mirror of life, the scope and realm of his pages is utterly new compared with the other two novels we discussed. Fogazzaro has none of the idealized respectability of De Amicis, nor does he have the *ante litteram* "dolce vita" of D'Annunzio. Instead, reading his book we read the first signs of democratic representation's degeneration—a type of decay that, as we know all too well, became much more widespread and commonplace over the following years.

3

LEOPARDI IN ROME

One fine autumn day I retraced the route Giacomo Leopardi took on his way to Rome more than a century before. He had set out in the autumn of 1822, at the age of twenty-four, and it was the first time he ever left the "despised tomb" of Recanati, his hometown in the Marche region.[1] The poet sought freedom but did not find it in Rome.

To reach the capital (of the Papal States, as Italy had not yet been unified) he spent nearly a week aboard a horse-drawn carriage that belonged to the Antici family, relatives on his mother's side. He ascended the Apennines along a tightly winding road carved into the bottom of a valley that still looks almost exactly like it did back then, nestled amid dense forests punctuated here and there by an ancient hermitage. He crossed the light-filled plains outside the Umbrian town of Colfiorito, descended toward Foligno, and visited the source of the Clitunno River.[2] The small group of travelers he was with stopped off in Spoleto and spent the night at the Albergo della Posta. From there he wrote his father Monaldo a letter that was so disjointed he felt obligated to follow up a few days later, after he had finally arrived in Rome, with another letter, swiftly sent to his brother Carlo: "Please have father read this letter, as I cannot be sure of what I wrote from Spoleto: you and he should both know that

I was writing from a table amid a bunch of scoundrels from Fabriano, rascals from Jesi, etc." From this correspondence we also learn that, even though he was barely into his twenties, Leopardi already enjoyed a degree of fame as a poet, which he rightly found gratifying. Another man seated at the same table of raucous folk from the vicinity was a priest who apparently liked to crack crude jokes. The letter describes him as follows: "A clever rascal of a priest, who was with the rest of them, tried to joke around with me as he had with the others; but believe you me, upon my first reply he suddenly changed his tone, and he and everyone with him became as kind and gentle as a bunch of meek sheep."

Leaving Spoleto he passed through Terni, Narni, Otricoli, Civita Castellana, and finally spotted Rome, whose ragged skyline of bell towers and domes dominated by Saint Peter's came into view as the road began to descend from the surrounding hills. The spectacle made a real impact on him, as he wrote to his sister Paolina (on December 3): "I myself saw the cupola, with my nearsighted eyes, from five miles away . . . and it appeared so very distinct, with its spherical shape and cross, looking much as the Apennines do from our hometown."

I followed his same route, but in the opposite direction, going from Rome to Recanati. I wanted to see the outlines of the mountains, the gorges, the stubbly ridges, the city walls that he saw—such as the "frightful" walls of Spoleto, which no longer fill anyone with dread, much as the enormous fortress known as the Rocca Albornoziana looming over the whole town no longer instills any fear. The fortress's history is quite strange. Pope Innocent VI had it built as a stronghold to defend the Church's territory. His ambassador, Cardinal Egidio Albornoz, summoned the architect Matteo di Giovanello (known as "il Gattapone") and commissioned him to design the castle. That was back in 1362, and for several centuries thereafter the fortress was the cornerstone of Spoleto's history. Its dominant position and the luxuries built into it made it fit for hosting many prominent guests, including Lucrezia Borgia, daughter of Pope Alexander VI, who was governess of the territory during the late fifteenth century, to name just one illustrious visitor. Later on the papal government turned it into a prison, and it remained in use even after Italy was unified, all the way up to 1982.

Italian history is so densely woven with echoes and interconnections that it is easy to go off on tangents, following multiple forking paths. Let's get back to Leopardi on his voyage toward Rome.

Obviously a lot has changed since his day, above all the quantity and density of buildings along his route. But, asphalt aside, I believe a few stretches of the road have remained exactly as they were, judging from the tight curves and steep rises and falls. And if you take a look around, here and there you can spot mountainous contours, patches of forests, meadows, and countrysides that must look much the way they did to him, with his poor vision and nearsighted eyes.

———————

Leopardi's idea was to settle into the capital and free himself of his father's suffocating tutelage. He was prepared to do anything, even enter the priesthood, to escape that prison. But in word only—and, as they say, actions speak louder than words. When Cardinal Consalvi, Pope Pius VII's secretary of state, replied to a request on behalf of Leopardi by offering him an opportunity to "don court garb"—that is, accept a mid-level position between the prelate and the secular authorities, which would have swiftly granted him a career in the Church—he declined in a fit of pride, or perhaps because of some deeper revulsion, writing that his life "had to remain as independent as possible."

Once in Rome he held up for about six months as a guest of his maternal cousins, who put him up in a chilly room on the mezzanine level or on the floor just below the attic—in any case, he wasn't staying in a nice room on the *piano nobile* with everyone else. The poor poet often complains in his letters of the chilblains he suffers that, once opened, remain painful sores that are very slow to heal.

The Anticis were a typical family under papal rule—neither too poor nor too rich, contented yet a bit bedraggled, unorganized and utterly devoid of any cultural interests, driven by sadly opaque tastes that Leopardi deemed "momentary, indefinable, unpredictable, incomprehensible." His reports of mealtime conversations with them paint a full picture of their narrow-mindedness.

From the letters to his siblings Carlo and Paolina we catch glimpses of a vast, chilly home with bare walls; as you read them you can picture waitstaff in threadbare livery and worn-down shoes, adept at pilfering leftovers from the Anticis' plates to make up for their meager wages.

The 945 letters of his entire correspondence, which tell the real story of his life, are filled with unforgettable characters and sketches. On November 25 he writes Carlo: "I'm forced to live life as our Antici relatives do—the kind of life that you and I, in our past discussions, had no idea of: neither what it consisted of nor how it kept afloat, nor, indeed, if it were any kind of life at all, in any sense of the word."

But life back in Recanati, in their fine ancestral home, couldn't have been that much different, aside from their father Monaldo's noteworthy erudition and the library he was so proud of, where Giacomo spent much of his youth.

Alfredo Panzini, a well-known novelist and lexicographer, wrote a great book titled *Casa Leopardi* on the home and its inhabitants, wherein he paints this expressive portrait of Count Monaldo: "One of the most singular men of his time, the throne and the altar—that is, the Church and the Sword—had few defenders as staunchly convinced as he . . . The count was neither tall nor short, neither handsome nor ugly; his face was clean-shaven, of course, and his wig was tied back. He always wore black, as if he were a member of the Ancien Régime, with short trousers even when longer ones were the fashion, black stockings, flat shoes with silver buckles, a white cravat . . . he took curious pride in wearing his sword each and every day, like an olden-day knight . . . He looked out on the world from his high palazzo atop Recanati. He constantly corresponded with all the most famous reactionaries, Jesuits, and other legitimists of the day."[3]

And yet, in his own way, during the suffocating years of the Restoration period that followed Napoleon's turbulent rule, Monaldo managed to be an affectionate father, at least as much as a man of his station could; he was unabashedly pro-Church, nostalgic, and fearful of any possible future. He loved his son, but never managed to understand him. As often happens, Giacomo reacted with mixed feelings, wavering between love and hate. In the end, judging from the letters' salutations, love won out. He addressed the first letters to "My father," then moved on to the less rigid "Dear father," and the last, most heartrending letters were lovingly addressed to "Dearest dad."[4]

Leopardi's feelings toward his mother, Adelaide Antici, were much more clear-cut. When Count Monaldo married her, in 1797, the young marquise was nineteen years old. She gave him ten children, five of whom survived past infancy, and soon became one of those "ladies of the house" with jingling keys latched to their belts, keeping a close eye on how much wine was in each bottle and how much food was in the larder. Monaldo, who punctually got her pregnant each year, was soon reduced to the status of a "closely watched, penniless ward." The prevailing atmosphere in the Leopardi household was rather gloomy. Paolina— poor, unpretty Paolina, oppressed by her parents, destined to become a melancholy old maid—saw her mother thus: "Everything I can see from my window is constantly under the surveillance of my mother, (who) incessantly roams the house, and is everywhere, at all hours."

In his *Zibaldone*, Leopardi provides an even harsher description of his mother:

> Not only was she unsympathetic with parents who lost their chil-
> dren in infancy, but she was profoundly and sincerely envious
> because they had flown to heaven without sin and freed their
> parents from the inconvenience of supporting them. Often find-
> ing herself in danger of losing her own children at the same age,
> she did not pray God to let them die, because her religion did not
> permit it, but she heartily enjoyed it . . . Nature had endowed this
> woman with a very sensitive character, and she had come to this
> [barbarous way of thinking] through religion alone.[5]

So how did Pope Pius VII's Rome look through Leopardi's eyes? Briefly, I'd say it struck him as a vast city that was poor in every sense of the term—culturally impoverished above all, with drawing rooms full of occasionally brilliant intellectuals who were nevertheless frightfully misinformed and provincial. On December 9, 1822, he writes his father:

> Intellectuals . . . honestly, I've met very few, and those few have quashed any desire I might have had to meet others . . . They seem to think the height of human knowledge—indeed, man's sole true science—is the study of antiquity . . . Philosophy, morality, politics, the sciences of the human heart, eloquence, poetry, literature, all such things are utterly foreign here . . . What's more, there is not a single Roman who really knows Latin and Greek; without those languages, just imagine how far one can get in his study of antiquity.

When he writes his brother Carlo about the learned historian Abbot Francesco Cancellieri, he describes him as follows: "Yesterday I went to see [Cancellieri], who is an absolute moron, a jabbering ass, the most boring, despair-inducing man on earth. He speaks of absurdly frivolous things with great interest, and of significant things with the greatest possible detachment."

Leopardi's perceptive take on Rome's cultural vacuity is even more striking than his description of the empty raving of that "jabbering ass" of an abbot. The well-informed philologist in him surfaces when he notes that anyone studying classical antiquity without a knowledge of classical languages is automatically barred from gaining any possible, true understanding of what it is he's studying.

That December he writes his sister Paolina:

> The frivolity of these beasts surpasses the bounds of credibility . . . This morning (to give you just one example) I overheard a group engaged in a weighty, long discussion of the excellent voice

of the high priest who had sung mass the day before yesterday, including talk of how he carried himself with such dignity while performing his function . . . The high priest replied that he had learned from years of working in the chapels and just watching, and that the exercise was very useful for him, so it is a necessary education for all their peers, and that he was not embarrassed in the least, and so on and so forth through countless other pleasantries. I later learned that many cardinals and other higher-ups were as happy as he was at the wonderful outcome of his singing at mass. Bear in mind that all conversations in Rome are of this sort, and I'm not exaggerating one bit.

But many other tales about Rome during that same period take a rather different tone. Stendhal, for one, who visited Rome a good six times, writes: "In Rome, spirited people have real zest . . . I can think of no other salons, in all of Europe, that I'd rather frequent than those in Rome."[6] So who is right, Leopardi or Stendhal? Is it possible, as nineteenth-century Italian critic Francesco de Sanctis maintained, that Leopardi's dark worldview was what tinged his Rome with such funereal overtones? Stendhal certainly provides proof of Romans' sense of humor, which Leopardi completely missed.

———

Stendhal, for instance, relates an amusing anecdote about an English tourist who rides into the Coliseum on horseback and sees a bunch of construction workers reinforcing its walls. That evening he tells his friends: "The Coliseum is the best thing I've seen in Rome thus far. I like it, and when they're finished building it, it will be truly magnificent."

But Leopardi occasionally speaks kindly when describing the people of Rome, the "hoi polloi" so dear to his fellow poet Giuseppe Gioachino Belli. In a letter to Carlo dated February 20, 1823, Leopardi describes this scene as he climbs the Janiculum to the tomb of Torquato Tasso and the church of Sant'Onofrio al Gianicolo:

Even the road leading up here prepares your spirit for emotional impressions. It is lined with craftsmen's houses, and is filled with the clamor of looms and other such instruments, as well as the songs of women and laborers hard at work. In this city— which is as lazy, wasteful, and unorganized as any capital—it is nevertheless nice to contemplate the idea that life can be collected, organized, and occupied by useful professions. Even the physiognomy and manners of the people as they meet up on the street have a certain something that makes them simpler and more human than others; they exhibit the habits and characters of people whose lives are based on truth, not on fiction—that is, they live by hard work, not by the scheming, posturing, and deceit practiced by most of this city's populace.

In a city where the poet sees "scheming and posturing" prevail (and he wasn't the only one either), he chooses to talk about the people he sees as dedicated to living a collected life devoted to "useful professions," people whose existence is based "on truth, not on fiction." This was certainly a conscious choice, since the great theater that is Rome offers onlookers a peek of absolutely any and everything.

———————————

The 2,279 sonnets penned by Giuseppe Gioachino Belli, which I briefly referred to above, deal with neither the city's intellectuals nor its bourgeoisie. He describes only Rome's commoners—indeed, he goes so far as to say he'd like to erect a monument to those commoners and their degraded, corrupt dialect. In the introduction to his sonnets he writes: "The form and matter herein will appear neither chaste nor occasionally pious, albeit undeniably devout and superstitious: but these are [Rome's] people, and it is they that I copy—not to offer up as a model, but rather to give the reader a faithful image of that which already exists and, moreover, has been abandoned to its own devices, with no betterment." This poor populace "abandoned to its own devices, with no betterment" is the flip side of the coin, the lesser relative of the bigoted, reactionary, equally superstitious, highly ignorant, neither chaste nor pious bourgeoisie that Leopardi found so displeasing. On December 16, 1822, he writes Carlo:

> Cardinal Malvasia laid his hands on ladies' breasts during confession, he was a debauchee of the highest order and sent the husbands and sons of the women who refused him off to the inquisition. Cardinal Brancadoro did similarly, as did all the cardinals (who are the most revolting people on earth), as did all the high priests, none of whom have any luck except with the help of women. Holy Pope Pius VII owes his rank as cardinal and pope to a Roman coquette ... and currently enjoys rambling on about the love affairs and other lascivious actions of his cardinals ... Some artist's daughter, I'm not sure whose, who was already [Count] Lebzeltern's favorite companion, used their relation to her advantage and now enjoys an annual pension of 800 scudi ... And Madam Magatti, the famous whore of Calcagnini, receives a pension of 700 scudi from the government.

These aren't just impressions, they're matters of fact. And anyway, the phenomenon of cardinals' (and other powerful men's) favorite women earning their "pensions" in bed was nothing new; that had been the case for centuries, it's the world's oldest profession—power has always brought with it such privileges, nor is it a given that they invariably end up doing damage. Giulia Farnese, for example, was fifteen when she became Pope Alexander VI's lover; he was fifty-eight. During one of their amorous encounters she put in a good word for her brother, twenty-five-year-old Alessandro Farnese, and the pope made him a cardinal. Alessandro in turn became Pope Paul III. During his reign he brought about several innovations: he agreed to recognize the Jesuit order, organized the Council of Trent, and instituted the Roman Inquisition. He also initiated the Church's unbridled nepotism, which happens to tie in with the events we'll read about in chapter 8, on Parma. Alessandro's favorites included his son Pier Luigi Farnese, probably his firstborn, to whom he granted governance of Parma and Piacenza in 1545 (the same year the Council of Trent began), officially separating those two cities from the Papal States. That marked the birth of a duchy that remained in the Farnese family's rule for over two centuries, and we'll read about how that developed in just a bit.

———————

In the meantime, I'll pose a worthwhile question: what kind of relationships did Leopardi have with women during his time in Rome? In a word, difficult, just as they were throughout his life. Although he was still young and not too ill at the time, as he later became, the poet couldn't have been any woman's idea of good company: he wasn't physically alluring, and it seems he often emitted a rather foul odor. You'd have to have gotten to know the man's immense soul before being able to love the man himself. But not many people were ready to make the effort to go beyond appearances, and fewer still were sufficiently perspicacious. As a result his relationships were primarily of the sort money could buy, and even those weren't easy to come by. On December 6 he wrote Carlo:

> Out for a stroll, at church, and even roaming the streets you find nary a hag who will so much as look at you . . . I've wandered all of Rome in the company of very handsome, well-dressed young men . . . It's as difficult to stop a woman on the streets of Rome as it is in Recanati—indeed, it's much more difficult, given the excessive frivolity and dissipation of these female animals who . . . love nothing more than strolling about, having fun God-only-knows how; they don't put out (believe me) unless you go to the same efforts necessary in any other town. It all comes down to the "public women," the prostitutes who I find to be more circumspect now than they ever were before, and remain just as dangerous, as you are well aware.

Being accustomed to Recanati, Leopardi was frightened by Rome's sheer size, even if it was still a modestly sized city compared with other European capitals. His worry, mistrust, and unhappiness in Rome were such that they almost overshadowed its great monuments, even as he strolled along Via dei Condotti and Via del Babuino from Piazza di Spagna to Piazza del Popolo. One of the few places that drew his attention was the Convent of Sant'Onofrio along the slopes of the Janiculum, where sixteenth-century Italian poet Torquato Tasso is buried. Even Chateaubriand, just a few years earlier, had been so struck by this special place that in his *Mémoires d'outre-tombe* ("Memoirs from Beyond the Grave") he wrote: "In case I have the good fortune of ending my days here, I've made arrangements to have a small chamber in Sant'Onofrio, right next to the room where Tasso died."

When I visited the convent, gardens, chapels, and scenic view out over Rome, I was overcome by a similar emotion, drawn in by the allure that, even today, remains almost fully intact. It must've been the same for Leopardi during his discouraging stay in Rome, when Sant'Onofrio made him, too, feel one of life's few true emotions. In a famous letter to Carlo dated February 20, 1823, he writes: "On Friday, February 15, I went to visit Tasso's tomb and wept. That was the first and only pleasure I felt in Rome." He goes on: "Many feel a sense of indignation when they see Tasso's remains, covered up and marked by nothing more than a small stone plaque measuring about a foot wide and high, set into a small side chapel . . . You can understand the mixed rush of emotions that comes about as you contemplate the sharp contrast between Tasso's sheer greatness and the utter modesty of his tomb."

Leopardi's time in Rome was troubled, and in late April, feeling defeated, he headed home. On April 26 he confided to his friend and fellow writer Pietro Giordani: "I'm no longer good for anything in this world."

An odd coincidence links Leopardi to Giuseppe Gioachino Belli, the Roman poet who had reluctantly married a rich widow fourteen years his elder and had a long love affair with the young marquise Vincenza Roberti (whom he affectionately called Cencia, a play on the pronunciation of her first name, as well as a riff on the word for *rag*). For several years Belli went to visit her in Morrovalle, the town where she vacationed each summer in the Marche region. She, too, was in a marriage of convenience with the municipal doctor, and could well be seen as an Italian Madame Bovary. So it's easy to imagine what a breath of fresh air Belli was—she couldn't have found his devotion displeasing—and the excitement he brought to town from a city like Rome. It's no accident that the sonnets he composed in Morrovalle (in September 1831) included some openly erotic verses. Just one brief example:

> Io sce vorrebbe franca una scinquina
> Che nn'addrizzi ppiù tu cor fa' l'occhietto,
> Che ll'altre cor mostrà la passerina.

> I'd be willing to bet a boatload of cash
> That you make more men hard with just a wink of your eye
> Than other girls do by flashing their pussy.
> ("A Nina," September 7, 1831)[7]

Morrovalle is just a few kilometers from Recanati, and young Vincenza and her family often visited the Leopardi household. Given this logistical premise, so to speak, many have wondered whether the two poets might have met each other at some point. There can be no certain answer, although it's possible they could have met in the winter of 1831–32 when Belli lived on Piazza Poli and Leopardi lived nearby, on Via dei Condotti. If indeed they did meet it was only in passing, which is a shame, because they had so much in common.

For starters, both were subjects of the papacy. Both were temperamentally inclined toward melancholy. Both fell victim to the narrow, backward-looking, discouraging cultural climate of papal Rome, which they sought to escape—each in his own way—through their written works. Who knows what they might've said to each other had they been able to sit down for a chat. But they were divided by age: Belli was seven years older, but outlived Leopardi by a quarter century. Leopardi died at thirty-nine, Belli at seventy-two. Leopardi was consumed by his sadness and illness, Belli was haunted by an oppressive hypochondria. To quote Belli: "I am as lonely here at home as time itself, which drags me with it." In response to a distant relative's letter that describes him as a "born poet," he writes that he feels instead like a "dead poet." Curiously enough, Leopardi used nearly the exact same words to describe himself, long before death freed him from his suffering on June 14, 1837. A few days later the author Antonio Ranieri wrote to a friend: "We mustn't regret that his suffering has come to an end; rather, we must regret that he spent 40 years wanting to die—that is the pain no medicine can alleviate."

4.

PALERMO, ON THE BORDER BETWEEN TWO WORLDS

Palermo is a 4-D city. In order to even barely touch upon its complexity, you have to view it in the context of its own highly unique spatiotemporal dimensions. Years ago Francesco Agnello—Baron of Siculiana, president of Amici della Musica, Palermo's main musical association, and a veritable legend in his day, dare I say a caliph of sorts—whispered to me in a flutelike timbre: "Our association patrols the farthest borders of the well-tempered tonal scale; just outside our doorstep lies the realm of Arabian pentatonic scales." Many Italian cities must be viewed in light of their spatiotemporal singularities, but in Palermo it's especially true: in this city, space is actually a dividing line between two worlds, maybe even three. Floating between the West, the Near-Eastern Greek and Byzantine worlds, and Islam, Palermo has lived alongside them all, taking something from each of them while at the same time giving up a part of itself. Its customs, social organization, mistrust of government, almost always unfounded hauteur, ferocious vendettas, hardheaded reticence, obsession with secrecy, and use of a dialect that is virtually unintelligible to outsiders—these are the results of a culture that has endlessly encountered and crossbred with various populations and conquerors. Many cities and regions throughout Italy have been dominated by foreign armies (up until the mid-twentieth century, anyway), and the same goes for Palermo and Sicily even more so: this is the land that has bordered the territories (and been a colony) of the Angevins, Aragonese, Spaniards, Savoyards, Austrians, Neapolitan Bourbons, and, most recently, "Italians."

When, in Giuseppe Tomasi di Lampedusa's novel *The Leopard*, the Piedmontese representative Chevalley di Monterzuolo offers the Prince of Salina a seat as appointed member of the senate, the prince declines, replying: "The sin which we Sicilians never forgive is simply that of 'doing' at all. We are old, Chevalley, very old. For more than twenty-five centuries we've been bearing the weight of a superb and heterogeneous civilization, all from outside, none made by ourselves, none that we could call our own... for two thousand and five hundred years we've been a colony."[1] In its status as "colony" the island experienced many abrupt shifts under various dominant powers. In a period of just over twenty years in the early eighteenth century it changed hands three times: in 1713 Savoy Duke Victor Amadeus II took it, then in 1720 it went to the Austrians, and in 1735 the Spaniards took it back under the Bourbon dynasty. Finally, in 1860, Garibaldi showed up with *i Mille*, his "thousand" supporting troops.

Centuries before, the Phoenicians, Carthaginians, Greeks, Romans, Berbers, Normans, and probably many others had chosen this island as their seat of power, stationing their headquarters under the shade of its palm trees, amid the scented air of its orange groves, the sound of its murmuring fountains, and the rush of waves breaking on its incomparable beaches. This prolonged servitude had its price—Palermo's history is rife with risks and opportunities, and only rarely did the latter gain the upper hand.

Its permeable, worn-out social fabric has reacted to the vexations of power in the only way it could, considering the circumstances and traditions shared by all oppressed populations: by cultivating the art of the vendetta—in other words, by establishing a parallel system of justice.

Anyway, before the idea of entrusting the legitimate use of force exclusively to the government, attempts at reestablishing some kind of "justice" by one's own hand—to spontaneously remedy all wrongs and to establish local heroes—was a common practice everywhere. Robin Hood, a character hovering somewhere between historic fact, legend, and faithful superstition, is one of the most well-known incarnations of the phenomenon: part bandit, part philanthropist, in the most popular version of the tale he lives like an elf in the woods, suddenly popping out to steal from the rich and give to the poor.

Provence, too, has its own hero hovering between history and legend, an analogous myth based on the real-life man known as Gaspard de Besse (named after his hometown, Besse-sur-Issole) who became known by a catchy couplet: *"Brigand pour la France, héros pour la Provence."*[2]

After recruiting a gang of men ready for anything from the narrow alleyways of Toulon sometime around 1775, Gaspard became a bandit. Posted along the town's main streets, his gang preyed upon the carriages of the wealthy, especially nonlocals. Gaspard continually changed his appearance and played pranks on the town's gendarmes. Such a tumultuous life soon burned him out: Betrayed by one of his own, he ended up hanged in the main square of Aix-en-Provence alongside his assistant, Joseph Augias, an ill-fated forebear of yours truly. Both were barely twenty years old when they went to the gallows.

And in Palermo? It, too, has its own Robin Hood, probably an ancient myth that became widespread in the eighteenth century. We'll hear about that in a bit. But beforehand I should explain why the local version of this archetype, unlike his parallels in England and Provence, acquired such unique and enduring characteristics.

Both Palermo and Sicily in general have their own unique religiosity, wherein displays of pain and death are paramount. Guido Piovene's unforgettable book *Viaggio in Italia* ("Journey Through Italy," 1957) describes the strange customs of this "Arab, baroque, dark, fantastic" city:

Here [children] receive gifts from the dead instead of from Santa
Claus, and kids express their wishes in letters written to their
dead uncles, grandmothers, fathers, or other late relatives. The
dead then give them, in addition to toys, dolls made of colorful
candy. Local shops are full of these dolls—paladins, jacks, fairies,
Amazonesque damsels on horseback—which the children then
gnaw on, breaking them apart limb by limb.[3]

Death is a constant and widespread presence, or perhaps I should
say mood or climate. This death is infused with the flavors of ancient
Spanish culture, highly baroque—it is the atrocious death of martyred
virgins, of Madonnas pierced by swords, of people flayed, burned at
the stake, hanged. It is the death of the immense religious processions parading down Sicilian streets each Good Friday leading up to
Easter, frightfully lumbering forward atop the shoulders of young men
crushed by tons of wood, plaster, ornaments, capes, candles, and ex-
votos, between a riveted and bewildered crowd of people making the
sign of the cross, staring at the statue, and counting its wounds, be it
a grieving Mary or an urn containing a realistic statue of Christ drip-
ping with blood, contorted in agony, just like the faces of the flagellants
whipping themselves as they march with the procession until blood
gushes from their wounds.

Palermo is also the place where the Inquisition's tribunals organized the most successful autos-da-fé.[4] Pietro Zullino—whose guide
to the city's mysteries and pleasures has never been translated into
English, and has become hard to find even in Italian—reminds us that
the Palermitan version of the auto-da-fé swiftly became a colossally
popular form of spectacle, a veritable street fair of sorts. Bleachers were
set up to seat prominent spectators, who festively ate and drank as they
awaited the executions: "For months afterward the chit-chat in noble
Palermitans' mansions focused on the physical and moral strength displayed by the condemned, much as Spaniards spoke of the brave bulls
of the *corrida*."[5] On August 15, 1573, a Muslim, a presumed Muslim, and

an old man "who maintained that the soul dies along with the body" were all burned at the stake together. The crowd's jubilation was enormous. The magnificence of such shows often struck even the Spaniards with a sense of admiration.

The bureaucratic machinery of the Santo Uffizio ("Holy Office," as the Inquisition's main institution was referred to in Italy) was merciless, relentless, and remarkably far-reaching. According to Zullino's accounts, in 1577 Viceroy Don Marcantonio Colonna calculated that no fewer than twenty-four thousand inhabitants of Sicily were officially working for the Inquisition, including fifteen thousand in Palermo alone. Altogether they were the so-called *Famiglia dell'Inquisizione*, the "Family of the Inquisition"; as Dominican spies, they enjoyed the privilege of full tax exemption. Comparisons with equally extravagant present-day regional institutions would appear to be warranted.

In the winter of 2012 Lisbon's Museu Nacional de Arte Antiga hosted an exhibition titled *"Cuerpos de Dolor"* ("Bodies of Sorrow"), featuring religious imagery in sixteenth-century Iberian culture, produced at the height of the Counterreformation and shaped by its religious tribunals and executions. It showcased statues tormented by pain, symbols of boundless affliction, a dark spirituality embodied in vivid visions of shaking virgin saints, in the severity of religious orders where obedience was to be observed *perinde ac cadaver*, "in the manner of a corpse," a term used to describe disciples' submission to their spiritual masters. This was the height of suffering, and the great seventeenth-century painter Francisco de Zurbarán captured it in his crucifixion scenes, where the body of Christ loses all sacred stylizations to become the mere cadaver of the executed, contorted in pain, nailed to his cross.

This was precisely the period when—in Spain and the many territories controlled by the Spanish crown, as well as Rome—the custom of religious processions became common. Such processions invariably included the display of a martyred body or the ecstatic rapture of a hermit staring into the empty eye sockets of a skull, spectacles that quickly became tools for putting the crowd on guard and, ultimately, for mass conversions.

———————————

From then on, year after year, these spectacular processions have continued to fill the streets of many southern Italian towns, with Palermo providing one of the best backdrops for such festivities.

The suffering of saints and martyrs contrasted with the fleeting pleasures of worldly life, the admonition of death and at the same time its alluring draw, to the point where it pops up even in colorful sweetmeats made for children. Such depictions offer the image of a severe god, ready to punish even the slightest transgression. But these weren't unique to Sicily. The American historian and mathematician Morris Kline wrote that in the seventeenth century, "Priests and ministers affirmed that nearly everyone went to hell after death, and described in greatest detail the hideous, unbearable tortures that awaited the eternally damned . . . God was presented not as the savior but as the scourge of mankind . . . Christians were urged to spend their time meditating upon eternal damnation in order to prepare themselves for life after death."[6] Such beliefs perpetuated the ancient role of religious faith as a force for restraining human passions. In one of his satirical dramas the ancient (fifth-century B.C.E.) Greek Sophist Critias outlined his famous theory that the gods were invented precisely to keep human behavior in check. Polybius, a second-century B.C.E. Greek historian who admired the rise of the Romans, wrote that the ancients had inculcated their populace with the idea of gods and an afterlife for precise reasons. Such ideas, he claimed, help to hold back the passions of the masses. He concluded by observing that modern thinkers trying to dispel such illusions were utterly ignored. Such ideas gradually fell into decline elsewhere, but held on tight in certain places, including Palermo and Sicily. It is as if such places needed an extra injection of admonishment in order to contain people's comportment, holding them back within the bounds of reciprocal tolerance.

The story of Saint Rosalia, Palermo's patron saint and protectress, is deeply significant. Rosalia was born in Palermo in 1128, daughter of the Norman count Sinibaldo della Quisquina, who claimed he was a descendant of Charlemagne. Rosalia's mother, Maria Guiscardi, also boasted of connections to the Norman court. Young Rosalia took the cloth at a young age, and then became a hermit on Mount Pellegrino, where she remained in solitary meditation until her death. She might easily have been forgotten in the seventeenth century, a period of harsh pestilence, famine, and poverty, were it not for the fact that the plague ravaged Palermo as well. Someone, apparently a plague-stricken woman named Girolama Gatto, claimed that in a dream (or perhaps in a feverish delirium) she had seen a young woman pointing her toward a cave on Mount Pellegrino. The cave was somehow found and, after a series of excavations, the bones of the pious young woman were also discovered. The Jesuits took up the task of verifying their authenticity. Since genetic analysis was not yet available, the research was entrusted to the goodwill and proven faith of a few doctors. On February 22, 1625, Rosalia's bones were turned over to the city council and, the following June, the virgin who had died five centuries before was proclaimed a saint. According to Zullino, the cult of Saint Rosalia's worshipers can be traced back to her connections to the imperial family of Frederick II, the Swabian, Norman, man, and king who for thirty years, from 1220 to 1250, had made Palermo the capital of the Holy Roman Empire, the political center of the world.

Even today it is commonly believed that Rosalia's remains, carried in a solemn procession through the city streets, are what stopped the terrible plague. Her cult became popular enough to eclipse her four predecessors (Saints Christina, Agatha, Oliva, and Nympha), and the veneration she enjoys elevated her to a level that is elsewhere reserved solely for Mary, Mother of Jesus.

———————

The story of Saint Rosalia is just one more instance reinforcing the importance Palermo grants its dead and their remains. The city also happens to be home to one of the largest and most macabre collections of mummies in Europe, and perhaps in the whole world. Somewhere between eight and ten thousand corpses lie at rest—in open coffins or swaying from the ceilings and walls in the dramatic, grotesque, obscene poses imposed by death and the passage of time—their jaws agape in one last mute cry, skulls half covered by strips of old skin, limbs contorted. Some are dressed in penitential sackcloth, some in evening gowns or gala uniforms. They include ladies in bonnets and hoop skirts, friars, merchants, baronesses, petty-bourgeois officials, virgins who died on the eve of their wedding in the gowns they never had a chance to wear while alive, now reduced to shreds, small children, and even babies. This army of the dead reminds the living of the fate that awaits us all.

The convent whose basement boasts this terrifying theater belongs to the Capuchin monks, one of the minor Franciscan orders, named for the hood (*cappuccio*) they added to the simple tunic worn by Saint Francis of Assisi, the order's founder. It is an annex of the church of Santa Maria della Pace in the Cuba neighborhood, and dates back to the seventeenth century. The first person to be buried there, at the very end of the sixteenth century, was a friar known as Silvestro da Gubbio. Many other friars followed, and then secular folk who wanted to leave a visible trace of their existence, including the possibility of family visits, were also included. The structure's microclimate favored the processes of embalming and mummification, but they were nevertheless rather costly, which explains why almost all the remains you see there are of aristocrats or well-heeled, upper-middle-class gentry. The deceased were eviscerated and then laid out in a dehydrating mummification chamber for up to a year; after that the remains were washed with vinegar or arsenic, filled with straw, sewn back up, dressed in their Sunday best, and set up along the walls, right next to or below whoever had preceded them on their final voyage.

———————

In many cultures the horrible spectacle of the body's postmortem decay is hidden from view. The baroque tastes of the seventeenth century, however, dwelled on it, and put it on display with the pretense of using it as an admonishment. At the entrance to another cemetery run by the Capuchins—the catacombs on Via Veneto in Rome—a brutal cautionary greeting reads: *"Ciò che fummo tu sei, ciò che siamo sarai"* ("We were what you are, and we are what you will be").

In Ecclesiastes, one of the bible's wisdom books, the phrase *"Vanitas vanitatum et omnia vanitas"* is repeated twice over—"vanity of vanities, all is vanity." The sentence can be read in multiple ways, and one radical reinterpretation of it can be found at the end of Giacomo Leopardi's canto "A se stesso" ("To Himself"), in the famous and inconsolable conclusion: *"l'infinita vanità del tutto"* ("the infinite vanity of it all").[7]

In art history the term *vanitas* refers to a still-life featuring the symbols of life's fleeting nature as portrayed through many objects, although a human skull remains one of the most eloquent and immediate. It is with skull in hand that Hamlet, in Shakespeare's tragedy, reflects on the brevity of life. The Clown turns to the prince and says: "This same skull, sir, was Yorick's skull, the king's jester." The revelation triggers Hamlet's memory: "Here hung those lips that I have kiss'd I know not how oft. Where be your gibes now? your gambols? your songs? your flashes of merriment, that were wont to set the table on a roar? Not one now, to mock your own grinning? quite chop-fallen? Now, get you to my lady's chamber, and tell her, let her paint an inch thick, to this favour she must come; make her laugh at that."[8]

The vanitas Hamlet performs—if we can call it that—is also interesting because of how it juxtaposes death and Yorick's folly, albeit a folly that was at least partially put on for the king's amusement, or in order to voice inconvenient truths by passing them off as buffoonery. Pirandello uses this same expedient in *Henry IV*, arguably the best play he ever wrote.

Set in the early twentieth century, it centers on a nobleman who takes part in a masquerade held as a group horseback ride. He dresses up as Henry IV, and is knocked off his horse by a rival as they both vie for the same woman. He hits his head and faints, and when he comes to he actually believes he's Henry IV, Holy Roman Emperor, not least because a few friends and family members play along. After many years he finally returns to his senses, but he keeps pretending he's crazy in order to get back at his rival with impunity, since the man had both struck him from his horse and stolen his beloved. The relationships between insanity and normality, as well as fiction and truth, play a central role in Pirandello's theatrical works. For example, we witness another feigned insanity in *Cap and Bells,* where the act of pretending serves to keep up appearances, thereby saving the reputation of the bourgeois protagonist. And Leonardo Sciascia, who was as Sicilian a writer as Pirandello, takes up the same theme in his aforementioned short essay "The Crazy Cord," where he quotes quips from both *Cap and Bells* and *Henry IV*:

> "You see, *Signora*, there is in all of us, something like a musical instrument—an instrument which has three strings or cords: the cords of intellect, civility, and madness."[9]

> "All right, then, I'm a loony! Well, by God, on your knees, then! Kneel! I command you to get down on your knees and touch the ground with your foreheads, three times. Get down! That's what you do when you're confronted by a maniac!"[10]

That essay was later collected in a book of the same title in which Sciascia outlines and explores his thoughts about *sicilitudine*, "Sicilian-ness," or rather that special mixture of contradictions, falsities, and exasperated, belted-out truths he considers hallmarks of the Palermitan personality, and the Sicilian character in general. Underneath it all, he notes, lies a geographic factor: "Sicily is an island in the center of the Mediterranean, but its strategic importance, so to speak, as the keystone that assured its conquerors' power and dominion was, paradoxically, mirrored by vulnerabilities in its own defenses, and a sense of insecurity . . . that exposed it to all kinds of military and political attacks." Later on, returning to the eternal subject of this small island set smack in the middle of the trade routes crisscrossing the world's oldest sea, he adds: "That sea washed all sorts of people onto Sicily's shores: Berbers, Norman knights, Lombard soldiers, Charles of Anjou's greedy Neapolitan barons, adventurers fleeing the 'miserly poverty of Catalonia,' the armadas of Charles V and Louis XIV, the Austro-Hungarians, Garibaldi's troops, the Piedmontese, the troops of Patton and Montgomery; and over many centuries it suffered the ongoing scourge of Algerian pirates, who swooped in to steal its goods and its inhabitants. In the process, the island's 'historic' fear has become an 'existential' fear."[11]

One of the most compelling tales of madness, which both Sciascia and Andrea Camilleri have written about, involves the Real Casa dei Matti ("Royal Home for the Insane"), an asylum founded in Palermo by baron Pietro Pisani, a man motivated by the loftiest ideals of progress who happened to have a slight streak of madness of his own. A famous example involves his disdain at the locals' vocal dismissal of Mozart's *Così fan tutte* at the Real Teatro Carolino, Palermo's main stage at the time. Nearly fifty years later, to make up for the offense committed almost half a century before, Pisani had the company mount a performance of *The Magic Flute* paid for entirely out of his own pocket, and at which he seems to have been the sole spectator. He also frequently signed his letters by inserting the title "Sicily's Number-One Madman" before his official title and name. Basically, Camilleri notes: "Baron Pisani is the classic example of a Sicilian who, as Pirandello described in *Cap and Bells*, has three cords in his head—the serious or intellectual one, the civil one, and the crazy one—and therefore acts according to whichever cord he feels it opportune to pull at any given moment."[12]

As chance would have it, Pisani ended up turning his ties to madness into a veritable profession. Actually, chance had little to do with it, because in 1824 Lieutenant General Marquis Pietro Ugo made Pisani director of the insane asylum then held in the convent of the Discalced Carmelites. At the time, insanity was often considered divine punishment for past sins, even sins supposedly committed by some long-dead ancestor. This superstitious belief partially explains the frightful conditions those unfortunate souls were kept in. But, to be absolutely clear, the conditions in mental institutions under the Kingdom of Italy and, later, the Republic of Italy, were not all that different, and real reform was only instituted by Franco Basaglia, a prominent psychiatrist, in 1978.

Pisani himself left us this terrifying report:

> Verily, had I heard about it from others instead of seeing it with my own eyes, I would never have believed the state of abandon in which I found this place. It resembled more a menagerie for wild beasts than a residence for human beings. As I looked about inside the narrow edifice a few dark, tiny, squalid cells came into view: one part was for madmen, the other part was for madwomen. Maniacs, demented folk, berserks, and melancholics were all locked up together, thrown in with no distinction. Some of them were filthy, and lay on the floor atop a bit of straw; most were on the bare floor. Many were completely nude, some were covered in tatters, others were wrapped in rags; all of them were chained up like animals, covered in irksome insects, pained by hunger, thirst, cold air, hot air; all suffered mockery, torments, and beatings. These hapless souls were worn out, and nearly destroyed. Their eyes stared at any man who suddenly appeared before them and, consumed by the fear felt when they suspected new sufferings, they suddenly surged with fury and rage. Then, reassured by the compassionate gestures of those who pityingly looked on, they achingly asked for mercy, showing their tight shackles, and the bruises from all the blows that covered their entire bodies.[13]

Pisani fought so hard to improve mental patients' conditions that, just a few months after his appointment as director, one of Palermo's newspapers, the *Giornale d'Intendenza*, proclaimed: "The mental hospital … under the care of a specialist full of philanthropic ideas, has greatly improved and, thanks to an increase in resources, is already well on its way to reaching a degree of perfection that will, one day, surely allow it to rank among the best such establishments in all Europe." The increase in resources primarily meant more money, but it also meant more doctors and clearer instructions aimed at reaching precise goals, set according to a new therapeutic and "cultural" vision. Incredible as it may seem, some of the measures taken by Pisani in 1825 anticipated the steps Dr. Basaglia had to introduce all over again in the 1970s: a ban on beatings, chains, straitjackets and other forced restraints, and the combination of treatments (in truth, rather scant) with an increase in recreation and leisure time.

Pisani was a meritorious representative of an enlightened nobility dedicated to ideals of secular, civic-minded progress that rejected the fatalistic concept of madness as a form of divine punishment, bringing it back to the realm of mental pathology, where it properly belongs. And Pisani didn't stop there; his humane instincts extended from the treatment of the insane to other fields—for example, he saved the sculpted metopes of Selinunte from being shipped abroad, thereby triggering a rethinking of the island's approach to its archaeological heritage, which led to legislative changes during Bourbon rule of the island.

Follies, extravagances, and eccentricities abound in Sicily and its capital. Sometimes they act for good, other times not. Perhaps the most riveting example of the latter is the infamous case of Giuseppe Giovanni Battista Vincenzo Pietro Antonio Matteo Balsamo, better known as Alessandro, Count of Cagliostro, or simply Cagliostro. I won't even try to sum up his dramatic life as a sharp-witted scoundrel, forger, huckster, miracle worker, and thief. He pursued far too many activities and lived in too many places to name—all this after fleeing from Palermo, where he had been born to poor parents in 1743 and partially orphaned when his father died soon thereafter. He made up for his humble beginnings by turning a bunch of tall tales into an autobiography he lived out to the fullest, weaving together Near-Eastern legends with his presumed magical powers and quasi-miraculous abilities. He spoke of having spent his childhood in Mecca and of having learned the secrets of ancient Egyptian priests, as well as the art of transforming metals and the alchemical principles that allowed him to turn lead into gold.

We mustn't forget that in the mid-eighteenth century ancient Egypt was still considered more of a mythical place than an actual geographic location. It was only after Napoleon's expedition (1798–1801) that Europeans began to get a clearer picture of the area and its ancient civilizations. For Cagliostro, Egypt must have seemed like a lucrative mirage of a place, an easy, low-risk ruse. He went so far as to invent an ancient Egyptian Masonic Lodge and made himself its "Gran Cofto," something like a high priest. The goal of his so-called Egyptian Rite was no less than the regeneration of humankind so it might be brought back to its pure state predating "original sin." He honed the idea in Lyon, where he founded the Mother Lodge called "La Sagesse Triomphante" (in keeping with the enlightenment zeitgeist, which he'd quickly intuited). The initiation rites and mysterious ritual practices, which he also dreamed up, combined with the magnetism he must certainly have exuded to enthrall intellectuals and leaders across Europe. He traveled absolutely everywhere, from faraway Russia to Malta, Lisbon, and London, sometimes sharing a table with kings at court, other times locked away in prison.

In Rome in 1768, when he was twenty-five, he married seventeen-year-old Lorenza Serafina Feliciani, who also had humble roots, and was illiterate to boot. But she was shrewd and up for anything, even prostitution when necessary, and she was a perfect honey trap that drew in countless suckers. In London, for example, in cahoots with her husband, she seduced a naive Quaker, and Cagliostro burst in on them in the heat of passion. Feigning indignation at his wife's betrayal, Cagliostro called for the man's life to repay her lost honor, but then happily accepted the man's offer of monetary compensation instead. The crafty young woman seconded her husband in much more complicated schemes as well. After changing her name to Princess Serafina and then Queen of Sheba, she proclaimed herself Grand Mistress of the Initiation Rite, which was a special Masonic Lodge reserved for women, who—back then, as today—were not allowed to join the Freemasons.

Cagliostro met a terrible end. After a close, albeit marginal, brush with the infamous Affair of the Diamond Necklace, which some consider one of the key causes of the 1789 French Revolution, and after having dodged the law countless times all over Europe, he fell into a snare set by the pope's secret service. One day in Rome two papal spies strolled up to him and requested permission to join his Masonic Lodge. Cagliostro began the usual initiation ceremony without paying much attention to the fact that it was in violation of local law, which in the papal territories forbade any association with freemasonry, punishable by death. The two spies promptly took off without paying the agreed-upon membership fee, giving Cagliostro a dose of his own medicine. This was back in 1789, a fateful year. His wife Serafina, who had been his accomplice on so many adventures, realized the tough spot they were in and quickly denounced him to a parish priest, who then sent notice to the Santo Uffizio, which in turn got the papal higher-ups involved. Pope Pius VI immediately summoned his secretary of state and several other cardinals. On the night of December 27 Cagliostro was arrested and locked up in Castel Sant'Angelo; his wife was confined in the convent of Sant'Apollonia; and a poor Capuchin friar Cagliostro had recruited into his lodge was detained in the convent of Ara Coeli, on the Capitoline Hill.

The charges against him were numerous and weighty: he was accused of being a freemason, a warlock, a heretic, a blasphemer— against God, the Virgin Mary, the saints, and all Catholicism—in addition to accusations of forgery, crookery, slander, and sedition. It was

more than enough to send him to the gallows. So how did the brilliant
swindler defend himself? He pled insanity, so to speak, acting crazy
enough that his case went from being one against a nobleman and
innovative genius to one against a mere charlatan. His lawyer, Carlo
Costantini, presented him as a poor, low-level con artist, a fraudster
who eked out a living by selling illusions, just as any con man would.
Sure, he was an undeniable cheat, but on a small scale, nothing that the
Church should worry about, and he certainly was no heretic (the grav-
est charge), since he displayed a clear lack of even minimal theological
knowledge. As for his wife, well, she was just a two-bit whore whose
accusations held no water whatsoever.

On April 7, 1791, the Santo Uffizio issued its sentence, which included the stipulation: "Granting extraordinary grace, his sentence is
to be commuted from the [death] penalty to a secular authority over-
seeing a life term in prison, to be served in a fortress jail, where he
is to be closely watched, with no possibility of pardon. And, having
abjured his status as formal heretic upon entering detention [in Castel
Sant'Angelo], the [papal] censors are to absolve him, enjoining due
penitence." The chosen fortress was one of the most terrifying prisons
of the time, the Rocca di San Leo, in the Apennine foothills southeast
of San Marino. The cell he was sent to was like a tomb. Referred to
as *il pozzetto*, "the little well," it was a tiny oubliette with a minuscule
window, its sole furnishing a bare table. The walls had no doors, just a
hatch in the ceiling, opened solely to lower the prisoner down by rope
and then promptly sealed shut again. Cagliostro tried one last trick: he
began acting highly devout so that his guards, who peeked through the
hatch every now and then, would find him deep in prayer, beating his
chest, drawing sacred imagery on the walls, or ecstatically staring at a
crucifix they had allowed him to keep. He ultimately refused food as
a final act of penance. In that grim place, passing day after day with no
hope of release, what started out as fakery probably turned into real
madness, from which death finally freed him in August 1795, at the age
of fifty-two.

His wife, whose testimony had been a deciding factor, was absolved in her own trial, but she never again left the convent. The hapless Capuchin was sentenced to ten years' detention in the aforementioned convent of Ara Coeli.

When Cagliostro's body was found dead, after three days of agony, the chaplain of San Leo wrote:

> He remained in that apoplectic state for three days, during which time he seemed obstinate about his errors, and would hear nothing of repentance nor of confession. At the end of those three days the blessed Lord, justly disdainful of such an ungodly blasphemer who had so arrogantly violated holy law, abandoned him to his sin and left him to die in that miserable state, setting a terrifying example for anyone tempted to intemperately indulge in worldly pleasures and the delirium of modern philosophy.[14]

In 2003 a brilliantly unhinged semimockumentary film titled *Il ritorno di Cagliostro* ("Cagliostro's Return"), by Daniele Ciprì and Franco Maresco, was released. Its plot centers on a failed director, Pino Grisanti, who casts an alcoholic old Hollywood star, Erroll Douglas, as the legendary Cagliostro. At one point the elderly actor unexpectedly jumps out a window and dives headfirst onto the ground. Although he doesn't die, he does go crazy, and spends the rest of his days in a mental institution. Grisanti's made-up filmography includes an earlier film titled *Gli invincibili Beati Paoli* ("The Invincible Beati Paoli"). It is no accident that Ciprì and Maresco brought these two legends— Cagliostro and his lunacy, and the secret medieval sect of the Beati Paoli—together in the same film. Both are mighty, long-lived myths that almost invariably surface in discussions of Palermo and Sicily.

In 1909 the Palermitan author and journalist Luigi Natoli began publishing work in the newspaper *Giornale di Sicilia* under the pseudonym William Galt. What began as a feuilleton grew into 239 episodes published between 1909 and January 1910, a serial novel titled *I beati*

Paoli ("The Beati Paoli"). It was an enormous success and its publisher, Flaccovio, kept it in print for many years, through countless editions. In the preface to one of the later editions, Umberto Eco draws a few distinctions between historic versus popular fiction. He sets Natoli's text squarely in the latter category, seeing Alexandre Dumas, Eugène Sue, and Pierre-Alexis Ponson du Terrail as his forerunners. The jumble of interconnected events is complex enough that I won't even try to sum it up here, but the same edition also includes a noteworthy essay by Rosario La Duca on the history of the sect and its attendant legends.[15]

———————

The Beati Paoli were members of a secret sect that has inspired countless imaginations and been extensively written about. Some believe the sect was founded as far back as the twelfth century, and its aim was to right the wrongs committed against the poor. Basically, it is believed that the sect was a private response, outside all extant laws, to the afflictions caused by the nobles whose feudal rule included, among other things, the power of administering justice—which, of course, they did in whatever way they saw fit. According to Natoli/Galt, the cloaked and hooded Beati Paoli convened in an underground tribunal beneath the streets of Palermo's Del Capo neighborhood. Its labyrinthine tunnels were part of a fourth-century early Christian necropolis dug between the church of Santa Maruzza and a street now known as Vicolo degli Orfani ("Orphan Lane"). And there actually is a spacious chamber twelve feet underground, complete with seating carved into the stone walls. This dark, mysterious place easily lends itself to vivid imagination, and it is not hard to picture a secret tribunal passing down sentences amid flickering torchlight.

No one has been able to prove whether the stories surrounding the Beati Paoli have any basis in historic truth or were simply born of popular legend and handed down through the generations as part of a rich oral tradition. The only thing we know for sure is that, from the late nineteenth century onward, a conviction that the sect and its avengers really existed spread throughout Sicily.

But in cases like this, historic factuality bears very little importance. As with all religious matters, what really counts is people's need to believe, the consolation they get from having faith that somewhere, be it some underground crypt or ancient palazzo, there are men who take action in order to reestablish a semblance of justice capable of making up for the many wrongs they have suffered. The reader of popular fiction, as Eco writes in his preface, "looks to the pages of fantasy for consolation, for portrayals of a justice carried out by others, capable of making him forget how little justice he enjoys in his own life." Similarly, a few years before Eco, Antonio Gramsci had written that serial novels stir the imagination of the everyday man, thereby helping to compensate for his "(social) inferiority complex."[16]

According to another popular hypothesis, the Beati Paoli were actually predecessors of the mafia, to such a degree that they not only acted as protectors of the weak, but were also hit men who murdered for money. La Duca denies any such connection, asserting instead that the mafia sprang from agrarian roots in the early nineteenth century, just as the feudal system began to crumble, and that the Beati Paoli had already been long defunct by then. But ties between the myth of the Beati Paoli and the historic reality of the mafia can nevertheless be found. As early as 1876 two enlightened politicians, Leopoldo Franchetti and Sidney Sonnino, had noticed the phenomenon. They coauthored a major report on Sicily's political and administrative conditions that for the first time gave a full picture of how the island actually functioned.[17] According to their description, the mafia stemmed from "a medieval sentiment among those who believed they could provide for the safety of themselves and their possessions through the use of their own wealth and personal influence, independent of any system of authority or law," a sentiment taken to its extreme in the tradition of *omertà*, the code of silence that says a man's primary duty is to regain justice by his own hand for the wrongs done him.

A mistrust of government no matter who runs it, an eternal sense of resignation counterbalanced by rapid vendetta, and the need to adapt to any circumstance are all key components of the mafia's modus operandi. Indeed, such descriptions appear not only in countless essays on the topic, but in the incredibly rich Sicilian literary tradition as well.

The most obvious example is *The Leopard*, Giuseppe Tomasi di Lampedusa's masterpiece published posthumously in 1958, whose plot centers on its characters' sense of resignation during the transition from the Bourbon reign to the unification of Italy under the Savoy monarchy. But, many years before the publication of *The Leopard*, another novel dealt with the same subject matter—Federico De Roberto's *The Viceroys*,[18] published in 1894. Its powerfully realist prose recounts the history of the Uzeda family. Giving a friend of his a preview of the work, the author described it as follows: "It is the story of a great family composed of 14 or 15 people, men and women, each stronger and more extravagant than the next. My first working title was *Vecchia razza* ("Ancient Pedigree"), which captures my ultimate goal of chronicling the physical and moral decay of an exhausted bloodline."[19]

The plot involves several generations, and concludes with the story of Consalvo Uzeda, son of Prince Giacomo XIV, who scales the rungs of political power. Even though he is a fiercely pro-Bourbon reactionary at heart, he senses the winds of change and pretends to be a leftist, thereby winning election as a representative in parliament. The Sicilian proverb *Chinati giunco che passa la piena* ("Bend like a reed with the floodwater for this, too, shall pass"—in other words, go with the flow) perfectly describes this mind-set.

———

Not everything, nor everyone, is like that. But the fact that such sentiments so frequently turn up in literature—from Pirandello to Verga, Sciascia, and Tomasi di Lampedusa—reveals certain symptoms. In his preface to the biography of Giuseppe Tomasi di Lampedusa, Salvatore Savoia, a scholar of Sicilian history, writes that early on Sicilians welcomed Italian unification with real enthusiasm. But all too quickly, "All illusions of miraculous redemption soured into a sense of failure, or were so diminished by the march of history as to become unrecognizable. And Sicily—a place that has remained staunchly ahistorical throughout its long history, spent centuries lauding its latest conqueror, and clung to its fundamental skepticism while at the same time ever-ready to embrace new illusions—remained utterly immobile, irredeemable even. So has it been since time immemorial, and so it will remain, perhaps forevermore. Up until today, at any rate."[20]

5.

THE DISCOVERY OF
THE SOUTH

In 1860 Luigi Carlo Farini (1812–66), a distinguished political moderate who had served as minister of the interior, followed Savoy King Victor Emmanuel II to Naples. On October 26 he was a witness at the so-called Handshake of Teano, whereby Giuseppe Garibaldi handed the regions of southern Italy that he and his troops had wrested from the Neapolitan Bourbons over to the king.

The following day Farini wrote to Count Cavour in the north. The letter is less famous than the meeting at Teano, but much more significant, as it includes his impressions of the South: "Molise and the 'Lands of Labor'—what kind of lands are these? There is such savagery here! Italy? No, this is Africa: compared to these oafs, the bedouins are the very blossom of civil-minded virtue." Farini was clearly shocked, and wrote of how the Bourbons had given the dregs of southern society carte blanche to do whatever they wanted, merely to maintain their teetering position of power. He also described how the populace had taken advantage of its unbridled freedom in the worst possible way: "Even the oafish womenfolk commit murder, and worse: they bind gents . . . by their testicles and drag them through the streets, and then, snip-snap! Unbelievable horrors . . ."[1]

The letter was upsetting, and the cognitive capacities of its author might already have been compromised—soon thereafter he succumbed to an unspecified mental illness. But not even he would have let himself write such things had they not reflected some aspect of reality, and his sentiments matched those of the ruling class in general, which was highly disconcerted upon suddenly discovering the worrisome conditions down South.

Silvio Spaventa, a statesman who had ancestral roots in Abruzzo and eventually settled in Naples after a series of adventurous travels, echoes Farini's same dismay in a letter to his brother Bertrando, also dated October 1860:

> Everywhere people beg and grab whatever they can—everything here is an endless messing about, scheming, stealing. One cannot imagine how this place could ever be brought to even the slightest degree of logical order; it is as if society's moral cornerstones had been dug up and tossed out. I fear that the arrival of the king and his government will be of little to no use here. But they must come, and come quickly.

In 1961 Senator Diomede Pantaleoni (father of noted economist Maffeo Pantaleoni) wrote to his fellow statesman Marco Minghetti: "In Calabria one must travel in caravans, as if crossing the desert, to defend oneself from the Arabs and bedouins." The author and journalist Giuseppe Bandi, one of Garibaldi's supporting troops, wrote a book about the unification campaign in which he describes the Sicilian language as "highly African." Even as late as 1921 the journalist Giuseppe Prezzolini wrote that Italy is divided into two main parts: "The European part, which ends somewhere around Rome, and the African or Balkan part, which goes from Rome southward."[2] In 1909 the great scholar and politician Giustino Fortunato—an expert on the South and on agriculture who was originally from Lucania (present-day Basilicata)—wrote, "The North belongs to Central Europe, while the South is part of the

Mediterranean zone. On the one side Europe comes to an end, and on the other side Northern Africa and Asia Minor begin." Traveling toward Palermo, he adds, he saw a group of men approaching, "all on horseback, wearing skullcaps, with muskets across their saddles, like a bunch of bedouins." Even our dear Leopardi described Naples as "a city of slackers, scoundrels, and buffoons, half barbarian, half African." In short, many found the discovery of the South highly traumatic. Cavour himself, father of the unification movement, had "descended" the boot only as far as Florence; he never set foot in Rome, and had only the vaguest notions regarding the rest of the peninsula.

The historic truth is that, after quelling the revolutions of 1848, Ferdinand II, king of the Two Sicilies, had enacted harsh measures of repression in an attempt to isolate his kingdom from any outside political and intellectual influences. In 1861 the first census under the united Kingdom of Italy confirmed that, while illiteracy in the North hovered around 67 percent, in the South it reached a frightful 87 percent. According to the noted linguist Tullio De Mauro, the use of Italian as a standard means of communication was limited to 0.8 percent of the peninsula's population—or, out of 20 million, approximately 160,000 people.[3]

Indeed, among all modern national languages, Italian is the sole language to have existed for centuries almost exclusively as the voice of the learned elite, of officials, of orators, of the justice system. It is a jumble of liturgical, pompous lingo, with an arduous syntax, jam-packed with odd mannerisms, or, as has often been said, *anchilosato*, "stiffened" like a bunch of rigid bones—which is precisely why the Neapolitan writer and patriot Luigi Settembrini wrote: "When a population loses its homeland and its freedom and is dispersed worldwide, its language takes the place of its homeland and everything else. . . . And that is exactly what happened in Italy; the first thing we wanted when we finally felt Italian, after three centuries of slavery, was our shared language."[4] Settembrini was also a victim of the Bourbon repressions enacted after 1848, and barely escaped the gallows.

In the newborn Kingdom of Italy the idea of a southern population marred by "repugnant vices" and "profound corruption" began to spread at every level, from Cavour's correspondences, which repeatedly return to the subject, to the shared opinion of the emergent middle classes. Thus a situation that was already compromised became decidedly critical as the phenomenon of brigandage spread and, alongside the "Roman Question" (the survival of a state run by a Church that had long since proved to be an anachronistic obstruction), was one of the tragic problems the kingdom's new government had to deal with. Newspaper articles and images of captured brigands reinforced the idea that the South was a sinister, mysterious place populated by outlaws. Terrifying, picaresque rumors of a decidedly medieval tone began to spread, sparking people's vivid imaginations with visions of thugs drinking out of human skulls, devouring the still-beating hearts of their slain enemies. But actual brigands really did exist—lots of them—and not just in the South. The Apennine mountains in Tuscany and Emilia-Romagna, as well as the Maremma area of Tuscany, were chock-full of such rogues. To this day the more rustic taverns in Maremma proudly display old pictures of dead brigands posed before the camera, gun in hand, propped up against a wall or tree trunk.

But the brigands down South remained a separate, much more vexing issue. Viewed within the broader picture of widespread illiteracy, abject poverty, and social degradation, they flourished in little-known territories, mixing in with populations whose loyalty to the new kingdom was often dubious, despite the institution of a "plebiscite." This phenomenon was aggravated by the persistence of an essentially feudal system in a sparsely populated, harsh, mountainous land filled with easy hideouts in dense forests, caves, and ravines.

In 1799, Bourbon King Ferdinand IV of Naples had called on a noble cadet from Calabria known as Cardinal Ruffo to win back Naples. His army (the *lazzari*[5]) consisted primarily of brigands and fugitives.

Once their mission was complete, a few ringleaders were decorated or promoted to general. One such man was Michele Arcangelo Pezza (1771–1806), an ambiguous character who became famous as a fearless adventurer, a cruel brigand, and a valiant warrior under the name Fra Diavolo ("Brother Devil").

He has been the subject of many films (even one starring Laurel and Hardy) and equally numerous texts. Alexandre Dumas's historic novel *La Sanfelice* (about noblewoman Maria Luisa Sanfelice) involves Fra Diavolo, and his *Count of Monte Cristo* includes a romantically vivid portrayal of one of his gangs.

———————————

Stendhal also wrote about Fra Diavolo in an impassioned essay on Italian brigands. His text is quite effective, even if it does not always hew to historic fact.[6] For example:

> All Italy trembled in 1806 at the very name of Fra Diavolo. Born in Itri, this brigand spread terror mainly along the Mediterranean coast, confining his activities to the Papal States and the Kingdom of Naples. The sun-blackened former monk and ex-convict killed his fellow brigands by taste and out of need, sometimes saving them on a whim or helping them out of kindness. In all he did, he was devoted to the Virgin and the saints. After a life of brigandage he went on to become a counter-revolutionary, rising to the rank of a senior officer in the army of Cardinal Ruffo and cutting throats in Naples out of a sense of duty to the altar and the throne. He was always covered in amulets and armed with daggers. After many deeds of astonishing boldness and courage, Fra Diavolo fell captive to a French detachment. He was tried and hanged.

Brigandage after Italian unification therefore had something to do with an established tradition that had fascinated foreign writers because of its adventurous, picaresque, colorful prose potential. And such brigands fit perfectly in an Italy that was viewed as a nation rife with bloody crime, betrayal, superstition, and intrigue. Their actions seem to be a mixture of ferocity and popular justice, authoritarianism and anarchy. Acting with utter indifference, brigands can just as easily right a wrong as they can deny someone his freedom by force—the sole means by which they act, unless of course some gentleman commissions them for his cause, handing them a uniform to don and a musket to wield.

But central/southern Italy, from Lazio down, was the region that became most familiar with large-scale brigands, such that popular customs were seeded with the germ of a criminality that grew stronger over time. The region's brigands flourished in step with its increasing wealth, such that a parallel, underground economy sprouted up next to—and often was far larger than—the legitimate economy. Once again, from Stendhal:

> The whole of Italy was infested by brigands, but it was mainly in the Papal States and the Kingdom of Naples that they held sway for the longest time and where they operated in the most constant and methodical way. There they had an organization, privileges, and a guarantee of impunity. If they became strong enough to intimidate governments, their fortune was made. It was therefore towards this goal that they constantly aimed throughout the period during which they plied their infamous trade. A man felt he was back in the days of the barbarians when, in the absence of any law, force was the only arbiter, the only recognized power. What kind of government is it that can be reduced to trembling before a handful of criminals! Twenty or thirty men could spread terror throughout a country and force all the pope's troops into battle.

Even as they committed their crimes or led lives of profligacy, the brigands never forgot their religious practices, although they usually took the form of simple superstition.[7] This coarse devotion, which the Church never decisively condemned, is also rooted in a centuries-long tradition.

> A bandit, accused of several murders, appears before his judges. Far from denying the crimes imputed to him, he admits others until then unknown to the law; but when someone asks if he observed the fast day, the devout rascal grows angry and is mortally offended. "Are you accusing me of not being a good Christian?" he says bitterly to the interrogating magistrate.

The ultimate motivation of this "faith" is that, because the brigand's actions continually involve risking life and limb, he wants some guarantee of eternal salvation. His uncouthness leaves him indifferent to the blasphemous disconnect between his crimes and the overall message of Christianity.

> In the course of such an adventurous life, the two things that comfort the Italian brigand and that he never lays aside are his gun for defending his life and his medallion of the Virgin for saving his soul. Nothing is more terrifying than this blend of ferocity and superstition. The outlaw is convinced that death on the scaffold, preceded by a priest's absolution, will assure him a place in heaven.

The following cruel episode, once again found in Stendhal, perfectly illustrates the primitive ferocity such brigands were capable of unleashing. It is no coincidence that similarly violent events have recurred over the years: in 1860 during the riots in Bronte, Sicily, under Garibaldi's push for unification; during the period of outright civil war in the wake of World War I; and still today in mafia-related vendettas, which have involved acts as heinous as disposing of a child's body by dumping it in acid.

The band known as Independence—commanded, I believe, by De Cesaris—reigned over Calabria in 1817 with absolute and terrible power. The group consisted of thirty men and four women. Landowners and farmers were the main tribute payers. They took pains not to fail to place, on a certain day at a certain hour at the foot of a tree or the base of a column, whatever was demanded of them. One farmer however wanted to rid himself of this heavy burden. Instead of bringing his tribute, he tipped off the authorities, and troops on foot and horseback surrounded the Independents. Finding themselves tricked, the brigands shot their way out, leaving the field covered with the bodies of their enemies. Three days later, they took the most terrible revenge on the ill-fated farmer. Having tortured him and condemned him to death, they threw him into a huge cauldron in which milk was boiled to make cheese. The bandits then forced each of his servants to eat a piece of their master's body.

For years on end such phenomena devastated Italy's southern regions. Their root causes have been analyzed from very different perspectives. In general it could be said that the various social, political, and criminal factors were so closely intertwined that it proved hard to isolate and evaluate each component without accepting specific preconceptions.

Many Southerners considered the arrival of the "Piedmontese," as supporters of Cavour and Garibaldi were referred to, an invasion. It is also worth noting that, considered from the perspective of international law (*ius gentium* or "law of nations" as it used to be known), Garibaldi's Expedition of the Thousand was an act of brigandage that, nowadays, would certainly be condemned by the United Nations: a thousand-odd unofficial soldiers attacked and invaded an officially recognized kingdom. To give the campaign the "legitimacy" it deserves, you have to look beyond the strictly legal level to consider the push toward territorial unification the way the more educated, well-informed people in the Papal States and Kingdom of the Two Sicilies saw it. In both cases the general populace had been left behind, as the economy languished and land management remained the way it had been in the Middle Ages, complete with vast tracts of unfarmed, undeveloped estates. To give just one example, in 1861 the Basilicata region had 124 townships, of which 91 had no roads.

In June 1862 several democratic representatives in parliament presented an official memorandum on the South, in an attempt to overcome the government's reluctance to confront the situation head-on. One theory maintained that brigandage was a consequence of the political line held by conservative supporters of Cavour (who had died on June 6, 1861) and Bettino Ricasoli, which was on the one hand repressive, but on the other took a conciliatory approach to the Bourbon regime. The proposed solution was to increase public-works projects to reduce high unemployment, and then entrust the peace-keeping process to Garibaldi, the only Northerner who enjoyed a degree of popularity in the South as well, perhaps because of his atypical temperament. Although his impetuousness and somewhat confused political ideas make him recognizably Italian, other aspects of his character are decidedly off-kilter for what you might expect from a model leader.

For instance, he was a great general—sharper and more courageous than most military figures throughout Italian history—but the end of his life, spent in exile on the small island of Caprera, revealed his eccentricity. He departed for the island with a bit of money gathered by a friend, some coffee beans, some sugar, a few seeds, and a sack of dried codfish. Compared with Garibaldi, Cincinnatus almost looks like a wastrel. But even within his lifetime Garibaldi had become a legend, and his nickname *"Eroe dei due mondi"* ("Hero of the Two Worlds") was not mere rhetoric.[8]

After having done combat on both sides of the Atlantic, trying to defend the glorious yet short-lived Roman Republic in 1849, losing his beloved wife (who had fought at his side) during their retreat from the besieging troops, and turning down the modest pension the government had offered him, he left for the shores of New York, where he landed in 1850. One of the Italians who had charitably pulled together some funds to help him out was a former stagehand from Florence who had also circled half the globe, a wild genius who was fighting to keep the Americans from stealing his patent for the invention of a strange gadget that let people talk across relatively long distances. He called it the *telegrafo parlante* or *telettrofono* ("talking telegraph" or "telectro-phone"), and if it really worked it would be revolutionary. In the end it did, and it was—but without his name attached.[9]

Antonio Meucci lived on Staten Island, the least accessible of New York's five boroughs, and invited Garibaldi to be his houseguest. The Meucci household was small, just Antonio and his wife Ester, who was gravely ill. The poor woman was virtually bedridden, so her husband divided his time between the kitchen and working at several trades; he had developed the "telectrophone" precisely so he could communicate directly between his workshop and their bedroom. He earned a living by various minor inventions, small jobs, and fleeting enterprises. His poor command of English was a real obstacle, and it is not hard to imagine the American lawyers making mincemeat of him when it came time to hash out the rights to his strange invention. He had recently set up a candle-making venture to produce a new kind of three-color candle using white, red, and green stearin. Garibaldi showed up, looked around, and liked what he saw—the little house was at the edge of a wood, ideal for early morning hunts. Seeing Meucci bent over a cru-cible melting wax, he did not think twice, and offered to help out. And so the Hero of the Two Worlds and the inventor who was about to be robbed of his best idea solely because he could not afford an adequate lawyer worked side by side, pouring wax into the casts and rolling out lots of fine tricolor candles. Thus these two men, from such differ-ent places, headed toward such different destinies, were momentarily united by their shared status as immigrants.

As Garibaldi wrote in his memoirs: —

I worked for [Antonio] Meucci for a few months and, although I was his employee, he treated me as family, quite lovingly. But one day, tired of making candles—and perhaps driven by my usual, natural sense of restlessness—I went out with the idea of finding a new line of work. I recalled having been a sailor, and I knew a few words of English, so I went to the shore [of Staten Island], where I came across a few coastal navigation boats busy loading and unloading goods. I went up to the first one and asked if I might be taken aboard as a sailor. They hardly listened, and everyone—at least, everyone I saw aboard—carried on working. I tried again, going up to another vessel. Same reply. Finally I went up to another, where men were unloading goods, and asked if they might allow me to help out—and received the reply that they had no need of help. "But I am not requesting any compensation," I insisted. Their reply? Silence. "I only want to work so I can shake off the cold," I said (there really was snow on the ground). More silence. I was mortified! I thought back to the time when I had the honor of commanding the entire fleet of Montevideo—I had commanded an immortal fleet at war! But what did it matter? They did not want me! I suppressed my sense of mortification, and went back to making tallow candles.

I bring up this touching, slightly off-topic episode because it helps us understand why Garibaldi was the only Northerner who earned widespread popularity in the South. He instinctively understood what its people were made of, and it did not hurt that the conditions he had experienced in the United States were similar to those that millions of emigrants would soon experience over the coming years.

———————

Italian or not, Rome and Naples were nevertheless destined to succumb to the winds of change and the rigid laws of economic development.

But that does not mean that the differences between Garibaldi's troops and the Bourbon military were quelled before turning into outright civil war, accompanied by the usual acts of violence that come along with such conflict. The Bourbon forces unleashed summary executions, pillaged and razed countless villages, and destroyed civilian homes as retaliation. On the opposite side, "Piedmontese" soldiers who were captured were often tied to a tree and burned alive or crucified and mutilated. Here, as before, the general population frequently viewed brigands as heroes of the common folk, since they were often local acquaintances, if not relatives or neighbors. And anyway, as soon as you go beyond the most vulgar and easily judged cases of brigandage, individual brigands were often complex mixtures of many conflicting aspects, both positive and negative. Sometimes their delinquent side might be redeemed by a vivid social vision, as well as the presumption that what they viewed as political tyranny could only be put in check by armed resistance. The famous, sometimes idealized case of Sergeant Pasquale Romano is a perfect example.

Pasquale Domenico Romano was born to a family of shepherds in the Apulian town of Gioia del Colle in 1833. After enlisting in the Bourbon army he swiftly rose to the rank of sergeant, but when his unit was then decommissioned following unification, he decided to launch an armed resistance against the Piedmontese forces. One of his most sensational actions was the occupation of his hometown, where, aided by the local population, he forced the Savoy troops to retreat. At the same time he continued his brigandage, destroying the farmhouses of local liberals and Garibaldi's former supporters, now considered "traitors of the Southern People." The hunt for Romano closed in on him, and in 1863 he was tracked down in the woods near Gioia del Colle, subdued, and executed. People say—although this may just be legend—that just before dying he shouted out *"Evviva 'o rre!"* ("Long live the king!"). But local farmers' veneration of his martyred remains is no legend; we have concrete proof of it. The French writer Oscar de

Poli compares him to a hero of the War in the Vendée, leaving us this vivid description of the scene:

> Sergeant Romano had been slashed with a sabre, torn to shreds on the road to Mottola, by the Piedmontese troops . . . All the townsfolk wanted one last glimpse of the unrecognizable remains of this heroic bandit; they showed up in droves, as if on a pilgrimage made holy by way of martyrdom. The men doffed their caps, the women knelt, almost everyone cried; the deceased went to his grave showered by the condolences and admiration of his compatriots.[10]

Compare that with a depiction of the same episode filed in a report sent to the parliament of the Italian kingdom, and you get dramatic, eloquent proof of how radically two views of the same event can differ:

> A gang of scoundrels led by one Pasquale Romano from Gioia, former Bourbon sergeant, saddened those delightful and fertile districts with all sorts of robberies and murders; early last January the cavalry of Saluzzo, commanded by the valorous Captain Bollasco and backed by Gioia's courageous national guard, assailed the infamous gang, killed its leader, destroyed its members, and from then on the area surrounding Gioia is free and safe.

Later that same year a parliamentary commission completed its investigation of brigandage, presided over by Giuseppe Massari (1821–84), a journalist and liberal Catholic who supported the historic Right and was himself from Apulia. Despite the sharp limits such commissions always have, the final report (known as the Massari Report), read at a secret session of the Chamber of Deputies on May 3 and 4, identified a few underlying causes of the phenomenon:

The bad counsel of abject poverty—untempered by any instruc-
tion or education, unhampered by the vulgar religion that is
preached to the multitudes, and corroborated by spectacularly
bad examples—prevails among those unhappy people, and delinquent habits become second nature. The faint voice of moral
sense is suffocated, and robbery, instead of inspiring a sense of
repugnance, appears to be an easy, legitimate means of subsistence and income. . . . The brigand's life abounds in aspects that
would attract any poor farmer, who, comparing it to the difficult
and wretched existence he is condemned to eke out, certainly
does not lead him to reach a conclusion favorable to the social
order . . . and the allure of the temptation to behave badly is ir-
resistible . . . Of 373 brigands who were imprisoned in the jail at
Capitanata [near Foggia, Apulia] on April 15, 293 belonged to the
low-level category of day laborers . . . He who has not an acre of
land to call his own, who has not a belonging to his name, and is
condemned to serve a wealthy landowner he sees grow richer by
the day through his own sweat—not only poorly paid, but forced
to labor under the harshest conditions—cannot possibly have
the slightest patriotic feeling, nor can he feel any sense of respect
toward society at large. But in those places where the relationship
between landowners and farmers is better—where the latter is
not reduced to a nomadic state, and feels some kind of connection to the land—in those places brigandage might attract a few
thugs, who can be found anywhere in the world, but it cannot
grow deep roots, and can be more easily defeated.

The poverty of this population, utterly unfamiliar with any notion of
organized society, was therefore seen as the primary cause of the ram-
pant brigandage and "habitual delinquency" that had cast such deep
roots as to become second nature. But the report also noted the phenomenon's underlying political implications and "causes of import."
One was the Vatican's underground actions that welcomed brigands

within its territories and financed their undertakings, fully aware that sooner or later the "Roman question" would be resolved by force, and that any step it could take to weaken the unification movement would at least postpone the inevitable. The bishops became the spokesmen of the Vatican's directives, which is another reason that the Jesuit magazine *La civiltà cattolica* issued a harsh review of the Massari Report. It emphasized how the text "greatly exaggerates reasons it refers to as social factors" in a vain attempt to find every possible cause for brigandage "outside political factors," since "Neapolitans will hear nothing of this fictitious 'unity.'"[11]

The magazine repeatedly returned to the topic. In 1874 it published an article claiming that "the Southern provinces consider themselves conquered, dominated, exploited." The Jesuits did not hesitate to hit where it hurt the most. But, years before—on August 2, 1861, to be precise—even Massimo d'Azeglio, the former prime minister from Piedmont, had written a famous letter to Senator Carlo Matteucci expressing similar views:

> In Naples we did indeed expel the sovereign in order to establish a government based on universal consensus. But it took 60 battalions, and it would seem that even those will not suffice to contain the kingdom. As is well known, whether they be brigands or not, no one cares to know. But one might say: what about universal suffrage? I know nothing about suffrage, but I do know that on this side of the Tronto River no battalions are needed, whereas on the other side of the river they are required. And so there must have been some error; and we must alter our actions and principles. We need to hear from the Neapolitans, once and for all, whether they want us—yes or no.[12]

Giuseppina Cavour Alfieri, Cavour's niece, left written recollections of the great statesman's final hours. Overcome by fatigue after days of agony inflicted by sudden illness, he muttered, "Northern Italy is complete, there are no longer Lombards, Piedmontese, Tuscans, Romagnans—we are all Italians. But there are still Neapolitans. Oh, there is so much corruption down there. It is not their fault, the poor souls, they have been so badly governed . . . One must set moral standards for them, educate their small children and youths, build nursery schools and military colleges: but one cannot change the Neapolitans through vituperation."[13]

The same problem pops up even today. What might the southern masses have said back then, had they been given the chance to express themselves? I am talking about the people who helped defeat the French-backed Parthenopean Republic of 1799, who in 1857 grabbed their guns and pitchforks and stalked Carlo Pisacane and his fellow patriots all the way to Sapri, who welcomed brigands who were staunchly against unification—the vast masses who were left in an abject state of utter ignorance for centuries on end. Had they been allowed to speak freely, and had they been able to choose, what choice would they have made? The authors of the Massari Report do not touch upon that, nor do they say much about the Italian army's actions, much less about the actions of the unified government. They merely flip the argument on its head, blaming the problem on the Bourbon government's misrule, its long neglect of even basic education for its subjects, its corruption, and its coarse and cruel dominion, the other main cause of brigandage. To again quote the Massari Report:

> Poverty alone would not produce such pernicious effects, were it not combined with the other evils that the inauspicious Bourbon reign created and left in its wake in the Neapolitan provinces. These evils are: a jealously preserved and ever-increasing ignorance; a widespread and substantiated belief in superstition; and, most markedly, an absolute lack of faith in laws and the justice system . . . The Bourbons did everything in their power to commit the most nefarious of patricides—that of denying an entire population its conscience regarding all that is right and honest.

In truth, there were situations even more dire that the text did not even hint at. For example, there was often a close complicity between the landowners and the groups of brigands, veritable "pacts of coexistence" in which you can already catch a glimpse of the kinds of extortion that are still widespread in areas controlled by organized crime. The brigands would let the landowners know what they required in terms of foodstuffs, horses, supplies; the landowners or *galantuomini* would then assemble the requested material in one of their farmhouses. After a few days the gang would then break in and plunder the place, thereby allowing the landowner to file a claim for reimbursement from the authorities. It was a win-win situation for everyone but the government, which found itself combating brigandage with one hand while indirectly subsidizing it with the other.

Many have tried to attribute southern brigandage to the sole cause of political revolt, chalking it up as a symptom, however bloody, of a secessionist desire for independence. The numerous underlying causes of the ongoing battle are complex, even though a 1927 letter from Giustino Fortunato to Nello Rosselli contains this blunt summary:[14]

> Down here, in the South, brigandage was not an attempt at restoration under Bourbon rule, nor was it an attempt at establishing a separatist autonomy . . . rather, it was a spontaneous movement that, historically, returned at the slightest sign of agitation and with each political change. This is because it is essentially primitive and savage in nature, and is the result of centuries of degradation stemming from the poverty and ignorance of our rural populations.

As always, the many factors contributing to the tragic situation included rising prices for staples like bread, oil, and salt, while at the same time people's broader expectations—some legitimate, others illusory—were invariably let down. It was clear, for example, that the administrative jurisdictions and systems of local government had not changed a bit in terms of the sheer laziness, inefficiency, and corruption they had been famous for under Bourbon rule. And then there was the new government's obligatory military conscription, which the southern farmers viewed as an abuse of power; more than a few decided it was better to become a brigand or cut off one of their own limbs rather than don the Savoy insignia.

But the Massari Report did have some direct consequences, including an influence in the passage of the Pica Act, named after Giuseppe Pica, the representative who authored it, originally from the southern region of Abruzzo. For four and a half months, from August to December 1863, the law that had been conceived of as an "exceptional and temporary means of defense" effectively put southern Italy under siege. It allowed for the arrest, without due process, of vagabonds, people with no permanent job, and anyone suspected of collaborating with brigands and organized crime.[15] In a word, all civil rights and liberties were suspended, and exceptional measures like collective punishment for the crimes of individuals and reprisals inflicted on entire villages were introduced. In practice, the Pica Act put a legal façade on the very same practices that had been used in the past, including summary executions, and sidestepped the authority of the slow, corrupt justice system in favor of resorting to the all-too-rapid court-martial.

More people were killed in combat under the repressions resulting from the Pica Act than in all the wars fought during the Risorgimento. Fifty-five people were sentenced to death, and another 659 were sentenced to hard labor—some for a few months, some for years, and some for life. The repression lasted from 1861 to 1865, a period that, once again, it would be no exaggeration to call a civil war. Admittedly, when it was all over a certain degree of peace had been attained. But the fragility of that peace, and its hefty cost, remain visible even today.

6.

PARADISE
AND ITS DEVILS

Everyone, over the centuries, has had something bad to say about Naples. As early as the first century C.E., Livy's *Ab urbe condita* (*History of Rome*) included an eloquent anecdote of the situation around Naples two centuries before, during the second Punic war: *"Cum Hannibal circa Tarentum, consules ambo in Samnio essent..."*

> Hannibal was still in the neighbourhood of Tarentum and both the consuls were in Samnium apparently making preparations for besieging Capua. Famine, generally the result of a long siege, was already beginning to press upon the Campanians, as they had been prevented by the Roman armies from sowing their crops.[1]

And so a few messengers were sent to Hannibal to ask for some corn. Upon Hannibal's orders the Carthaginian general Hanno marched his troops into Campania, carefully avoided the Roman consuls' encampments, set up his own camp about three miles from Benevento, and ordered allies in the area to bring all the corn they had stored up. Then, Livy continues: "A message was despatched to Capua stating the day on which they were to appear in the camp to receive the corn, bringing with them all the vehicles and beasts they could collect." And what happens after all these complicated maneuvers to help out the starving Campanians? According to Livy:

> The Campanians carried out his instructions with the same slackness and carelessness that they showed in everything else. Hardly more than four hundred country carts were sent and a few draught cattle. Hanno scolded them severely, telling them that even the hunger which rouses the energies of dumb animals failed to stimulate them to exertion. He then fixed another day for them to come for corn provided with much more efficient means of transport.

So it seems that Naples and its environs had already earned a bad reputation in ancient times. Livy, originally from Padua, way up north, was writing in the first few decades of the Common Era. Years later, the sixteenth-century Calabrian philosopher Tommaso Campanella wrote his own masterpiece, *La città del sole* (*Civitas solis / The City of the Sun*), and put these words in the mouth of an imaginary Genoan sea captain, a stand-in for the author himself:

> [T]here are three hundred thousand souls in Naples and not fifty thousand of them work, and these work so hard that they destroy themselves. Meanwhile, the idle ruin themselves in pursuing idleness, avarice, lasciviousness, and usury; and they ruin still others by keeping them in impoverished servitude or by making them parties to their own vices. As a consequence, the public services are not sufficiently attended to. The tasks of the fields, of the camps, and of the crafts are badly performed even with great effort.[2]

More time passes, and by the eighteenth century the Age of Enlightenment has dawned. Yet Naples appears to remain the same as ever:

according to legend, a German philologist known only by the Italian version of his name, Giovanni Andrea Bühel, claimed that Naples is full of cheats and swindlers, especially when it comes to gambling, and that the Neapolitans' general temperament is so vile that all other peoples of Italy rightly consider them the worst of the worst.

Later that same century the Marquis de Sade admits that Via Toledo is one of the most beautiful streets anywhere, but he is quick to add: "[It is also] fetid and filthy . . . Good Lord, look whose care it is in! Why in the world does Heaven hand such riches to people so incapable of appreciating them?"[3]

Matilde Serao—a profoundly Neapolitan writer even though she was born in Patras, Greece—experienced and described Naples from within. Each and every emotion she felt was closely tied to the life of the city and its inhabitants. Here is how she saw it toward the end of the nineteenth century (*Il ventre di Napoli*, 1884):

> Crumbling houses, dead-end streets, a haven for filth of all sorts: everything remains as it has always been, so dirty it is disgusting, not a street cleaner nor garbage collector in sight, not a soul to peek in and safeguard the city's sanitation . . . A writhing maze of alleyways and blackened lanes where even the noonday sun never shines, not a ray of light penetrates. The ground is covered with years of accumulated muck, and rubbish collects in great piles, in every corner—everything is dark and depraved.

How curious it is, then, that seventy years later the lead character of Anna Maria Ortese's book *Il mare non bagna Napoli*[4] (1953) describes an almost identical scene: "[The streets are dotted by] arched niches, blackened by time, with brightly lit candles encircling the grieving Virgin Mary; the ground is white with soapy water, strewn with cabbage leaves, bits of paper, litter, and—in the middle of the courtyard—the usual group of wretched souls dressed in rags, their faces pock-marked by poverty and utter resignation."

Benedetto Croce, a major philosopher and adoptive Neapolitan, published an essay titled "A Paradise Inhabited by Devils" in the early twentieth century.[5] This proverbial saying about Naples dates back as far as the fourteenth century. Croce's text tries to explain the roots of the phrase, perhaps inspired by "the spectacle of feudal anarchy that the city represented to citizens coming from the peninsula's central and northern towns and republics . . . the spectacles of poverty and sloth and their attendant vices, all of which made an impression on the merchants coming to Naples from Florence and Lucca and Pisa and the Veneto and Genoa to conduct trade." He concludes:

> If we still accept this ancient criticism today. . . it is solely because we feel it might act as a whip to prod us into shape, a lash to keep us consciously aware of our duty. Viewed from that perspective, we are not so concerned about how true the saying is; it is to our benefit to believe it absolutely true, such that it becomes increasingly untrue.

This list could go on forever, as it seems most voyagers who embarked on the grand tour generally had a strongly negative reaction to Naples. But there are a few exceptions—illustrious ones, at that. Stendhal, for example, called Naples the most beautiful city in the universe. Goethe wrote that he spent his entire time in Naples contemplating magnificent things. Norman Douglas compared the city to an ancient amphora extracted from the depths of the sea: it is covered in algae and incrustations that make it nearly unrecognizable, but the eye of an expert immediately sees the beauty of its original form.

———————

Who are we to believe? Who most accurately captured the city's core features, which—like any complex place—can be viewed from many different perspectives? The Neapolitan writer Raffaele La Capria calls his hometown a *città bifronte*, literally a two-faced city, much like the ancient Roman god Janus, with one face looking to the past and one peering toward the future. Depending on how you look at it, Naples can be either completely desperate or absolutely happy—sometimes both.

Perhaps the real dilemma of Naples is the fact that whatever judgment you make about it could be considered correct. Its magnificence and abjection, its beauty and horror, its kindness and cruelty all seem to come from the distant past. But if Naples were only a place of horror and savagery, as news reports often lead us to believe, then it wouldn't even be worth the slightest consideration; we would not bother to even wonder how what goes on there can go on.

In a book titled *Le strade della violenza* ("Streets of Violence"), the Salerno-born writer and politician Isaia Sales uses cold hard numbers to expose the extent of Naples's ongoing massacre: more than 3,500 people killed by the camorra over twenty-five years, a number that would warrant the label of civil war. The city is in the grip of criminal gangs that are at once both archaic and postmodern, whose rites are modeled on ancient traditions, primitive pagan cults, and Christian practices as well as movies and television shows. They express themselves through pop singers and poets, and live in a realm quite far from any semblance of civil society. Sales describes the culture, the lifestyle, and the world that produced this socially perverted phenomenon. The same things Sales portrays in terms of economic sociology are also addressed by Roberto Saviano in his bestselling book *Gomorrah*, a voyage into the economic empire and power-hungry aspirations of the camorra.[6] The book is even more shocking than one might expect, since its episodes are taken from the lives of men, women, teens, and even children. Saviano himself grew up in the area, where the only valid laws are those set by the camorra, where every teenager dreams of getting his hands on a gun, money, women, fast cars—and of dying like a "real man": being shot by someone.

———————————

It is true, as the Neapolitan essayist Enzo Golino wrote a few years ago, that in Naples and throughout southern Italy "the camorra's code of silence and amoral familism, in both politics and among circles of relatives, have been a defining aspect of society for many centuries."[7] This is a point worth keeping in mind, and we will come back to it later. But Naples has never been, nor is it today, shaped solely by that. In the eighteenth century it was one of the main musical and theatrical capitals of Europe. Its musicians' refined performances were widely renowned, as were the innovative stagings produced in theaters, churches, private institutions, and the homes of the wealthy. The Neapolitan operatic tradition—with its school including Giovanni Paisiello, Alessandro Scarlatti, and Domenico Cimarosa, to name only the most famous— set the tone for the entire century. These composers' subtle use of the human voice and joyous melody are unrivaled. It took the arrival of Mozart for the Neapolitan school to fall from its first-place ranking.

During the Enlightenment, shifting attentions—the rediscovery of antiquity through the ruins of Herculaneum, Pompeii, and the temples at Paestum; the enchantment of the Neapolitan seaside, the Amalfi coast, and the gulf islands; as well as the area's golden light, lush gardens, and scented breezes—once again gave the city the aura so aptly captured by the ancient Roman name for the region, *Campania felix*, "fertile countryside."

While all that was happening and the area's natural beauty unveiled itself to the eyes of ecstatic visitors, the flip side of the coin was that, with equal eloquence, Naples's other face—its darker, more evil side—began to surface as well. It moved the great Victorian writer Charles Dickens to write to his friend John Forster: "What would I give that you should see the lazzaroni as they really are—mere squalid, abject, miserable animals for vermin to batten on; slouching, slinking, ugly, shabby, scavenging scarecrows!"[8]

These *lazzari* or *lazzaroni*, which I briefly mentioned in the previous chapter, seemed to live on nothing, doing nothing. They were often covered in rags and eked out an existence doing occasional odd jobs, pulling scams, pickpocketing, and thievery. The city's tempered climate, sunshine, and lavish nature certainly helped them out a lot. Among the upper classes, enlightened citizens attempted to establish a Partheno-pean Republic in 1799, and some of the city's best intellects joined in the effort: Vincenzo Cuoco, Domenico Cirillo, Mario Pagano, Gennaro Serra, Francesco Caracciolo, and courageous women like Luisa San-felice and Eleonora Pimentel Fonseca. But it did not last long, and, like the Roman Republic of 1849 a half-century later, was destined to remain a brief yet glorious experiment. The Neapolitan writer Enzo Striano made the Portuguese-born Eleonora Pimentel Fonseca the heroine of his superb novel *Il resto di niente* (1986). In one of its toughest scenes, some of the aforementioned enlightenment thinkers turn onto a filthy side street in an attempt to convince the riotous populace to rebel in the name of liberty. The noble progressive's speech is met with ridicule and scorn until the lead *lazzarone* gives his brutal dismissal, in dialect: *"La libertà ve la tenite pe' vvuie! Sai addo' l'avit'a mettere? Dinto a lo mazzo de màmmeta!"* ("You can keep your freedom to yourself! Know what you can do with it? Shove it up your mother's ass!"). As Vincenzo Cuoco wrote in his book about the short-lived revolution, *Saggio storico sulla rivoluzione napoletana del 1799*: "The Neapolitan patriots were great ide-alists but terrible politicians. They held their tottering republic upright by way of outsized illusions and minuscule accomplishments, ardent proposals and insufficient means. Thus it vacillated between comedy and tragedy, until the latter finally prevailed."

As we saw in the last chapter, this unrealistic republic was ulti-mately crushed by the troops of the so-called Army of the Faith led by Cardinal Ruffo, supported by Horatio Nelson's naval fleet and the many *lazzari* who almost unanimously lined up in favor of restoring Bourbon rule, which they felt was more fitting for them than that word they found so unsettling: liberty.

Another sixty years passed before Garibaldi and his legendary army of volunteers finally brought the Kingdom of the Two Sicilies to an end.

It has often been written—even recently—that Garibaldi's famous expedition and fight for Italian unification was actually an act of oppression, a huge overthrow, a criminal trespass. But even a thousand men, valiant as they may have been, would certainly not have been enough to defeat an entire kingdom were it not already rotting from within; all it took was a little push, and it toppled.

From September 27 to 30, 1943, Naples starred in yet another major historic event. Groups of civilians—including many teenagers, with assistance from pro-southern militants known as *badogliani*[9]—rose up against the Nazi occupation of the city. By the time the Allied troops arrived on October 1, the people of Naples had already kicked the German troops out, becoming the first European city to rise up against the occupying army during World War II. Sporadic revolts against the occupiers had begun with the announcement of the armistice on September 9. The period of confusion that followed was punctuated by acts of great cowardice and unprecedented courage, in almost equal measure. To give just one example: on September 9 on Via Foria, a group of soldiers captured a German tank, taking twenty prisoners. The Italian military command, upon learning of the capture, ordered the Germans' release. It was total chaos, no one knew who to obey anymore. The Italian soldiers had thought they were undertaking a commendable action, and instead found themselves literally tied up in the Bianchini barracks, a building already partially destroyed by the bombardments, risking an unfortunate end.

The city and its port were repeatedly bombed by British and American forces. More than twenty-five thousand people were killed, and the city's buildings and monuments were significantly damaged as well. One of the buildings hit was the eighteenth-century barracks designed by Luigi Vanvitelli for the Bourbon cavalry, later renamed in honor of the Neapolitan military captain Edoardo Bianchini. The uselessly heroic act of those young Neapolitan soldiers ended up with their brief imprisonment amid its crumbling walls.

The damage already done by Mussolini's disastrous war and all the bombardments was then aggravated by the Nazis' harsh reprisals following the declaration of armistice. German colonel Walter Schöll proclaimed a state of siege and ordered that anyone acting against the German troops be executed. For every German killed, one hundred Neapolitans would pay with their lives. The ferocious acts of terrorism that followed included the execution of a young sailor on the steps leading up to the university, with German troops forcing hundreds of people to watch. Neapolitan acts of sabotage against the occupiers were sporadic yet incessant, while the Germans continued their summary executions, round-ups, and sacking. Colonel Schöll stood rigid in his uniform, utterly unaware of basic human psychology, and reacted in the worst way possible. On September 22 he ordered the evacuation of the city's coast, clearing out a swath of land three hundred meters wide all along the seashore. In just a few hours, thousands of people were forced to abandon their homes, and you can imagine how they felt about that. A few hours later all men between the ages of eighteen and thirty-three were ordered to report immediately to the German prefecture, to then be sent to do forced labor in Germany. Basically, it was a mass deportation. Anyone who failed to report would be executed. Only a few hundred men, out of an estimated thirty thousand, responded.

On September 27 the Germans forcibly rounded up nearly eight thousand men, whereupon the Neapolitans' accumulated exasperation finally exploded. A few hundred people who had stolen arms from the Germans' depositories launched an attack that raged on for the next four days, amid clashes, skirmishes, and improvised tactics of urban guerrilla warfare. People of all socioeconomic levels—doctors, priests, young women, students, and the city's street urchins (known in dialect as *scugnizzi*)—took to the streets, driven by sheer misery, hunger, fear, and the desire to end the nightmare by any means necessary. The lower- and middle-class citizens were joined by soldiers from troops that had disbanded on September 8.[10] The men who had been imprisoned and slated for deportation were freed. They were under no directives, nor did they have any contact with organized partisan groups—their battle was general, spontaneous, impassioned, and led primarily by self-appointed commanders representing their own apartment buildings, city blocks, and neighborhoods.

Despite the Germans' superior weapons capabilities, armored cars, and discipline, Colonel Schöll understood he would eventually have to negotiate a deal. His counterpart was a young lieutenant from the Royal Italian Army, Enzo Stimolo. Schöll was granted a route by which to withdraw from Naples in exchange for releasing his hostages. But the retreat was not painless. He continued his path of destruction right to the very end, complete with ferocious, pointless, and criminal acts, such as torching the priceless documents held in the state archives. The Germans, generally known to be highly respectful toward culture, behaved like barbarians blinded by wrath, but for the first time in their broader European occupation they were forced to deal with insurgent civilians as equals. In recognition of the Four Days of Naples, as the uprising became known, the city was awarded the gold medal of military valor.

———————————

After Liberation, during the postwar period the city seemed to have lost the impassioned energy of those exceptional days. In his reportage-infused novel *La pelle* (*The Skin*, 1949),[11] the controversial writer Curzio Malaparte illustrates the Neapolitans' conditions and state of mind with the vivid, macabre colors of a prose that deftly mixes the blue of the sea with the red of blood—buffoonery and obscenity with tragedy, inventiveness, resignation, hunger, and abuse. In the chapter "The Virgin of Naples," the author and an American lieutenant enter a tenement where visitors are invited to admire an actual virgin, laid out, legs splayed apart. For a dollar, they are allowed to test her virginity with their own fingers. All the book's episodes have a similar tenor: Neapolitan women's pubic wigs are blond because the American "negroes" like blondes; one scene describes a homosexual orgy with a strap-on; another scene portrays a group of monstrous dwarfs as if they were painted by Hieronymus Bosch. The overall impression is that of a city populated by thieves, ruffians, and whores where any- and everyone is ready to sell their body for a song or some basic staple. All traces of dignity are gone, and rather than returning to its usual flow, life in the city slithers along instead, in the most degrading way possible. Malaparte's stories are based on his actual experiences, expanded by his vivid imagination, his expressionistic and lush prose, and the dreamlike distortions by which his writing reshapes reality. I do not know whether Fellini ever read his work, but many of their characters' "monstrosities," deformations, and excesses (at least from *La dolce vita* onward) reveal that these two men had a similarly attentive, distorted, realistic yet hallucinatory vision.

The natural question, at this point, would be to ask how in the world the attempted revolution of 1799 and the revolt of 1943 had opposite endings, with the former turning out to be a total failure and the latter resulting in relative victory. The two events betray stark differences in terms of their historic time period, political context, armies on the ground, the duration of conflict, and the presence or absence of the masses' support. History, including historic fiction, pushes us to try to compare the two circumstances, but in this case that is not possible, with the exception of one key aspect: There is a degree of coherence hidden within the social mechanisms at work, and their tendency to repeat themselves sometimes allows us to read them as behavioral constants.

The late eighteenth-century intellectuals aiming to establish a republic were asking illiterate masses to make a profound political decision involving a demanding series of changes, all of which was too advanced for your average Neapolitan back then, who viewed such propositions as just a bunch of highfalutin hot air. But 1943 was a different matter—it was a rapid, violent flare-up, the enraged rejection of an occupation that had been not only arduous, but utterly stupid to boot. Colonel Schöll's comportment in Naples exhibited the same blindness Pontius Pilate displayed in the ancient Roman province of Judaea; both were incapable of understanding what kind of people they were dealing with.

In 1799 there was a prospect of enacting radical change, the end of a monarchy—of that particular Bourbon monarchy. But just a few years earlier in Paris, the French Revolution had turned into the Reign of Terror, and the king and queen had been guillotined in public.[12] Naples was under the reign of Ferdinand IV and his wife Maria Carolina of Austria (a stronger ruler than her husband), sister of the beheaded Marie Antoinette. In light of those recent tragedies, the term *republic* easily assumed the same sinister air that twentieth-century people later associated with the word *communism*.

To the contrary, in 1943 it was all too easy to think that nothing could be worse than that blind, cruel, hopeless German occupation, no one worse than its hardened, precise, merciless soldiers. The year 1799, in all respects, promised revolution; 1943, on the other hand, brought true revolt. It did not matter what would come after; the only thing of any importance was putting an end to what was going on, no matter what it would take, no matter what the price to pay.

––––––––––

Once upon a time in Italy there was a phenomenon known as *maschere*, "masks." This term referred not to the carnival masks you might be familiar with; rather, it described the characters who embodied—in their repetitive gestures, vices, and tics—a specific region or city, keeping its ancient traditions alive. Maybe *guise* is the term that best captures the sense of these stock characters. A few examples: Arlecchino (Harlequin) was a *maschera* from Bergamo's commedia dell'arte, an astute, ribald, agile servant with a talent for playing tricks and pranks; his accomplice Brighella was equally slick; his mistress Colombina (Colombine) was yet another sly servant. Bolognese theater boasted Dottor Balanzone, a know-it-all busybody; Piedmontese theater had Gianduja, a peasant with a penchant for good food and drink; Venetian theater starred the stingy, rich, senile Pantalone; and Roman theater had Rugantino, a quarrelsome braggart ready to flee at a moment's notice. For centuries on end these stock characters brought to life countless interwoven plots and intrigues, broke and reinforced every rule, and generally entertained, as the barkers outside the theater claimed, young and old alike. Naples, too, had its own, who was in turn one of Italy's most famous: Pulcinella (Punch), born in the sixteenth century, or perhaps even earlier, was a descendant of the ancient Roman shows known as Atellan Farces, filled with fun, scurrilities, and copious sex. He traditionally wears a large white cassock and a black mask with a long nose, leaving only his mouth uncovered; he is often portrayed with a protruding belly, and sometimes as a hunchback. He is simultaneously both stupid and clever, he seems like a devil but can also be an angel, he knows he is in a tough spot but also knows he will eventually get out of it, somehow, with some game, some twist, some imbroglio, and that it will all end with a huge feast of macaroni. He talks, shouts, dances, sings, flails about, and gesticulates; but he also often spends a long time without making a move, lazing about, sleepily resting, all the while ready to pounce like a cat to catch whatever prey chance might have to offer. He is an amicable, amusing, generous character, ready to share whatever it is he has stolen with his companions in both adventure and misfortune. But he is also no stranger to betrayal and sudden sadness, whereupon he begins to philosophize, looking for a way out through dream or song.

Of all the quintessential Italian stock characters, Pulcinella is the richest, most intense, and most nuanced. His roots run deep into the terrain underlying the city and its common folk, some of the liveliest in all the Mediterranean. Indeed, *too* lively according to some—so lively they are apt to ignore even the most basic rules governing collective behavior, the kinds of rules that make it possible for all of us to deal with one another on a daily basis. Neapolitans' vivacity lets individuals' energy explode, boundless, as blood boils and quick, impatient thoughts arise in the face of life's many obstacles, be they people or laws; whatever gets in the way, person or law, is to be gotten rid of or deftly circumvented. A lot of what is both good and bad about Naples, a lot of its vitality, enchantment, and damnation, all comes together behind the mask of Pulcinella.

For a few centuries Naples was a true capital, certainly more so than Rome, which had been reduced to a veritable village, its population a mere 250,000 (70 percent of whom were illiterate) when it became a part of unified Italy. Rome was overrun by backward-looking clergy who lived off the Church's accumulated wealth, surrounded by neglected territories ridden by malaria and brigands. Sure, it had its glorious ruins, but even those were in terrible shape, stripped of every last bit of marble or iron ready to be reused by residents who had shed any pretense of dignity and respect for ancient craftsmanship. Naples, on the other hand, enjoyed its rank as a bona fide capital and carried out its role with a culture that, at least for a while yet, held its standing among the main courts of Europe.

The Kingdom of the Two Sicilies had a convoluted political history, as its name implies. It included the present-day regions of Abruzzo, Campania, Basilicata, Molise, Apulia, Calabria, Sicily, and a good portion of southern Latium (the district of Gaeta). One of the kingdom's peculiarities was that King Ferdinand, from the Congress of Vienna in 1815 onward, held two crowns, reigning as Ferdinand IV in Naples and as Ferdinand III in Palermo. Another curiosity: his relative territories were referred to as "on this side" and "on that side" of "the lighthouse," meaning on the mainland or on the island side of the lighthouse marking the Strait of Messina.[13]

The island itself was referred to as *Sicilia ulteriore,* and the peninsular part of the territory was called *Sicilia citeriore,* which combined to create, voilà, "two Sicilies" encompassing a total of twenty-two provinces: fifteen on the mainland, seven on the island.[14] Over the years a few fleeting attempts at unifying the crown and its various territories had been made, but they were ultimately brought together only after the Congress of Vienna.

Today the former Kingdom of the Two Sicilies has become the (in)famous *Mezzogiorno,* the southernmost, least developed, most problematic part of the Italian peninsula. The area has been subjected to numerous attempts at development that rarely ever succeeded. Countless narratives, essays, articles, books, and political initiatives have centered on this very area—and from that heap of pages, words, and proposals a few significant studies have surfaced, almost always sparking heated debate.

––––––––––

In 1958 the American sociologist Edward C. Banfield published a book titled *The Moral Basis of a Backward Society,* wherein he advanced the hypothesis that the village in Basilicata he had studied at length was characterized by an ethos he termed "amoral familism."[15] In such a society, individuals maximize the immediate material advantages of their family to the detriment of the broader community. It is as if their world ended at their own doorstep. According to Banfield such behavior has anthropological and cultural causes, and is relatively unrelated to economic structure. In other words, in a backward society like the one he describes, the poor and the rich behave the same way, because both come from a "culture" that is more prevalent than class distinctions. A rich man might construct a villa without bothering to observe local building codes, whereas a poor man might cobble together an illegal shack. "Amoral familists" develop behaviors that are not community oriented because they have no faith in collective society or its individual members; they cooperate with others only if they stand to make personal gain. So amoral familism is the opposite of civic-mindedness, the condition created when a community considers its own "social capital" a "public good" that establishes shared rules and values, inspiring faith in a collective that everyone (or most people) identifies with, including its historical and value-based characteristics. Thus social capital becomes a shared characteristic, held together by a shared history and the network of relationships between individuals. According to Banfield, all those things are lacking in the backward societies of southern Italy.

Another noteworthy book is *Making Democracy Work*, published by the American sociologist Robert Putnam in 1993.[16] Over a period of twenty years Putnam (and his colleagues Robert Leonardi and Raffaella Nanetti) studied the way various Italian regions work, roughly modeling his approach on the one employed many years before by Alexis de Tocqueville as he prepared his famous text *Democracy in America*. The idea was to analyze how the new regional administrations, which were fundamentally identical but operated within vastly different environments, would act across the peninsula's various regions. Their research centered on how local traditions of social association, civic engagement, and cooperation would influence political action. Once again, the results showed significant differences between the central/northern and southern regions. Moreover, in retrospect it seems obvious that Campania and Piedmont established substantially different administrative approaches.

Putnam, like Banfield, emphasizes the greater or lesser presence of "civic sense" as it affects the functioning of government, citizens' participation, and the correct use of public money. Any time scholars try to rank Italy's regions, for each and every issue regions like Emilia-Romagna, Lombardy, Umbria, and Tuscany are always in the lead, while Calabria, Campania, and Sicily always bring up the rear. When researchers look for possible causes, they usually look to the local history of each specific place. In the South, for example, Putnam asserts that public life is organized hierarchically. Very few people make decisions with an eye to the collective good. In such places, people's interest in politics comes not from civic commitment, but rather stems from a sense of deference toward others or outright careerism and profiteering. Almost no one is involved in social or cultural associations. Corruption is considered the norm, even by politicians, and truly democratic ideas are viewed with cynicism.

Putnam goes on to observe that the North, however, exhibits greater, more intense interpersonal ties, and these stronger "civic communities" are the result of historically rooted, ancient municipal institutions. It is as if the North was somehow better able to reconcile individual and family interests with those of the broader community.

Back in the South, from the Middle Ages onward there has been little sense of shared, civic-minded experience. As a result, the North developed horizontal relationships between citizens through mutual exchange and cooperation, whereas relations in the South remained vertical—that is, between subjugated individuals and those in power.

All these conclusions have been strongly criticized. Researchers have been accused of setting up a hypothesis that, taken to their extremes, could easily escalate into anthropological profiling or outright racism. It has also been noted that such studies ignore the more recent causes of underdevelopment in the South, everything from the rest of the country's exploitation of the area to its imposition of a hasty industrialization that such areas, now plagued by the pollution of chemical plants and steel factories, were neither ready for nor able to accommodate. In light of recent discoveries, we might well add that over the last few decades both North and South have jointly hammered the last nail into the coffin by colluding to smuggle toxic waste southward, where gangs of local criminals dispose of it, poisoning everything from the topsoil to the groundwater table.[17]

One of the more noteworthy studies of these phenomena was led by the Italian anthropologist Carlo Tullio-Altan. His book *La nostra*

Italia ("Our Italy," 1986) gives great weight to familism, understood as the root of certain values and behaviors, virtually to the exclusion of other forces. In other words, familism establishes its own realm of values, which almost always oppose those of the city and, even more important, the nation. Altan goes a step beyond Banfield, and views Italian familism as a veritable moral metaphysics capable of directing people's behavior to benefit their own families at the expense of the broader society's interests. Empirical proof of this hypothesis can be seen in the attitudes of political leaders like Umberto Bossi who—while claiming to be a true *padano*, or at least a "non-Italian"—when it comes to their own families and children, act like the staunchest of southern godfathers.[18]

————————

Can such analyses ever suffice to explain the South's perennial under-development, or Naples's emblematic decay? Even more important: are their primary assumptions even accurate? Any possible answer is necessarily hypothetical, and could easily be refuted by a different viewpoint. For example, in his latest book the historian Rosario Villari deploys many years of archival research to show that the history of Naples and southern Italy as a whole parallels the slow incubation of a reformist project, a "dream of freedom" (his book is titled *Un sogno di libertà*, Mondadori 2012), which has succeeded in engaging even the humblest members of the population. That is certainly a part of the overall picture, but on the whole the area's prevailing traits seem so dissimilar from the rest of the country that people have even begun to talk about "two Italies." Some time ago the Milan-based think tank Fondazione Edison summed up the situation as follows: "According to Eurostat data, Northern Italy has a higher per-capita GDP than the UK, while central Italy surpasses that of countries such as Sweden, Germany, and France. . . . The South, on the other hand, with its 20.7 million inhabitants, is the largest low-income area in all of Europe, comparable to that of Greece and Portugal combined."[19]

Is it possible for a country to remain truly "united" when its financial inequalities are so significant? The answer is not necessarily negative: economic performance is not everything, and by many other criteria Italians in both North and South share similar values and destinies. It is just a matter of knowing how to spot those other criteria.

7.

HE LINGERED A LITTLE, THEN LEFT THE WORLD

Umbria is a special region. It is Italy's sole landlocked region, and is also the only one that does not border another country; all other regions have at least one international border, on land or at sea. Its one million inhabitants make it one of the least populous, and its primarily hilly landscape is crossed by the Tiber, a medium-sized yet well-known river, and the Via Flaminia, an ancient consular road dating back to 220 B.C.E., which led from Rome to the Adriatic coast. At first glance, then, it would appear to be a region that lends itself to being bypassed, rather than lingering in for an extended stay. The fact that it is enclosed in a relatively small area (3,300 square miles total), as well as the gothic character of its towns—from the capital, Perugia, to Orvieto, perched atop a high rocky outcrop—gives Umbria an invariably authentic, ancient feel that is only rarely marred by an affected sense of complacency. Spoleto, Todi, Cascia, Gubbio, Norcia, Montefalco, and Montecastello di Vibio are little cities of various size, almost always built atop a hill. Each is different from the next, but all are enriched by some artistic treasure, be it the very urban fabric, the ancient stone structures of the historic city centers, the steeply winding cobblestone lanes, the narrow spaces, or the surrounding countryside with its rolling hills, lush with olive groves, vineyards, and forests of oak and chestnut trees. The histories of other regions speak of domination and conquest, violence and clashes; not Umbria, where the most important military episode was the famous Battle of Lake Trasimene in 217 B.C.E., between Hannibal's troops and Roman consul Gaius Flaminius Nepos's legions. More than a battle, it was an outright massacre: Hannibal pulled off an almost Napoleonic maneuver by waging a surprise attack, striking the Romans from the sides as they were lined up to march, and were therefore particularly exposed. Thousands of Romans died that day.

I have not mentioned Assisi yet because that is where we are headed. The view from the valley is impressive because Assisi rises in stages up the terraced slopes of Mount Subasio. And in Assisi, as in Jerusalem, you immediately get the feeling you are entering an extraordinary place, thanks to its unique colors, contours, the contrast between the mountains and the sky, and the foothills of the Sacred Convent, whose large arches support the town's many houses, domes, steeples, and basilicas above.

When Giovanni Bernardone, son of Pietro Bernardone, was born here in 1182, the scenery was obviously different—the woods were denser and there were fewer houses. But the transparency of the air and the many shades of colors were likely exactly as they are today, from the polished white of the main fortress to the green fields, shaded woods verging on black, and the intense blue of the summer sky.

The story of Giovanni's life has been told many times, though you probably know him by a different name, as I shall soon explain. The main events of his time on earth are well known, but—despite his fame—his undeniable allure remains intact, because his existence represents one of human nature's most poignant enigmas. His mother was the one who named him Giovanni (John), but his father insisted on calling him Francesco (Francis), meaning "the Frenchman," in honor of his connection to Provence, where he had become a success-

ful textile merchant. Another hypothesis for the name is that Francis's
mother, Pica, was originally from Provence. Even as an adult, Francis
sometimes used his mellifluous voice to sing in French.

So he came from a rich family and had a wealthy upbringing,
with all the leisures that his given time period, companions, and local
places had to offer. In his twenties he took part in the war between the
Guelphs of Assisi (loyal to the papacy) and the Ghibellines of Perugia.
He was not much of a warrior, and was quickly captured and imprisoned in the enemy city. Might this period of imprisonment—his first
exposure to loneliness, starvation, darkness, and the discomfort of a
cell—be what sparked his radical shift? Many of his biographers (it is
probably more accurate to call them *hagiographers*) have written as
much. In truth, we have no way of knowing. We know almost nothing
about his early years, at least nothing of any historical reliability.

Francis is one of the tiny minority of Italians who managed to
direct their entire lives toward the affirmation of a principle, if you
will, an ideal. Even during his lifetime he had been called a madman,
a fanatic; it is possible that he suffered from anorexia and hysterical
attacks, but even those are not enough to explain the ideals that so
deeply pervaded him. Ultimately, he is an example of how consistency
and conviction can shape a man's entire existence. Francis's life harbors
a secret, and that secret is his very life.

When the war ended in 1203 he was twenty-one years old. He
had been in prison for about a year, and had been released after his
father had paid an adequate ransom. His health had always been fragile, and imprisonment certainly had not helped. He spent a period of
convalescence in the family estate, surrounded by Umbria's restorative
greenery, as sweet back then as it is today. Thomas of Celano, one of
what I like to call his "mythographers," described his early years before
conversion:

> This is the wretched early training in which that man whom we
> today venerate as a saint—for he truly is a saint—passed his time

from early childhood and miserably wasted and squandered his time almost up to the twenty-fifth year of his life. Maliciously *advancing beyond* all of his *peers* in vanities, he proved himself a more excessive *inciter of evil* and *a zealous imitator* of foolishness. He was an object of admiration to all, and he endeavored to surpass others in his flamboyant display of vain accomplishments: wit, curiosity, practical jokes and foolish talk, songs, and soft and flowing garments. Since he was very rich, he was not greedy but extravagant, not a hoarder of money but a squanderer of his property, a prudent dealer but a most unreliable steward. He was, nevertheless, a rather kindly person, adaptable and quite affable, even though it made him look foolish. For this reason more than for anything else, many went over to him, partisans of evil and inciters of crime. Thus with his crowded procession of misfits he used to strut about impressively and in high spirits, making his way through the streets of Babylon.[1]

Whether it was the result of his exposure to the horrors of war, or from meditation during his convalescence, or from his prolonged contact with nature, or perhaps, as Thomas of Celano asserts, that the hand of the Lord touched and transformed him, the fact is that his previous behavior—that of a financially and emotionally rich young man—suddenly changed. Within a few months the formerly reckless, arrogant young man became Francis—the man the Church later beatified a mere two years after his death. A reversal of this kind could not happen overnight, nor in a peaceful manner. His father was the first to worry about it. He wanted, like any loving father, for his son to carry on the lucrative family business, hewing to the prescribed customs of the time for a young man of his status. For example, Francis had wanted to join Walter of Brienne's military expedition. His father had no objections, since such military service was a normal addition to the résumé of any young man from the wealthy merchant classes. His departure, dressed in lavish armor, was duly celebrated.

In fact, Francis barely made it to Spoleto, a mere thirty miles away, where he fell ill and had to turn back, now intent on changing his life path. This was bad news for the family, and Francis's sudden, inglorious return was a source of shame. Soon thereafter he began avoiding his father, and was simultaneously burdened and enlightened by a series of new intentions he kept absolutely secret, as his family would have considered them mere whims. There were disagreements and a few violent arguments, whereupon Francis ran off and hid in a cave for over a month. When he returned to Assisi he was shaken, ragged, and pale as a corpse, so passersby began throwing stones and fistfuls of dirt at him, mocking him and calling him crazy. His father was shocked, dragged him home, and locked him up in a secret room, bound by chains so he could not flee. But somehow he did escape, likely with the help of his mother, and took refuge with a friend of his who was a priest at San Damiano, a church on the outskirts of the city.

At this point Francis's father had to give up the fight; his son was clearly lost, cut off from the family and the world, or *his* world, at least. And so he denounced his own son to the bishop, who instigated a trial of sorts. When Francis appeared before the judges, he was ordered to turn over all the money he had to his father. They went on to assert that it was against God's will for him to spend his father's earnings in support of the Church.

And now we come to the famous scene, repeated and commented upon countless times, first illustrated around 1306 by Giotto in a series of frescoes adorning Assisi's main basilica. Francis turned over not just the cash, but everything: every last object, every article of clothing down to his britches, and he topped it all off with the little bundle of money.

According to Thomas of Celano:

> When he was in front of the bishop, he neither delayed nor hesitated, but immediately took off and threw down all his clothes and returned them to his father. He did not even keep his trousers on, and he was completely stripped bare before everyone. The

bishop, observing his frame of mind and admiring his fervor and determination, got up and, gathering him in his own arms, covered him with the mantle he was wearing. He understood completely that this was prompted by God and he knew that the action of the man of God, which he had personally observed, contained a mystery.[2]

Deep down, its meaning is not really all that mysterious. Apart from the burst of pride or perhaps emotional instability that such radical behavior betrays, it is clear that, given the circumstances, Francis's gesture also had an allusive meaning. He stripped down to his birthday suit so that the act took on the appearance of precisely what he wanted it to signify: a complete and total rebirth.

———————

I have briefly summarized Francis's early years, up to the existential, symbolic episode that signaled the start of his new life. That is when he began helping lepers, overcoming his repugnance at the horror and stench of their festering sores. He shook their hands, welcoming the embrace of these poor souls who were forced to wear cowbells on their ankles so others would know to run the other way. He even discarded the basic clothes he had been given and, seized by a feverish rapture verging on madness, kicked the shoes from his feet, dropped his staff, and was content with just one tunic, replacing his leather belt with a length of rope. He then made the garb whose form echoes the shape of the cross, in order to remove all the temptations of the devil. It was coarse—for *they that are Christ's have crucified the flesh with the affections and lusts* (Galatians 5:24)—and of such roughly hewn cloth that no one in the world dare envy it.

This marked his marriage with poverty and his total abandonment of the world. He spoke of this abandonment quite eloquently in his testament, from which I also took the title of this chapter.[3] From that moment on, Francis lived solely to proclaim the word of the Lord, the spirit of the gospel.

Strong as the mystic love that had possessed him was, his behavior cannot be entirely understood without seeing it in historical context. During those years a few monastic trends arose that required their members to make, among other things, a vow of poverty. Not only individuals, but entire groups and convents were forbidden to own anything; what little sustenance they required had to come from charitable handouts or manual labor. A few "heretical" strains—the ones we now refer to as the Protestant Church—were the first to espouse this message: the Cathars and Waldensians, for example, popular among the humblest and poorest levels of society, were openly shocked by the ecclesiastical hierarchs' ostentatious wealth. The Dominicans, named after founder Dominic de Guzmán, and the Franciscans, named after our dear Francis, rose up to combat such heresies. The vast movement focused on pauperism inspired many within the Church, and Francis's enthusiasm certainly contributed to its success. Once again, to quote Thomas of Celano:

> At this time he wore a sort of hermit's habit with a leather belt. He carried a staff in his hand and wore shoes. One day the gospel was being read in that church about how the Lord sent out his disciples to preach. The holy man of God, who was attending there, in order to understand better the words of the gospel, humbly begged the priest after celebrating the solemnities of the Mass to explain the gospel to him. The priest explained it all to him thoroughly line by line. When he heard that Christ's disciples should not *possess gold* or *silver* or *money*, or *carry on their journey a wallet or a sack, nor bread nor a staff*, nor *to have shoes* nor *two tunics*, but that they should preach *the kingdom of God* and *penance*, the holy man, Francis, immediately *exulted* in the *spirit of God*. "This is what I want," he said, "this is what I seek, this is what I desire with all my heart."[4]

There are versions of Francis's story that tend to gloss over the events and the reactions they met with. Such accounts do not mention the dramatic atmosphere in which Francis made his first choices, the suspicion his movement aroused, and, consequently, the difficulties the Franciscans had in becoming an officially recognized order. In order to have real impact and attract new brothers, Francis needed the pope's approval, and knew full well that it would not be easy to obtain. His natural inclinations and conscious choices had led him to adopt a way of life that sharply contrasted with the values of the pope and curia. In 1209 Francis and a few of his brothers went to Rome to give Pope Innocent III the first draft of his Rule, outlining a few indispensable directions for leading a holy life—its contents are reported in Thomas of Celano's text. The pope had it examined and reacted cautiously, approving it only orally; he did not consecrate it with a bull, the official papal seal.

Those few pages contained revolutionary ideas regarding current mores, and proposed a complete renewal of the human spirit. Those very pages are what make Francis not only a saint for his Church, but a great, humane spirit worthy of everyone's veneration. The first rule sets the tone for all the others: give up all worldly possessions. When asked about the reasons underlying such a radical choice, he once pointed out that the ownership of private possessions would necessitate the possession of weapons by which to defend them. Wealth leads to the disputes that impede one's love of God and neighbor. This very radicalism is what set the movement apart from the luxurious lifestyles embraced by the papal curia.

One day Bernard, Francis's first disciple, was preaching in a Florentine church and gave an enlightening reply to a generous man who wanted to give alms. "It is true that we are poor," he said, "but for us, poverty is not a burden as it is to the needy; we opted to become poor, through our own free will." This freedom is what allows Franciscans to face the inconveniences of poverty with a sense of "joy." As Matthew (6:16) instructs: "Moreover when ye fast, be not, as the hypocrites, of a sad countenance: for they disfigure their faces, that they may appear unto men to fast. Verily I say unto you, They have their reward." And in the first version of his Rule (chapter 7), Francis advises: "Let them [the brothers] be careful not to appear as sad and gloomy hypocrites but show themselves joyful, cheerful and consistently gracious in the Lord."[5]

This is the core of the Franciscan way, focused on voluntary sacrifice, living an outwardly miserable life that is instead all the richer in terms of meditation, prayer, and the redemptive action of helping the world's excluded, its forgotten, the "wretched of the earth," to use the term coined by the twentieth-century philosopher Frantz Fanon.

There is only one other movement that, in one respect (and one only), comes close to the Franciscans', and that is the early twentieth-century kibbutz movement established in what later became Israel. The kibbutz or collective farm, much like the Franciscan communities, abolished private ownership of goods. This radical form of communal life included, as long as it lasted, a shared rearing of children, who lived in their own separate homes and visited with their parents only a couple of hours a day.

The kibbutz movement's Communist and Zionist ideals gradually declined over the years, for various reasons. Israel's economic development made the tough life of the kibbutz less and less attractive to younger generations, much the same way as the Franciscans' tenets gradually grew less rigorous than the original rules set by the movement's founder.

These two movements, from distant places and times, are united by the unique importance they place on free will. One entered a kibbutz by choice, and was also free to leave at will. Similarly, people submitted to Francis's strict rules by choice, and had to really want it—their conviction became an indispensable condition for withstanding the severity of that particular way of life.

In the words of Thomas of Celano:

> As followers of most holy poverty, since they had nothing, they
> loved nothing; so they feared losing nothing. They were satisfied
> with a single tunic, often patched both inside and out. Noth-
> ing about it was refined, rather it appeared lowly and rough so
> that in it they seemed completely crucified to the world. They
> wore crude trousers with a cord for a belt. They held firmly to the
> holy intention of remaining this way and having nothing more.
> So they were safe wherever they went. Disturbed by no fears,
> distracted by no cares, they awaited the next day without any
> worry. Though frequently on hazardous journeys, they were not
> anxious about where they might stay the next day. Often they
> needed a place to stay in extreme cold, and a baker's oven would
> receive them; or they would hide for the night humbly in caves
> or crypts.[6]

This and yet another anecdote, bordering on the insane, perfectly
capture the extreme to which the ideal of voluntary poverty could be
taken. In chapters 1 and 8 of the *Fioretti*, as *The Little Flowers of St. Francis of Assisi* were first known, we read how Francis explained to his most
trusted companion, Brother Leo, what the truest, most perfect joy is.
It was a hard winter day and the two were walking in a wind that froze
their rough clothes stiff. Francis offers Leo a few examples of admirable
charity and conviction regarding conversion: "Brother Leo, though the
Brothers Minor throughout all the world were great examples of sanc-
tity and true edifying, nethless write it down and take heed diligently
that therein is not perfect joy." He follows up with some increasingly
detailed and lofty instances: "albeit the Brother Minor should speak
with the tongue of an angel, and know the courses of the stars and the
virtues of herbs; and though all the treasures of the earth were revealed
unto him and he understood the virtues of birds, and of fishes, and of
all animals, and of men, and of trees, and of stones, and of roots, and

of waters, write that not therein is perfect joy."[7] Finally, we come to the point his entire peroration was building up to. For Francis, the perfect joy would be to reach the threshold of the church of St. Mary of the Portiuncula after a long journey on a cold night, knock at the door, and be brutally rejected by the guardian friar: "Get ye gone hence, vilest of thieves, begone to the alms-house, for here ye shall find nor food nor lodging." To bear such a harsh rebuke with patience—therein lies the truest joy.

Although in many respects this parable might seem utterly sense-less, there is, of course, another explanation. The historian Chiara Frugoni points out that this parable contains "a clear model: Christ betrayed by his own people, beaten, and insulted at the beginning of the Passion."[8] Here, Francis is cast as a new incarnation of Jesus. Many theologians have picked up on this parallel.

———————————

A recent book by the Italian philosopher Giorgio Agamben points out how, in its original form, the monastic ideal is ultimately an individual's escape from the world. The penitent, the hermit, and the Stylite (or pillar-saint) are all examples of men turning away from a community—an escape, we might even say, from the body itself—to immerse them-selves in meditation and prayer. Later on, however, as more and more people opted to participate in this sequestered kind of life, the commu-nity required concrete rules, schedules, discipline, divisions of labor, and hierarchy. In a monastery everything is shared—meals, religious services, the set hours of prayer, work, and rest. The rigor of such a schedule, Agamben writes, "not only had no precedent in the classical world, but, in its uncompromising absoluteness, has perhaps no equal in any modern institution, even in Taylorist production lines."[9] It is not just a question of being poor, denying oneself anything beyond the strict minimum required for survival (a bit of food, a shelter); rather, it is a revolutionary rethinking of how goods are used, arrived at by stepping outside of the norms regarding material possession. Being born poor or forced into poverty by external circumstances is one thing—spontaneously embracing poverty is something else entirely. He who is poor out of necessity and he who is poor by choice only appear to share the same condition, but each perceives his own status in a very different way. Poverty, like chastity and humility, falls within a set rule, but many people have adhered to that rule so completely that they have ultimately appropriated it. Agamben quotes canon regular Stephen of Tournai (1128–1203), who boils this idea down to a few words, concluding that the so-called books of Rules issued by some ascetic movements *"non Regula appellatur ab eis, sed vita"*: followers referred to them not as the *Rule*, but rather as *Life*.

An anonymous text about Francis titled "The Sacred Covenant with Lady Poverty" clarifies the relationship the early brethren had with the act of self-denial, which resulted in an unprecedented serenity. The allegory speaks of how Francis and some of his companions spent a day in the company of a lovely lady referred to as Madonna Povertà, or "Lady Poverty." They lead her up to a place of great natural beauty, offer her some stale bread, give her some spring water to quench her thirst, and offer her a place to rest on the bare ground. Upon awakening she asks them to show her the cloister where they spend a portion of their day, whereupon they lead her to a hilltop and point to the surrounding territories, as far as the eye could see, telling her that is their cloister.

It is a touching anecdote, but above all it helps us understand the distinction between the mendicant friars of Francis and all other monks. The latter shut themselves away in convents and cloisters, isolating themselves in places from which even the faithful were usually excluded. For the Franciscans, on the other hand, the world itself was their cloister. Each of them had, in a sense, fled from the world, but that flight was about the follower and him alone—his actions and the example he set were projected out into the world, viewed as a free space, wide open to his perpetual wandering.

This undeniably revolutionary impulse could not but be viewed unfavorably by a Church that practiced the exact opposite behavior: its use of wealth was often conspicuous, and it behaved according to the rules imposed by the dynamics of established power. Another fourteen years had to pass until, in 1223, Innocent's successor Honorius III agreed to officially grant the Rule of Francis a papal bull; even then, it had been modified to such an extent that it now reflected only a small portion of his initial intentions. Chiara Frugoni summarizes the differences between these documents: "Most of the evangelical quotes were omitted, and the language became dry and legal instead of effusive and poetic. The document no longer speaks of the duty to cure lepers, take a strict vow of poverty, or rebel against unworthy superiors," and so on and so forth. Francis won official recognition, but clearly felt the weight of the compromises it required. According to some biographers, 1223 marked the beginning of the period of his so-called great temptation: He abandoned everything, stopped caring for his community of brothers, and retreated into a solitary conversation with God.

With or without the papal bull the order still spread and the Franciscans, as they are now known worldwide, exuded great charm wherever they went to preach, attracting new members—perhaps too many, judging by the fact that the movement soon sprouted different philosophies or "strains," as we might say today. Toward the end of his life Francis was forced to repeatedly denounce the involution of the order he had created, knowing that it had come to contain too many divergent positions. In terms of sheer number, the so-called spiritual strain took on particular importance. Its adherents claimed to want to live in absolute poverty, in imitation of Jesus Christ and in obedience to the testament of Francis himself. This sect grew particularly strong in southern France/Provence and central Italy, especially Tuscany; its friars were known not only for their impassioned preaching and devotion to poverty, but also for their pronouncements regarding the imminent arrival of the apocalypse, which would put an end to the corruption of the Church and herald its renewal.

The barely hidden contrast between the Church hierarchy's official line and these "alternative" precepts exploded ninety years after Francis's death, with the ascent of Pope John XXII. Born Jacques Duèze in 1249 in Cahors, an ancient Gallo-Roman town in the Midi-Pyrénées, the new pontiff was consecrated in September 1316 at the rather advanced age of sixty-seven. In this period (1309–77), the papal seat was located in Avignon. Disputes within the Franciscan order, especially those raised by the spiritual branch, were one of the problems the new pope had to deal with. And deal with them he does, in his own way—that is, decisively, avoiding further fracturing by other pauperistic movements through harsh repression. One year after his election, Pope John banned the spiritual Franciscans: all dissidents were sent before the Inquisition to be condemned as heretics.

The disagreement centered mainly on the issue of poverty, which became such a controversial topic that the spiritual Franciscans and the pope ended up accusing each other of heresy. In 1389 (more than 150 years after Francis's death!) the Franciscan preacher Michele da Calci, a member of the "little brothers of the poor life" (*Fratres de paupere vita*) from the province of Pisa, was burned at the stake in Florence. The story of his trial and martyrdom, told by an anonymous monk as "The Story of Minor Brother Michael," is considered one of the great texts of fourteenth-century Italian literature.[10] Like any eyewitness report, it even records the screams of the crowd urging the monk, as he is led to the gallows, to recant his ideas: "Deny it, deny it!" they shouted, and even "You should not die willingly, you fool." He did not recant and, like the philosophizing Dominican friar Giordano Bruno, he died at the stake.

Umberto Eco's novel *The Name of the Rose* makes one character, Adso of Melk, another witness of this event, paraphrasing the text of the anonymous monk:

They set fire to the wood. And Brother Michael, who had chanted the "Credo," afterward chanted the "Te Deum." He sang perhaps eight verses of it, then he bent over as if he had to sneeze, and fell to the ground, because his bonds had burned away. He was already dead: before the body is completely burned it has already died from the great heat, which makes the heart explode, and from the smoke that fills the chest. Then the hut burned entirely, like a torch. . . .[11]

During his life Francis had long understood that the movement he founded had become too large to maintain the compact inspiration it had at the outset, a fact that became broadly evident a few decades after his death. In 1266, exactly forty years after his passing, the leaders of the Franciscan order gathered in Paris to select, for reasons of discipline and doctrine, the sole authorized biography they would allow to remain in circulation, dismissing the many others. They chose the one written by Bonaventure of Bagnoregio (born Giovanni Fidanza, 1221–74), a theologian, philosopher, professor at the Sorbonne, and minister general of the order. Also known as Doctor Seraphicus because of his theological wisdom, he was the best man for the job, and could write what had to be written. His text became known as the *Legenda maior*, with the first word taken literally: a must-read book.

In addition to these skills, however, Bonaventure also had a precise vision of who Francis had been, and wanted to set straight the considerable confusion caused by the many rumors about the saint's life, including Thomas of Celano's two different "biographies." Therefore the committee convened in Paris ordered the destruction of all the other "Legends" in circulation, and many texts that diverged from the official line were seized and burned. With a swift process of elision and editing, the life of poor, glorious Francis was purified of its most dramatic aspects and at the same time elevated to a level not far from that of Christ.

Francis was certainly a "good" man in the broadest sense of the term, and that quality must have struck all who encountered him. His presence must have been fraternal and reassuring, his expression intense and kind, since many people had already begun to call him *Alter Christus*, "another Christ."

But his goodness went hand in hand with his unwavering vision of the true path to holiness, and an indifference to the tortures and sacrifices it might entail. His vision gave precedence to the very last moments of Jesus's life, his Passion: the whip, the thorns, the nails, the blood. And the last few years of Francis's own life were a conscious, willful replica of the Passion: his liver, spleen, and stomach failed him, his sores spread, he was frightfully thin, he caught an intestinal infection after drinking contaminated water in Egypt, and was nearly blinded by a trachoma contracted in the Near East. Suffering was his constant companion, day and night.

Then there is the controversial legend of the stigmata, which I will not dwell on, given the many different versions of the story and their complex theological implications.[12]

Bonaventure's *Legenda maior* sealed the fate of Francis's legacy by elevating him to an unreachable height, such that no one could feel guilt at being unable to match his sacrifices. According to the novelist and historian Alessandro Barbero, "It was a matter of showing that the order's strength, its hundreds of monasteries, its thousands of monks, its leaders' ideological and political influence, and its perfect integration in the Church's balance of power did not contradict the ideal of poverty by which the inimitable Saint Francis had chosen to live."[13] To have his movement welcomed into the Church, he had had to make serious compromises, and his legacy in turn had to be stripped of any potentially excessive or dramatic aspects. Chiara Frugoni believes that Bonaventure was the one who imposed this new Francis, well aware that he ran the risk of reducing him to the sweet, slightly cloying character we have become accustomed to.

During the last few agonizing years of his short life, Francis was aware that the movement was shifting away from the ardent faith with which he had built it, veering away from the search for simplicity and peace that was the foundation of his "gospel." His pain would have been even more bitter had he been able to foresee that his own brothers—the Franciscans, alongside the Dominicans—would become the harshest judges in the courts of the Inquisition.

In September 1220, during a general chapter at the church of Saint Mary of the Portiuncula attended by Cardinal Ugolino, he said he was too ill to fulfill his role as guide, and entrusted the job to his friend Pietro Cattani. In a Latin manuscript of unknown origin known as the *Compilatio assisiensis* or "Assisi Compilation" (and also referred to as the "Leggenda antica di san Francis," the "Ancient Legend of St. Francis"), we read that his decision was based not so much on his illness, but more out of disappointment. He felt that, once upon a time, the brothers observed holy poverty with great commitment, but then its purity and perfection became corrupted, and the brothers used the excuse that they could not stick to the ideal because there were just too many of them. Francis knew he had lost authority as founder, and his health was also getting worse by the day. His final hours are particularly moving. At forty-four he was a relatively young man, even by the standards of the time, but his pains gave him no respite and his physical exhaustion was compounded by spiritual suffering, which is perhaps even crueler than bodily suffering. He had also botched an attempt to cure his trachoma by himself, using a red-hot iron, which only resulted in severe facial burns; naturally, his eyesight got no better.

During the night between October 3 and 4, 1226, laid out on the bare ground, Francis left his earthly life and entered the realm of legend.

The somewhat saccharine image of Francis that is so prevalent today does not do justice to the dramatic power of his message. But you can still catch an echo of it in Assisi's Franciscan community, which welcomes and unites all different kinds of people.

In June 1939 (the tenth anniversary of the Lateran Accords), Pope Pius XII proclaimed Francis patron saint of Italy. His announcement featured an infamous play on words that—intentionally or not we do not know—toed the line of the Fascist regime in power at the time, declaring Francis the most Italian of all the saints and the saintliest of all Italians. Even Benito Mussolini tried to appropriate the image of the pauper saint, who had become very popular in a country filled with paupers. In a magazine article titled "Messaggio francescano" ("Franciscan Message"), he praised Francis with belabored phrasing: "The prow of the ship that carries the immortal doctrine of this standard-bearer Eastward greets the infallible destiny of the race, retracing the steps of its forebears. And the saint's disciples who, following him, moved to the Levant, were both missionaries of Christ and missionaries of the Italian character."[14]

Issues of race aside, both Catholics and non-Catholics would probably agree on another aspect of Francis's legacy, the poetic spirit emanating from the *Laudes creaturarum*, better known as "The Canticle of the Creatures" or "Canticle of the Sun." It is a key text of early Italian literature, and was innovative in comparison to prevailing views on the penitential life back then; it was also quite prophetic, foreseeing the precepts behind the science we now know as ecology. In it, Francis joyfully sings the praises of the world, of animals, and of natural elements such as water, wind, sun, and even death itself, considering it a divine gift. Here, his religiosity morphs into a harmonious ode to nature in its entirety.

> Praised be You, my *Lord*, with all *Your creatures*,
> > especially Sir Brother Sun,
> > Who is the day and through whom You give us light . . .

> Praised be You, my *Lord*, through Sister *Moon* and *the stars*,
>> in heaven You formed them clear and precious and beautiful.
> Praised be You, my *Lord*, through Brother *Wind*,
>> and through the air, cloudy and serene, and every kind of
>> weather . . .
> Praised be You, my *Lord*, through Sister *Water*,
>> who is very useful and humble and precious and chaste.
> Praised be You, my *Lord*, through Brother *Fire*,
>> through whom You light the night . . .
> Praised be You, my *Lord*, through our Sister *Mother Earth*,
>> who sustains and governs us,
>> and who produces varied fruit with colored flowers and herbs.
> Praised be You, my *Lord*, for those who give pardon for Your love,
>> and bear infirmity and tribulation . . .
> Praised be You, my *Lord*, through our Sister *Bodily Death*,
>> from whom no one living can escape.[15]

Anyone familiar with the life of Francis will have noticed that these brief notes omit numerous episodes. I make no mention of Saint Clare, his "sister" in poverty, nor do I delve into the most famous legends, from his preaching to the birds to his taming of the wolf, nor have I mentioned the advent of the nativity scene tradition and its inclusion of two animals, the ox and mule, which there is no trace of in the scriptures. And I have only barely touched upon the difficulties he had in getting his Rule and new order accepted by a papacy that had long been suspicious of such a radical call to the gospel.

A recent book by the philosopher Massimo Cacciari explores Francis's journey, arriving at divinity only after starting out from the most forlorn human condition.[16] In this chapter, I have taken a rather different approach, casting Francis in an entirely earthly dimension so as to fully grasp his heroic intensity. Cacciari's essay examines Giotto's and Dante's interpretations of Francis. In the frescoes of Assisi's main basilica (as well as in the Bardi Chapel in the church of Santa

Croce, Florence), Giotto portrays Francis according to Bonaventure's *Legenda maior*. His life appears somewhat softened in the paintings: scenes of his dramatic encounter with the lepers and his death, which he insisted take place outside, on the bare ground, are both omitted. In short, Giotto seems to stick to the "correct" interpretation of his life as requested by the Church. Dante's portrayal, on the other hand, is a profound homage, and the poems tell of a man who submits his Rule to the pope without bowing—making him a Ghibelline, so to speak, or better yet, a true *Alter Christus*. Dante writes (*Paradise*, canto 11, verse 50) that "a sun was born to the world" in Assisi and that Lady Poverty, after losing her first husband with the death of Jesus, had to wait eleven centuries before finding, in Francis, her second.[17]

In this chapter our story has focused on our hero's exceptional "civility," since Francis belongs in the same circle as many other great spirits—such as Michelangelo, Giordano Bruno, Galileo, and Dante—all of whom fought, with all their strength, to assert their individual worldviews. Some sacrificed their lives for their ideals, and all pushed them to the very limits.

People of this temperament are a minority everywhere, not to mention in Italy. Italians have a widespread reputation for being accommodating even when they should not be, more inclined to compromise than to courageously break from the ranks, more apt to forget their word than to keep it. They inhabit a land, after all, that has never successfully staged a revolution, as we have already seen. Riots, rebellions, and uprisings yes, but never real revolutions. This is the country's "character," and its history has followed suit. But it has also had its share of greats, all those who, like Francis, tenaciously carried out their given task, without trembling: magistrates who died defending justice, courageous priests who sacrificed themselves to fight crime, lawyers who resisted the criminal underworld's incessant blackmail, politicians who rejected the shame of the abuses of power, volunteers and freedom fighters who braved torture to reaffirm the nation's dignity. They are the select few, the noble minority, the brothers and sisters of Francis.

8.

THE GOOD DUCHESS

It is hard to believe that a city with fewer than 200,000 inhabitants and a territory of one hundred square miles boasts so many quality goods and talents. Parma, better than any other Italian city, exemplifies how the different events and historical phases a place experiences can potentially become an intolerable burden or a unique opportunity.

In Parma, the latter has prevailed. The past, its legacies, and their implications for the present are perhaps more visible here than elsewhere. Here it could be said, without too much exaggeration, that you breathe the city's rich past in through the beauty of its streets and squares, its theatrical traditions, and its unparalleled cuisine—symbolized by its delicate prosciutto and exceptional Parmigiano Reggiano, king of cheeses. One of the most beloved local dishes, turkey breast with a prosciutto and parmesan filling, is called *Duchessa di Parma*, "Duchess of Parma." Then there is Stendhal's succulent favorite, anolini, a type of hand-made pasta stuffed with breadcrumbs, eggs, and parmesan cheese—a must for lovers of fine food. As for the local talents outside of the kitchen, just consider painters like Correggio and Parmigianino, musical masters like Verdi and Toscanini, and, more recently, visionaries like the poet Attilio Bertolucci and his film-director son, Bernardo.

And just think, it all began as an act of pure political and military calculation around the mid-sixteenth century, when Pope Paul III Farnese
appointed his illegitimate son Pier Luigi, Duke of Parma, in order to
establish a safe buffer zone between the Papal States and the Spanish
powers ruling Lombardy, threatening expansion.

The Farnese family has an odd history, and after rising to power
in Parma they went on to become owners of one of the most beautiful Renaissance palazzos in Rome, now home of the French embassy.
As the nineteenth-century German historian Ferdinand Gregorovius
wrote in a book chronicling his travels throughout Italy, they started
out as just "a small, predatory, feudal dynasty in Etruria," (northern
Latium).[1] Just picture the scene: herds of sheep, milk, cheese, fields
granting only meager harvests, their patrician residence surrounded
by miserable hovels, stunted children, hardships, people worn down
by barely remunerated labor. Giulia Farnese, as we will see, was one of
the people who brought about real change. She was a beautiful young
woman, and helped to better the family's fate by ushering it into a larger
story that, strange as it sounds, was destined to merge with that of
Parma. These obscure, quintessentially Italian tales combining lust,
love, money, power, intrigue, illegitimate children, and personal predilections inspired nineteenth-century writers and artists just as the
early romantic movement began to dissolve into atmospheres steeped
in melodramatic plots, poisonings, and betrayals.

Pier Luigi Farnese was an illegitimate child. His father was still
a cardinal when he fathered him with Silvia Ruffini, a Roman noblewoman who went on to give the future pope three more children. The
nobles of Piacenza and Parma used to contemptuously call him "the
pope's bastard," which certainly did not improve his ability to govern,
and also worsened the steely temperament Titian so perfectly captured
in his famous portrait. It ended badly, as the trustworthy account left
by the chronicler Lorenzo Molossi tells us. Molossi's text also contains

the first historical mention of Marie Louise, Duchess of Parma, Piacenza, and Guastalla and former French empress. We will discuss her fascinating life in a little bit; for now you need know only that in 1832 Marie Louise commissioned Molossi, an economist and geographer, to draw up a history of these places, including key events in the area. According to Molossi, this is how Pier Luigi met his miserable end:

> On the fateful day of September 10, 1547, Pierluigi was in the old citadel of Piacenza. The conspirators had taken their positions, the few German guards had been bound and gagged, and some had even been killed. Count Anguissola resolutely stormed into the room where the duke was and repeatedly stabbed him until he showed no more signs of life. Anguissola and Landi then opened the window that most directly faced onto the square below and showed the corpse to the people, shouting "Freedom" and "Empire," and then tossed it down into the pit. Once this tragedy was completed, imperial soldiers stationed nearby marched into the city, and the following day Don Ferrante Gonzaga came to take possession of the city in the name of Caesar.[2]

So it was a political assassination, followed by defenestration. The conspiracy was organized by Don Ferrante Gonzaga, governor of Milan, who briskly did away with anyone who annoyed him. In this particular case, Pier Luigi had annoyed Emperor Charles V. As a loyal imperial subject, Don Ferrante Gonzaga did not hesitate to enlist Anguissola and, with his help, other nobles who lent a hand in the assassination. The civic museum in Palazzo Farnese in nearby Piacenza houses a nineteenth-century painting by Lorenzo Toncini depicting the moment the daggers strike the duke, who has already collapsed on the floor. The lights, colors, and mood all look like they come straight out of the backdrop of a Verdi opera.

Despite this, the Farnese family ruled the territory for another two centuries, up until 1731. In their own way, as much as the times allowed, they led rather well: They reorganized government, founded a university, and restructured the justice system. A series of events then followed that made their mark on the duchy and its history, alternately pushing it toward conservative reaction followed by periods of fervid enlightenment, complete with the expulsion of the Jesuits, confiscation of Church property, and suppression of the ecclesiastical tribunals.

But the period that most heavily shaped the history and destiny of the city was the more than thirty-year reign of the young woman whose name appeared a few lines above, a woman history both favored and frowned upon at the same time. She was the firstborn child of Francis I, future emperor of Austria, in 1791 (the same year Mozart died). She was named Maria Ludovica Leopoldina Franziska Therese Josepha Lucia von Habsburg-Lothringen, so all her parents and grandparents were represented. At eighteen, her virginity intact, she was promised in marriage to the forty-year-old Napoleon to seal the truce between the two countries after the Austrian defeat at Wagram (1809). She had not wanted to move to Paris. Throughout the courts of Europe, Napoleon, a Corsican social climber who had ascended to the throne with a coup d'état, was considered an ogre—a violent man born into a rustic family on a semisavage island. He had usurped the imperial throne and invaded Vienna twice—once in 1805, and again in 1809—forcing the entire court to flee all the way to Hungary in search of refuge. Furthermore, Marie Louise could not forget that less than twenty years before, those same people had sent her great-aunt Marie Antoinette, nicknamed "the Austrian bitch," to the guillotine. Nevertheless, she did go to Paris and successfully gave Napoleon the son his first wife, Joséphine de Beauharnais, had been unable to conceive.

At twenty-five she took possession of the Grand Duchy of Parma, Piacenza, and Guastalla. The price she paid to get there, and how it happened, is one of the most exciting stories of the century, on both the political as well as the personal level. So many events happened, and with such speed, that in many respects her tale seems closer to fiction than to reality.

Marie Louise, or Maria Luigia as she was referred to in Italy, entered the city mid-month, on April 18, 1816. You could certainly say that she had already experienced a lot, for someone only twenty-five years old. And since she had left Vienna on March 7, you could also say that the voyage was slow going, even considering the means of transportation back then. She had very low expectations for Parma, a provincial town where (as she once wrote her father, now emperor of Austria) "I am told that there are no resources and no society, few educated women, and even fewer of any real value."[3] Her harsh judgment was confirmed soon thereafter by direct observation: "Here, society is even more boring than you might expect. I have not been able to wrest a single sensible word from the women."[4]

The archduchess was certainly no intellectual, and she had always had only the most general idea of culture. But she had lived in two imperial courts where everyone, especially her ladies-in-waiting, excelled at the brilliant art of conversation, interweaving fine chit-chat with the occasional spicy bit of insinuating slander, the occasional provocative detail—in short, everything at the atmospheric core of courtly life, where anyone unfamiliar with the art of being in the world is quickly cast aside, and those who remain know no other way of life. These idle, astute little ladies spent much of their time chatting about this and that, gossiping (circumstances permitting) about the prowess, tastes, preferences, and prerogatives of the men they knew, all accompanied by complicit giggles, mischievous reticence, gracious little gestures, and allusive smiles quickly masked behind their fluttering fans.

All this was clearly lacking in Parma, although Marie Louise only occasionally expressed worry over it. Indeed, in another letter to her father she wrote: "My sole desire is to spend my life here in the greatest calm possible."[5]

Her marriage to Napoleon had been difficult, nor could it have been otherwise, when you consider the tempestuous tumult that rained down on her indomitable husband between 1810 and 1815.

The emperor probably had loved, in his own way, the timid young woman who had given him his much-desired son, king of Rome, *l'Aiglon* ("The Eaglet," as he was nicknamed), the boy he dreamed would one day be crowned Napoleon II. But the status of their marriage was disputed by many, and Pope Pius VII actually considered it null and void, as if it had never happened. In this sense, Napoleon found himself in the same bind as the English king Henry VIII. He, too, had been unable to raise a male heir from his marriage to Catherine of Aragon, and he needed a son in order to ensure the continuation of his dynasty. The Spanish-born Catherine was six years older than her husband and had had numerous pregnancies, but all except one ended in miscarriage. The one she carried to term resulted in the birth of a female queen, who later earned herself the nickname Bloody Mary.

Henry had solved the problem by making a clean break with the Church. When Pope Clement VII refused to grant him a divorce from Catherine, he simply declared a schism and founded his own church, headed by the king of England—himself—and his successors. Napoleon could not afford to do the same. Henry knew that, in so doing, he was also following the deep desire of his people, who supported the idea of cutting all ties to the Church of Rome, which they considered so far away, so corrupt, and ultimately too "Mediterranean." Things were different for Napoleon because his subjects had different religious sentiments. Pope Pius VII's excommunication of Napoleon had damaged his standing—we must not forget that (outside of England, at least) the coronation of a king took place "by the Grace of God," and that the pope was God's representative on Earth. A schism would have been too much. And so he resorted to an oft-used stratagem within the bounds of the Roman Rota (the Roman Catholic Church's highest appellate tribunal), even for less illustrious men. The ecclesiastical tribunal in Paris annulled Napoleon's marriage to Joséphine, using the simplest, most abrupt way of working the system to avoid a formal divorce decree.

Back in Vienna, however, things were not so simple. Sigismund Anton von Hohenwart, archbishop of the Austrian capital, reminded

Emperor Francis I that his daughter would not have been able to marry Napoleon without concrete proof that his previous marriage to Joséphine was null and void. They called upon the skills of Prince Metternich to ensure that their union was within legal bounds.

I bring all this up not to add biographical color to the story's characters, but simply because this episode—in which Marie Louise was a passive subject, rather than an active participant—ended up affecting her life until the day she arrived in Parma.

In any case, the woman had fulfilled her primary duty to Bonaparte by giving birth to an heir. The wedding was celebrated by proxy in Vienna on March 27, 1810. The crown prince and king of Rome was born in Paris on March 20, 1811, after twelve hours of labor. The process had been so painful that afterward the poor girl had fainted, and the child was left on the floor for a few minutes because the doctors thought he was stillborn. When the obstetrician finally lifted him up, just to follow protocol and scrub him off a bit, he noticed the baby's heart was beating.

But lingering doubts about the legitimacy of their wedding never entirely dissipated. At the Congress of Vienna in 1815, which sought to restore the balance between the European monarchies following Napoleon's turbulent sweep across the continent, the legitimists continued to cast doubt on whether Marie Louise could really be considered the wife of the emperor, instead of his concubine—which would make her the mother of a bastard.

Such a situation would have been a source of deep pain for any mother, and it certainly was for Marie Louise as well—but that was only partially due to the circumstances of her life between March 29, 1814, the day when she had to leave Paris after being appointed regent, and the final collapse following Waterloo on June 18, 1815.

Chateaubriand paints the details of her flight from Paris in vivid detail. It was as hasty and humiliating as the fall of any dying regime, and took place amid great pressure from the Austrian Uhlans and Tsar Alexander's Cossacks:

The Regency had retired to Blois. Bonaparte had given orders
for the Empress and the King of Rome to leave Paris, saying he
would rather see them at the bottom of the Seine than taken to
Vienna in triumph; but at the same time he urged [his brother]
Joseph to stay in the capital. His brother's flight made him furious, and he accused the King of Spain of ruining everything.
The Ministers, the members of the Regency, Napoleon's brothers, his wife and his son arrived in disorder at Blois, swept away
by the debacle; wagons, baggage-vans, carriages, everything was
there; even the King's coaches had been brought along and were
dragged through the mud of the Beauce . . . Some of the ministers
did not stop there, but went on to hide in Brittany. . . .[6]

How did Marie Louise react to the trauma of those terrible events?
Some claim that her emotional, sensual, and externally determined
relationship with Napoleon, which had never been entirely resolved,
finally broke off. On March 30, 1814, Paris capitulated, and the next day
the Allies marched victoriously through the city.

———————

The Cossacks were led by Tsar Alexander himself, and even Frederick
William III of Prussia wallowed in the victory, followed by his retinue.
Francis I of Austria was not present, and sent Field Marshal Schwar-
zenberg in his place—a delicate gesture in recognition of his fugitive
daughter and grandson, and perhaps even of his defeated son-in-law.

Bonaparte, exiled to the island of Elba, wrote to his wife several
times, first asking and then ordering her to join him. There was a significant precedent that allowed the former emperor to hold out hope:
When he took off on the Russian campaign in May 1812, Marie Louise
had accompanied him to Dresden before he went onward en route to
Moscow with his 600,000 troops, the largest army ever assembled.
Once again, Chateaubriand portrays the scene for us:

> Whenever Bonaparte walked through the palace at Dresden to
> go to a reception which had been prepared, he went first, in ad-
> vance, his hat on his head; Francis II followed, hat in hand, ac-
> companying his daughter, the Empress Marie-Louise; the crowd
> of princes followed behind, randomly, in respectful silence.[7]

This masterful sketch conveys the situation in the court, as well as
the hierarchical differences between father-in-law and son-in-law. But
those days were now over. The Russian campaign—where 400,000
men died, a full two thirds of the army—marked the end of Napoleon,
and Waterloo was nothing more than the tragic confirmation of his
fall. Those grand days are over, and the situation has radically changed.
Napoleon is exiled to Elba and asks his wife to join him, but she refuses,
replying that she would rather go to Vienna to look after their son and
safeguard his future. Chateaubriand goes on to say:

> Marie-Louise hastened to join her father: indifferently attached
> to Bonaparte, she found the opportunity to console herself and
> rejoiced at being freed from the double tyranny of a husband
> and master.[8]

"She found the opportunity to console herself," the author wryly
remarks. Indeed, that "consolation" accompanied her all the way to
Parma. Marie Louise often consulted General Neipperg, whom her
father had sent her as counselor, for advice. His full name was Count
Adam Albert von Neipperg, and he was a brilliant hussar officer. He
had lost his right eye in battle, and was distinguished both in combat
and as a diplomat—first at the Swedish court in Stockholm, then for
the king of Naples, Joachim Murat, whom he had (temporarily) per-
suaded to abandon Napoleon. He had been the married father of four
children, but became a widower in his early forties. He wore a showy
black patch, covering his eye socket with ostentatious pride—such

was the man who was to guide the inexperienced Marie Louise. He performed his task with great skill, accompanying the deposed regent first to Aix-les-Bains, then on the return journey to Vienna. While they were in Switzerland, during a hike on Mount Rigi, known locally as the Königin der Berge or "Queen of the Mountains," the couple was caught in a heavy rainstorm. They took refuge at an inn promisingly named Zur goldenen Sonne, "Under the Golden Sun." Soaked to the bone, they dried off in front of a robust fire and sipped a glass of wine to warm up. Meanwhile, night had fallen. In the darkness between September 25 and 26, 1814, the event that had been a long time coming finally took place, and it changed Marie Louise's life forever.

This explains why the doubts surrounding the legitimacy of her marriage only troubled the archduchess up to a point. If, as the legitimists claimed, her marriage to Napoleon had never really occurred and was null from the very start, then by becoming General Neipperg's mistress she was not committing adultery, she was simply a free woman pursuing a relationship with the man she loved. During the Congress of Vienna the papal ambassador Antonio Gabriele Severoli distributed a memorandum that reiterated the fact that the marriage between Napoleon and Marie Louise had never been valid from the canonical point of view, because the pope had not officially annulled his previous marriage to Joséphine. Furthermore, some informants had reported that the former emperor had received visits from his former lover, Maria Walewska, in his residence on Elba. She had apparently traveled all the way from Poland to alleviate his exile. These two reasons more than sufficed to cure Marie Louise of any guilt she might have felt for having succumbed to the attentions of the bold general.

This, then, was the woman who entered Parma on April 18, 1816. She left the turmoil of recent events behind her and looked squarely ahead, fostering some tentative hopes for greater tranquility.

She had had to leave her son in Vienna; the victorious powers had sent his father off to rot on an isolated rock in the middle of the ocean, and did not want the child to remain in Parma, for fear he might attract attention from potential pro-Bonaparte nostalgics. They thought it best he return to Vienna, where he would be brought up as an Austrian archduke and forget all about his father and mother. They even changed his name: he was no longer Napoleon, but became Francis, just like his grandfather—Franz for short. For a while Marie Louise hoped, in truth without much conviction, that the boy might one day succeed her. But she soon had to abandon the idea and settle for what her new life offered, which was quite a lot. Neipperg became de facto ruler of the duchy and stayed in close contact with Vienna, but made sure that Marie Louise retained the power granted her as duchess. She proved to be an enlightened ruler, not least because Neipperg held much more liberal positions than those that prevailed in the Austrian capital. Indeed, his differences with Vienna were often stark enough to trigger serious dispute. As for Marie Louise, as soon as she got to town she had to deal with an outbreak of typhoid fever. She rose to the occasion, and even ventured out to assess the situation firsthand. Almost five hundred people died, but the epidemic was eradicated in just a few short months. She was also committed to bettering the lives of women, and since she had suffered so horribly during childbirth she decided to found a new clinic for obstetrics and gynecology. She also displayed an endearing sense of imagination, a rather unusual quality in your average government functionary, and commissioned a new bridge over the Taro River, inaugurated in 1819. Twenty-five "girls of marriageable age" were summoned for the occasion, and each was given a dowry of 250 lire. A few days later Marie Louise wrote to her governess and confidante Vittoria Colloredo: "The party was superb, thanks both to the weather and the number of spectators, and although my health remains fragile I nevertheless rejoiced because that bridge and another one across the Trebbia River, as well as some of my charitable ventures, are the only monuments I want to leave behind; I shall leave luxury to my successors."[9]

Marie Louise came from Vienna, the capital of music at the time, and she devoted great attention to music and similar initiatives in Parma as well.

The "good duchess" renovated the magnificent Teatro Farnese and built the Teatro Ducale (today's Teatro Regio) from the ground up. It was inaugurated in May 1829 with Bellini's *Zaira*, composed for the occasion. A few weeks later *Mosè e Faraone* by "the acclaimed master Gioachino Rossini" (as a contemporary poster proclaimed) was staged. It was a promising start. She also founded Parma's famous music conservatory. Its alumni included Arturo Toscanini, who earned a diploma as cellist in 1885. Just one year later, at age nineteen, he picked up the conductor's baton and brandished it for the rest of his life. The composer Giuseppe Verdi, born near Parma in Roncole di Busseto in 1813, received a scholarship from Marie Louise. He dedicated his opera *I Lombardi alla prima crociata* to her; it features the chorus "O Signor, che dal tetto natìo," a slightly less melodic, darker version of the famous chorus "Va, pensiero" in his previous opera, *Nabucco*.

———————

Here I must veer off into another short yet essential aside. The opera *Nabucodonosor* was first staged (to great success) in March 1842 at La Scala in Milan, with a libretto by Temistocle Solera. Just two years later its title was shortened to *Nabucco*. It tells the story of Jewish prisoners exiled to Babylon, and in the justly celebrated chorus they travel, in their mind's eye, back to the hills and hillocks "where the warm, scented, gentle breezes of the native land blow." Up in Milan, which in 1848 was on the verge of an insurrection against the Austrian occupation that became known as the Five Days of Milan, that chorus poignantly evoked not distant Babylon, but instead current events in Lombardy and Italy. The comparison was apt. Therefore, one would have to be utterly ignorant of the history of music, and history on the whole, to try to turn the chorus of Nabucco into a hymn to so-called Padania, a small "country" spun out of thin air on the basis of often sordid commercial interests and tax breaks.[10]

Going back to Parma, these musical initiatives show the direction the duchess was working toward, and also attest to the richness of talent in her territory. But we cannot discuss her years in Parma without considering the importance, and in some cases the weight, certain aspects of her private life had.

On May 1, 1817, at the age of twenty-six, Marie Louise gave birth to a daughter, followed by another birth on August 8, 1819, this time a son. Both Albertine and William became countess and count, respectively, of Montenuovo, so that there could be no doubts regarding their parentage (Neipperg becomes Neuberg in German, and Montenuovo in Italian). Napoleon was still alive at the time, unhappily imprisoned at St. Helena under the watchful supervision of his merciless jailer, Sir Hudson Lowe. No one knew anymore whether his marriage to Marie Louise was valid, annulled, or had been null and void from the very start. As a precaution the two children were entrusted to a doctor, Giuseppe Rossi, who was also their tutor. Their mother and father paid them a visit each evening. Meanwhile, Marie Louise's first son, l'Aiglon, was growing up in faraway Vienna. Thus the duchess spent her years, missing the son she only saw during rare visits to Vienna, as well as the two children with whom, though they lived in the same town, she could not be seen in public.

Napoleon died on May 5, 1821, aged fifty-one. His widow, who had reached her thirties by then, wrote a very realistic funerary ode for her late spouse: "He was the father of my son and—far from having abused me as is generally believed, he granted me every respect. When all is said and done, that is the most one can ask for from an arranged political marriage."

Three months later, on August 8, 1821, Marie Louise finally married the father of her other two children. Theirs was a secret, morganatic marriage in the sense that neither Adam nor the two children ever shared the rank, status, and assets of their respective wife and mother.

———————

How did all these people end up? Adam Neipperg died of heart problems eight years after their wedding, in February 1829. Marie Louise grieved for him with sincere sorrow; she would have preferred to observe an official period of mourning, but an unexpected order from Vienna prevented it. Her first-born, the would-be Napoleon II, died of tuberculosis while still in his twenties, in July 1832 in Schönbrunn, officially unmarried and childless. The court had long kept Marie Louise in the dark about his condition. When she finally learned of his illness, she sped to Vienna and arrived just in time to embrace the unfortunate boy before he died, calling her name. As for the duchess herself, what was her fate? Aged beyond her years, she died prematurely at fifty-six, in 1847, of "rheumatic pleurisy," as the official report stated. Her body, prior to being transported to Vienna, was embalmed by the same Dr. Rossi who had tutored the two children she bore out of wedlock. Field Marshal Radetzky, commander of the Austrian troops in Lombardy, sent a squadron of 150 hussars as an escort of honor. But perhaps the most significant fact is that, upon hearing of her death, a large crowd of Parma's citizens gathered in front of the palace and stood in sorrowful, perplexed silence.

———————

What, then, does the court of Marie Louise and her beloved General Neipperg have to do with the small court of Prince Ranuccio Ernesto IV? Very little, perhaps nothing whatsoever. The two tales have not a single historical point of contact in common, nor did this man I just mentioned bear any resemblance to the city's earlier leaders. Prince Ranuccio reigned over an invented city, a place that is both Parma and not Parma, a town that, historically speaking, looks more like Modena but in any case is undeniably set in the Italy of those years— and perhaps set a bit in our present day as well. By bringing up Ranuccio Ernesto IV we have gone from real, historical Parma to a town transfigured by Stendhal, around which he built his masterpiece, *The Charterhouse of Parma*. As we saw at the beginning of this journey, Stendhal adored Italy precisely because of its shortcomings—that is, the impetuous passions found all across the Peninsula, in both North and South, that can drive people to commit crimes of passion or lose their minds by loving to the point of desperation. In the preface to his novel, which he dictated in a flurry over the course of only fifty-two days (November–December 1838), Stendhal wrote:

> Italians are sincere, honest folk and, not taking offence, say what is in their minds; it is only when the mood seizes them that they shew any vanity; which then becomes passion, and goes by the name of *puntiglio*. Lastly, poverty is not, with them, a subject for ridicule.[11]

They are beautiful words, especially the last few, where he separates the state of poverty from the possibly attendant feelings of inferiority or ridiculousness. Slightly farther down he adds:

> To what purpose should I give them the exalted morality and other graces of French characters, who love money above all things, and sin scarcely ever from motives of hatred or love? The Italians in this tale are almost the opposite.[12]

The principality might be fictional, but the environment conjured up by the author is rather realistic: a small court held afloat by delicate balances, where love, deception, jealousy, and blackmail intertwine on a regular basis. Fabrizio del Dongo—the handsome young protagonist agitated by erratic passions and sometimes grotesque thoughts—moves within the circles of that court, as well as on the battlefield of Waterloo. He has the archetypal romantic hero's typical lack of awareness, and so he is naive but also aware of the protection his aunt, the alluring Duchess Sanseverina, grants him. She is the official mistress of the powerful prime minister, Count Mosca, but actually nurtures an incestuous love for her nephew. Italo Calvino correctly considered this a "melodramatic" plotline, which is undeniable, and accurate insofar as lyric opera (particularly of the most melodramatic sort) was one of the keys through which Stendhal had discovered, described, imagined, and come to love Italy. But the author combines this transfiguration of a small fictional kingdom in the post-Napoleonic Restoration period with the gloomy shadows of Renaissance history—in this case, the life of Alessandro Farnese.

Things went like this: While in Rome, hunting for source documents that would help him reconstruct Italian history, Stendhal had discovered some random loose annotations regarding the origin of the Farnese family. He was so struck by the document that he scrawled in its margin: "Tale full of truth and spontaneity in Roman dialect. Rome, 1834." In fact those records held hardly any truth—they were littered with historical inaccuracies and outright inventions: mangled names, wrong dates. On the other hand, this was exactly what the writer sought for inspiration. He additionally notes: "Most noble families made their fortunes with the help of a whore or two. Such a thing would be impossible in New York, but then New York is so boring you can easily dislocate your jaw from all the yawning. Here the Farnese family has made its fortune thanks to a whore."

Stendhal is alluding to Giulia Farnese, who had entered a marriage of convenience solely so that she could then become the mistress of Rome's most powerful cardinal, Rodrigo Borgia, the future Pope Alexander VI. Cardinal Rodrigo lost his head the very instant he first set eyes on Giulia. She was fourteen, he was fifty-eight, but no one dared dream of resisting such a powerful man. Indeed, Giulia posed no resistance, in part because her mother strongly pushed her to yield to his will. She was first married off to a mediocre man named Orso Orsini, who officially rid her of her maidenhood. Once she had become a woman, she was offered to the cardinal. Within a few months all of Rome knew about it, and chroniclers openly wrote that Giulia had become "the concubine of the (future) pope." As soon as Rodrigo ascended the papal throne he repaid the favors of his young lover by making her brother Alessandro a cardinal at the age of just twenty-five. Alessandro in turn became Pope Paul III, thereby forever establishing a connection between his sister Giulia's adulterous passion and the city of Parma.

The truth is, Stendhal loved whores, and had known many in his day. He once confessed that the hypocrisy of "good women" made him nauseous. He also felt strong "elective affinities" with adventurous characters like Alessandro, who had spent his youth "among women and wine," and he must have done something big indeed to deserve being locked up in the dungeons of Castel Sant'Angelo—apparently he had become his stepmother's lover. He managed to escape that horrible cell, however, by climbing down a long rope—which is exactly what Fabrizio del Dongo does when, in a fictitious Parma, he is locked up in the nonexistent Farnese Tower.

Stendhal uses Fabrizio del Dongo as a means for setting Alessandro's sixteenth-century adventures in his own time, the nineteenth century. According to Italo Calvino, Stendhal aimed to demonstrate that there was "a continuity in the Italians' vital energies and passionate spontaneity, which he never tired of believing in." There is no Farnese Tower in Parma, nor has there ever been, but by creating that lofty, enchanted place in his imagination the writer allows the story to move even deeper into the realm of adventure. It also allows Fabrizio, and us readers, to enjoy a dizzying view out across all of northern Italy. As soon as Fabrizio gets to his appointed cell:

> He ran to the windows. The view that one had from these barred windows was sublime . . . There was a moon that evening, and at the moment of Fabrizio's entering his prison it was rising majestically on the horizon to the right, over the chain of the Alps, towards Treviso. It was only half past eight, and, at the other extremity of the horizon, to the west, a brilliant orange-red sunset

showed to perfection the outlines of Monviso and the other Al-
pine peaks which run inland from Nice towards Mont Cenis and
Turin . . . Fabrizio was moved and enraptured by this sublime
spectacle.[13]

To enjoy such a scene in real life, you would have to get on a plane and
fly a few hundred meters into the sky. It is a fantastic, fictitious point
of view, but precisely because of that it impresses upon us the equally
fantastic, fictitious realm in which Fabrizio lives.

The other made-up place is the Charterhouse itself, which gives
the novel its title, and is where Fabrizio retires at the end of his countless adventures. Stendhal settles the issue in two short lines at the
very end of the novel: "On the following day, having forwarded to the
proper authorities his resignation of his Archbishopric and of all the
posts . . . he retired to the *Charterhouse of Parma*, situated in the woods
adjoining the Po, two leagues from Sacca."[14] Scholars have wracked
their brains trying to locate this place, and finally found its model in
the Charterhouse of Paradigna, currently home to the archives of the
University of Parma. The location of the actual place does not really
matter. The Charterhouse imagined by Stendhal is inaccessible, hidden
in the woods near the Po, more a spiritual place than a real building in
which you could feasibly live. Moreover, not even Fabrizio del Dongo
lived long enough to enjoy many years in the imaginary Charterhouse,
since his earthly existence came to a close, so to speak, not long after
he retired there. But the memory of his seductive presence lives on,
and has come down to us intact through Stendhal's text. Both these
figures—the fictitious Fabrizio and the very real duchess—helped
make Parma a unique, kind, and profoundly human city.

9.

MILAN,
BOTH GOOD AND BAD

Try to imagine, for a moment, what Milan looked like on April 25, 1945, when it was liberated, just as World War II came to a close. Consider this: 60 percent of the city's homes had been destroyed or damaged by the bombings; 1,400 buildings, 250,000 properties were in need of repair; much of its industrial infrastructure was completely destroyed or rendered unusable; and the main monuments—the Castle, the opera house at La Scala, the Brera art academy and museum, the main hospital, the glass-covered Galleria Vittorio Emmanuele right near the duomo, and the Triennale exhibition space—had all sustained major damage. Milan paid a high price for its dense industrial development, and had lived the last months of the atrocious Nazi-Fascist occupation under tragic conditions, rife with gunfights and sudden raids, searches and seizures of goods by militia officers (both real and fake), three or four partisans sentenced to death each day, and relentless hunger everywhere.

Nowadays it is not so easy to convey what those months and years were like. Whenever I try to tell younger generations about it, I get the feeling that they cannot fully relate to the sheer weight with which those circumstances affected people's lives on a daily basis. It was a very material weight, inflicted by hardships and privation, but also a psychological burden, the nightmare of leaving home in the morning without being sure you would return that evening. Imagine what it meant for families, for children, to know that bread—stale and tightly rationed—was distributed only three days a week, and basic staples like milk, rice, butter, and sugar were virtually impossible to find. Sometimes you could get them on the black market, but only at horrifyingly high prices, or at the cost of having to barter off some valuable family heirloom. Any word that a certain store or unmarked door had some scrap of food for sale became a ravenous secret, swiftly whispered from person to person. Electricity was limited to a few hours a day; otherwise people relied on candles, lanterns, and odorous acety-lene lamps, which occasionally exploded. Although I grew up in Rome, not Milan, I still have vivid memories of running my hands along the walls as a young boy and feeling heat from the pipes running through them—now that the war was over, the heat was beginning to work again. No more chilblains, nor the need to wear fingerless gloves to do our homework. Mozart wrote his music with gloves like that, in even colder temperatures, but I only learned that many years later, and it only consoled me up to a certain point.

Things were worse in Milan than they were in Rome, and not just because of the harsher climate. Rome was liberated on June 4, 1944; the liberation did not reach Milan until the following spring, and winter of 1944–45 was the cruelest of all, in all respects.

But even though Milan was starving and lay in partial ruin, each evening the curtains opened up on new theatrical performances, cin-ema lights dimmed, and, amid the thick smoke of scrounged cigarettes, film screenings lit up the dark. The La Scala opera house had been bombed, but the company staged performances just the same, at the nearby Teatro Lirico.

Let us journey back to a frosty February day back in 1947, as Paolo Grassi and Giorgio Strehler stop to look at a few spaces in the center of Milan, on Via Rovello, a small side street off Via Dante. One building has an illustrious past, having belonged to the Count of Carmagnola, a fifteenth-century adventurer. By the early twentieth century it had become the seat of an amateur theater company founded by a group of city employees. During the occupation, members of the Legione Autonoma Mobile Ettore Muti—a renegade Fascist military corps—had commandeered the space and turned it into barracks where they detained and tortured people.

As legend has it, the door was either locked shut or stuck so it would not open, so Paolo Grassi, who was born in Milan to an Apulian family, gave it a good hard kick. It gave way, revealing a scary sight. The soldiers of the Muti corps were known for their cruelty, and had turned the former theater's dressing rooms into prison cells. Chilling invocations, prayers, and traces of blood covered the walls.

Paolo Grassi was twenty-eight years old, Giorgio Strehler twenty-six. They both had theatrical experience, but neither had any idea they were about to establish a tradition. Grassi became the model for all major Italian theatrical impresarios to come, and Strehler forever revolutionized the art of theatrical direction throughout the peninsula. Together, the two founded the country's first modern public theater.

It took immense courage to decide, almost on the spot, to take those bare, sinister spaces and turn them into a real theater. The stage was tiny—just six yards deep by five yards wide—it had no wings, and only a laughable lighting system. But there were a lot of courageous people back then, both in Milan and all across Italy. La Scala had been rebuilt in record time, and on Saturday, May 11, 1946, just a year after Liberation, it reopened with Arturo Toscanini directing the opening concert of all-Italian composers: Puccini, Arrigo Boito, Rossini, and Verdi. Naturally, the set list included Verdi's "Te Deum" and the chorus from *Nabucco*, "Va, pensiero," which for the first time since the Risorgimento made a comeback to once again move people's hearts and inspire hope for the future.

Right as Grassi gave that door his energetic kick, equally courageous men were at work in Parliament. They had been elected on June

2, 1946, and a year and a half later they had drafted a new constitution. It constituted the best system of guarantees and civil liberties the Italian peninsula's inhabitants had ever had—a more thorough defense against the abuse of power than at any other point over the course of their troubled history. One of its first articles (the ninth), read: "The Republic promotes cultural development, as well as scientific and technical research. It shall protect the Nation's landscape, as well as its historical and artistic heritage."

It is simply put, in dry language—but considering the context, it took a particularly enlightened set of minds to draw up an article granting such importance to the role culture and research play, and to defend the natural landscape as part of Italy's cultural and artistic heritage at a time when much of the country still lay in pieces and its trains moved in fits and starts. It was an utterly unprecedented principle and foresaw, several decades before certain kinds of industrial damage were even possible, the pollution that unfortunately came all the same.

One of the miracles of the "Reconstruction" following the terrible ravages of the war was its awareness that not only the houses, streets, factories, public buildings, electrical infrastructure, and railways had to be solidly rebuilt, but that cultural sites and initiatives also had to be revamped. Such sensitivity was crucial, if Italy was ever to recover from the blindness and fury through which Fascism and the occupation wrought their havoc, stunting the country's conscience and openness, holding it back and steering clear of healthy debate. Many of the city's cultural centers—the Società Umanitaria, the Casa della Cultura, the Centro Ambrosianeum—were reopened, and the Museum of Science and Technology was founded as well. Angelo Rizzoli, who had grown up poor and worked as a typesetter before becoming a publisher, launched the BUR imprint (Biblioteca Universale Rizzoli), a series of small paperbacks printed in tiny type on cheap paper, recognizable by their gray covers. It was a stroke of genius, and its catalog showcased literature from around the world at prices within everyone's reach.

The creation of Milan's Piccolo Teatro (literally, "Little Theater") was part of this overall climate. Strehler once wrote: "We must sweep the old stuff from the stage and produce works that speak to our time, replace the 'dictatorship of the great actor' with the abilities of a great director. The recent rediscovery of democracy makes the liberation of the theater even more urgent than before."[1]

Grassi expanded on that concept to aim for not just a theater that respected its directors' visions, but one that could serve and satisfy "a collective need, a civic duty, becoming a key public service on a par with the subway and firefighters."[2] It was to be a *teatro stabile*, a "stable theater" with a fixed group of actors, but that idea of stability would go well beyond the theatrical company itself: it would become a city institution, a resource set up not for the purpose of making money, but rather to give the community what it needed to live an existence that was something more meaningful than mere material subsistence.

This overturned two cultural traditions in one fell swoop: the eighteenth-century tradition centered on producers who regarded theater as a money-making commercial venture; and the artistic tradition centered on often capricious lead actors who simply followed their own whims. Instead, this new theater would focus on staging works through unified criteria, emphasizing the mise-en-scène and, ultimately, its direction.

There used to be a famous anecdote about a great nineteenth-century showman who waltzed into his dressing room just before the evening's performance and asked the stage manager, "What is tonight's performance?" "*Hamlet*, sir." "Well then, bring me the black costume." This perhaps ungenerous anecdote nevertheless captures a certain climate, a lazy habit, an approach to theater that remained unchanged through the first few decades of the twentieth century.

In short, Milan was the first place to foster a more socially aware theater, one that really holds a mirror up to reality, one capable of catering to the public's intelligence and sensitivity rather than its fickle moods. To once again borrow Strehler's words: "Theater can be contemporary even when it stages the classics, the works that are our guiding lights as we journey into history and the artistic experience."[3]

But there is another equally important aspect that should be emphasized. Amid the misery of those years, as the city slowly came back to life, Milan's municipal council somehow found the energy, wherewithal, and money to fix up the small theater on Via Rovello and allow the city's new public theater to finally open. The idea was first announced in the January 26, 1947, issue of the *Corriere della Sera*, and it opened less than four months later, on May 14, fixed up in a hurry, just like La Scala.

Grassi and Strehler had hoped to open with a great sixteenth-century classic, Niccolò Machiavelli's *The Mandrake*. The author, famous for having invented political science with *The Prince*, wrote this text in five acts in 1518. Its basic plot is Boccaccioesque, with the usual cheeky prankster playing a hoax to get up a woman's skirt and mock her gullible husband. Callimaco burns with love for Lucrezia, but she is married to a simpleton named Nicia. The couple would like to have a child, but has no luck. Callimaco poses as doctor who has just come to town from Paris, and says he has the solution: a mandrake potion that will make the woman fertile, but will kill the first man who sleeps with her. Nicia is clearly puzzled, so Callimaco immediately offers his next solution: he suggests finding some poor bloke out on the street, getting him to sleep with her, and then sending him for a walk—to go off and die. Nicia eagerly accepts, and although Lucrezia is reluctant at first, her confessor—Fra' Timoteo, in cahoots with Callimaco—convinces her it is for the best. The "poor bloke" they find on the street is, of course, none other than a freshly disguised Callimaco, whose ruse enables him to enjoy the beautiful Lucrezia. After their union he reveals himself to her and professes his love.

This archetypal plot continued entertaining audiences through the end of the nineteenth century, and was then passed on, virtually unchanged, into the new medium of comedic film. The trope of the cuckold and his beautiful, sexually frustrated, available wife has been a source of comedy since ancient Greek times, and if the Assyro-Babylonians ever staged plays they would almost certainly have had a similar plot, just like everyone else. But *The Mandrake* could not be staged in Milan; the Church considered it blasphemous because the priest character is a sinful enabler. That said, Machiavelli's opinion of Italians' religiousness is clearly spelled out in his other works, too.

At that point they fell back on Maxim Gorky's *The Lower Depths*, in which Strehler himself played the part of Alyosha. This makeshift solution had two positive results: the show was memorable; and it set the tone for the theater's future path, devoted to socially engaged plays, especially the works of Bertolt Brecht. I think it is safe to say that Strehler's productions of Brecht's work are the best, even on an international level.

That assessment also stems from my personal experience. Once, when I was just over twenty, I went for a Sunday-afternoon stroll along Via Nazionale in Rome. Passing in front of the Teatro Eliseo, I stopped to read the poster for that evening's performance, Brecht's *Schweik in the Second World War*. I had a vague idea of who Brecht was, but I had never heard of Strehler. The title, in particular, piqued my curiosity. I bought a ticket for the nosebleed section, and my love for the theater was born that night. I had no idea that a stage setting could so powerfully convey the sinister idiocy of a regime (in that case, the Nazis' Third Reich) and at the same time capture, with ironic precision, the lucky stupidity of a man who is always about to be cornered but invariably manages to get off scot-free thanks to his imbecility. I later found out that literature and film are full of guys like this, who strut unharmed amid the whir of bullets (real or metaphorical) whizzing by all around them, simply because they fail to grasp what is actually going on.

Although Strehler had been forbidden to stage *The Mandrake*, he made up for it by finding a play with an equally "secular" spirit for the 1962–63 season. This one, Brecht's *Life of Galileo*, did not have the same echoes of Boccaccio, and had a more tragic tone. The great Tino Buazzelli played the title role, as he had in *Schweik*. A frenzied anticipation built up before the show's debut, and it once again sparked controversy, especially among Catholics. Strehler had tended to every single detail: the sets and costumes were by Luciano Damiani; Hanns Eisler did the musical score; and Donato Sartori designed the masks. Postwar Italy gave us only two directors capable of stirring up such high expectations: Strehler in theater and Fellini in film. On the eve of the premiere the special Sunday edition of the *Corriere della Sera* dedicated one of its famous full-page illustrations to the work. Paolo Grassi had a hand in its success as well. Despite keeping a close watch on the budget, he kept the theater closed for forty-three days straight, so as not to hinder rehearsals. No one had ever done such a thing before, and I doubt anyone has done it since. Nowadays such a decision would be utterly inconceivable. But it was worth it. Of all the plays I have seen in my time, *Life of Galileo* remains one of the dozen-odd shows that, both in Italy and abroad, truly left its mark.

The tragedy is centered on the abjuration the great scientist was forced to recite before the Inquisition on June 22, 1633, in order to save his own life. He was almost seventy. Kneeling on the bare stone, wearing penitential garb, he recites a humiliating negation of his scientific discoveries. It sounded something like this:

> [A]fter an injunction had been judicially intimated to me by this Holy Office, to the effect that I must altogether abandon the false opinion that the sun is the center of the world and immovable, and that the earth is not the center of the world, and moves, and that I must not hold, defend, or teach in any way whatsoever, verbally or in writing, the said false doctrine . . . Therefore, desiring to remove from the minds of your Eminences, and of all faithful

Christians, this vehement suspicion, justly conceived against me, with sincere heart and unfeigned faith I abjure, curse, and detest the aforesaid errors and heresies, and generally every other error, heresy, and sect whatsoever contrary to the said Holy Church, and I swear that in the future I will never again say or assert, verbally or in writing, anything that might furnish occasion for a similar suspicion regarding me.[4]

A church parish in Milan held a vigil to pray that the play not go on stage. In the end, it was a success not only for Italian theater, but for European theater as a whole. Brecht's portrayal implies that Galileo agreed to recant, and betrayed the scientific truth, solely in order to stay alive and continue his experiments. Just thirty-three years earlier the philosopher Giordano Bruno, who had refused to abjure, was burned at the stake in Rome's Campo de' Fiori. Galileo, therefore, is portrayed as a hero of Machiavellian dissemblance—but only up to a point. Later on he seems to realize that entering into pacts with the powers that be is too risky, lest injustice and oppression contaminate the disinterested logic of science.

Brecht had rewritten the ending several times. In August 1961 a wall rose up to split Berlin (and, by extension, the world) in two for almost thirty years. Then came the Cold War, and the threat of nuclear disaster seemed imminent. The playwright sought to weave two major themes into his finale: the power and responsibility scientists hold, as well as the freedom of research. It was probably a mistake, because toward the end the two themes muddy the waters a bit, and the play's overall meaning gets a little bogged down. But, over a half-century later, the final scene remains etched in my mind: Galileo is under house arrest. Despite constant surveillance by the Inquisition, he manages to finish one of his most important works, the one that earns him the title "father of modern science": *Discourses and Mathematical Demonstrations Relating to Two New Sciences*, relating to mechanics and motion. He entrusts the text to one of his students, who gets it printed outside papal territory up in the Netherlands.

———————

The theater on Via Rovello is only one example of the sheer vitality of a country that had seemed dead at the end of the war but instead managed to pull itself back up and start walking, even running. Several times over the course of history Italians have given a name to this phenomenon, talking about the *Renaissance* in the sixteenth century and the *Resurgence* in the nineteenth. A similar idea applies to the years after 1945 as well, as factories *re*sumed production and the Italian aesthetic *re*volutionized industrial and furniture design, fashion, food, and technological innovations worldwide. Never, in modern times at least, had Milan and Italy had known such creative ferment—it felt like something from another era.

But the relative "purity" of that sudden momentum did not last long. The breath of fresh air and enthusiasm that had brought the country back to life gradually vanished. The slow spread of a higher quality of life than Italians had ever before experienced also favored the spread of corruption: for the first time in recent history, political ambitions and crime began to intertwine.[5]

Around the same time that *Life of Galileo* was hitting the stage Federico Fellini's masterpiece, *La dolce vita*, also premiered, and Pier Paolo Pasolini followed up his book *Ragazzi di vita* (*Hustlers*) with his first film, *Accattone*. Fellini was spit at during his film's premier in Milan, and Pasolini was indicted for obscenity.

All three of these artists worked in different, complementary registers, and all three were censored in one way or another. The Church went after Strehler and Fellini, and Pasolini was pursued by what was somewhat lazily referred to as the *borghesia benpensante*, the "well-intentioned, conformist bourgeoisie"—a class we might actually miss nowadays, since the acts of the well-intentioned, conformist bourgeoisie can be compensated for, whereas the acts of the ill-intentioned have no remedy.

In any case, artists were the ones who first saw the dangers posed by increased standards of living, consumerism, the loss of certain values (be they old-fashioned or otherwise), and the sudden, feverish obsession with money and consumption. They were especially insidious in a country as culturally fragile as Italy, which was ill prepared to cope with the shock of modernity.

Strehler, Fellini, and Pasolini are all dead, and they never had a chance to see how correct their intuitions were. They did not live to see how things ended up. We have, and all we can say is that they were right. Many attempts have been made to understand why the postwar momentum faded so quickly, never to return. A definitive answer has yet to be found—maybe there is none.

———————————

I have touched on theater and film, two highly significant yet relatively marginal fields when compared with the many other phenomena that ensured the country's recovery after the war, ushering in a veritable economic boom. Italy's industrial production grew as never before, along with everything else feeding into the famous gross domestic product, the index that measures a country's standard of living by mixing both positive and negative forces into a single equation—people's general well-being, health, education, exchange, and trade, as well as traffic accidents, on-the-job injuries, speculation, and crime. Everything that can be bought and sold is factored into the GDP. Separating the bad from the good would mean picking and choosing, and that would in turn imply some degree of moral and political judgment; such things fall outside the domain of economics, so all eyes remain glued to the ambiguous and sometimes deceptive GDP.

No matter what you think of the postwar boom, Milan was long the engine behind it, earning the city the title "Italy's moral capital"— a moniker that today, after all that has happened, sounds a tad too emphatic. While Rome was Italy's political and bureaucratic capital,

Milan was its real capital, the place the entire country's standard of living largely depended upon.

If we set aside Fiat (based in Turin) and the network of small and medium-sized enterprises that were sprouting up all around the country, a large part of the GDP was produced in Milan or thanks to Milan. Not only heavy industry, but also the lighter, sometimes intangible industrial activities like fashion, product design, architecture, photography, and graphic design. Those represented the visible, important face on the bright side of the coin. But that coin also had another, darker side, which we shall discuss shortly.

Milan and Lombardy's entrepreneurial class continued to desert public life even after the war, turning its back on public government and, by extension, on the general interests of the community. One of the criticisms that is occasionally leveled against northern entrepreneurs in Milan is that they dove headlong into the pursuit of profit (be it for their family or their business), neglecting all civic duties and commitments. From Alcide De Gasperi onward, postwar Italy has had many brilliant politicians from the North. More rarely have its public administrators of equal stature been Northerners. Northern entrepreneurs walked away from such duties and, absorbed in their own businesses, they left everyone else to worry about everyone else's business.

According to Carlo Galli, professor of history and political science in Bologna, the relationship between Italy and its elites has never been fully resolved.[6] The country's ruling classes, including intellectuals and entrepreneurs, have only rarely and in exceptional periods played an active role in bringing people together for the purpose of working in favor of everyone's mutual interest. On the contrary, these classes have often distinguished themselves by short-sightedly defending their own privileges, when not forming outright pro-business lobbies. Galli analyzes the backstory with his usual interpretive acumen. One remarkable example is the reversal of the cliché that claims so-called civil

society is far better than political society, often referred to as a "caste."
According to Galli these two layers of society, if they are even distin-
guishable, instead reflect one another like a funhouse mirror, giving
each other a distorted image of themselves. It is no coincidence that in
Parma, back in 2001, Silvio Berlusconi received a standing ovation from
Confindustria, the country's most powerful industrial association, with
his famous phrase: "Your program is my program." Here, the politician
who ought to have defended the interest of the general public—not
only one narrow category—acted like just another self-interested en-
trepreneur among fellow self-interested entrepreneurs. It is no coincidence that those entrepreneurs' enthusiasm declined, to the point that
they let him fall from political power, when they (finally) realized that
Berlusconi's program was in fact only "his" program, nothing more.

According to Galli, just a few of Italy's greatest—he includes
Giacomo Leopardi and Alessandro Manzoni, an atheist and a liberal
Catholic, respectively (we could also add Antonio Gramsci)—managed to describe in detail the regressive characteristics that plague the
country's ruling classes. Those characteristics are a chief cause of its
backwardness, its failure to modernize, and even its inability to come
together as a unified nation.

And to think that the history of unified Italy had begun in such a completely different way . . . Throughout the nineteenth century most
high-level administrators for the Kingdom of Italy were Piedmontese,
ostensibly for reasons of efficiency and integrity. Cavour himself had
willed it: he considered his fellow Piedmontese the most solid guarantee that the government would be able to deal with the disintegration
and corruption that were so widespread in southern society. In an article published in *La Stampa* on June 23, 1900, the prominent Piedmontese economist and politician Luigi Einaudi wrote: "We [Piedmontese]
have had a greater percentage of government employees—both high-
and low-level—than most [regions]. But that had been necessary early

on, in order to cement national unity under a bureaucracy imbued with the spirit of unity and a devotion to existing government institutions; such a bureaucracy could only be found in Piedmont."

There have been many studies on this topic, and practically all have come to the same conclusions. One of the most enlightening is by constitutional-court judge Sabino Cassese, and its title sums up the essence of this "historical" problem: *Questione amministrativa e questione meridionale* ("The Administrative Question and the Southern Question," Milan: Giuffrè, 1977). These two "questions" are cast as the two sides of a problem that has remained unsolved over the last century and a half of Italy's postunification history. To put it simply, that problem is the division (according to some, the deep rift) between the "productive" North and the "unproductive, bureaucratic" South.

Even the Piedmontese predominance in public administration did not last long. Remarkably, by the end of the nineteenth century most government administrators and employees were from southern regions. In a speech given June 26, 1920, marking the final term of Prime Minister Giovanni Giolitti, the Socialist Filippo Turati (born near Como, Lombardy) famously stated:

> The South is the largest supplier—virtually the only supplier— for the entire Italian bureaucracy at all levels, from department heads down to prison guards ... In Northern Italy, the industrial area, it is safe to say that not a single graduate of our polytechnic schools or upper schools aspires to hold any government office. These offices have become hiring halls for what I would call, if the phrase did not sound too immature, the unemployed desk-job workforce, unfit for any useful service.

The phrase did not "sound too immature"—quite the contrary, it was a rather harsh judgment that reflected current opinion, which has remained virtually unchanged ever since. Just a year earlier, in 1919, the great jurist and historian Arturo Carlo Jemolo, born in Rome, observed more or less the same: "The administration of the state is besieged by inopportune requests from many members of the petite bourgeoisie who are unable to find a profitable job in the professional world and lack the energy required to don laborers' overalls."

I mention all this because numerous later studies have confirmed that, after the first few years of primarily Piedmontese governance, the "southernization" of government has been a key characteristic of unified Italy, straight through Fascism and World War II up to today. In the sixties, for example, the Left was widely convinced that the Christian Democrats occupied government, facilitating the entry of "consensus bureaucrats" on every administrative level. Eighty to 90 percent of Italy's administrative "leaders" came from the South; 80 percent of the applications for police and other public-service jobs came from central and southern Italy, and only 20 percent from the North.

All that is true, but it is also true that this clear division would not have existed, at least not to this extent, if the ruling classes from the North had been more attentive to the *res publica*, to public affairs. That could have been a part of the postwar wave of energy and creativity that swept in—indeed, for a few months people had the feeling that even this seemingly entrenched geopolitical aspect of the country was changing. The boom hit Milan head-on, and the city made the most of it. Consider, to return to this chapter's first anecdote, how the city government reacted to the idea of opening a new theater at a time when most of the houses and factories destroyed by the bombardments had yet to be repaired. Just compare that with current administrations' inability or unwillingness to act on today's pressing issues and cultural projects, and you can see the stark difference. The courage, bold vision, and momentum of those years is distinctly lacking.

That spirit perished all too quickly, unable to maintain the necessary energy. Oftentimes people's criticism focuses, rightly, on the bad public behavior so prevalent in the South; more rarely are similar criticisms leveled against Milan and the North. Obviously there are visible differences, but underneath those differences lurks a more general problem concerning the country as a whole: the ruling classes (in both the public and private spheres) often seem unsuited to fulfill their professional and moral duties.

10

LAST JUDGMENTS

The first time I ever saw a painting of the Last Judgment it was not in the Sistine Chapel, as you might expect for a boy born in Rome, but in the Scrovegni Chapel, up in Padua. It was by Giotto. I was there with my parents, and of course that was a key stop on our itinerary, as no civilized traveler dare miss it. But the explanations of the work bored me: I did not really understand its beauty, nor was I capable of grasping how revolutionary it was. I could not appreciate how it marked a clean departure from all previous paintings in terms of sheer quality, as well as the way it depicted space and the perspectival solutions Giotto had come up with to portray the many narratives involved: the stories of Joachim and Anne, Mary, the story of Christ from his birth up to his torture on the cross, and many others. Inspiration for this vast cycle of images was drawn from various sources—not only the four canonical gospels, but also the saints' lives of the *Golden Legend* compiled by Jacobus de Voragine, and the Gospel of James and the so-called Gospel of Pseudo-Matthew, both from the apocrypha.

Amid the splendor of that space, evident even to the eyes of a child, I was struck by one detail in particular: the two angels at the top, on either side of a three-mullioned window, whom Giotto depicted in the act of "rolling up" the sky. You read correctly: they are rolling up the sky as if it were a theatrical backdrop, in strict keeping with a long visual tradition (which I only learned about many years later) devised to signify the end of days after the Last Judgment. This evocative medieval iconography was inspired by the Apocalypse scenes in the book of Revelation, one of the greatest visionary texts of all time, the archetype of all other flights of fancy into the uncharted realms of the unconscious and of guilt. After an impressive procession of terrifying apparitions, the end is announced by four angels sounding trumpets to usher in the final calamities.

> The first angel sounded
> and there followed hail and fire mingled with blood,
> and they were cast upon the earth:
> and the third part of trees was burnt up,
> and all green grass was burnt up.
> And the second angel sounded,
> and as it were a great mountain burning with fire was cast into
>   the sea:
> and the third part of the sea became blood;
> And the third part of the creatures which were in the sea,
>   and had life, died;
> and the third part of the ships were destroyed.[1]

This frightening description continues until catastrophe consumes the entire planet and the firmament, including all the stars and planets. But here is how it sounds in Belli's folksy retelling in Roman dialect:

> *All'urtimo usscirà 'na sonajjera*
> *D'angioli, e, ccome si ss'annassi a lletto,*
> *Smorzeranno li lumi, e bbona sera.*[2]

In the end a gaggle of angels
Will appear and, as if going to bed,
They'll snuff out the lights, and that'll be *good night*.[3]

A similar scene of the rolled-up sky appears in Rome, in the tiny oratory of San Silvestro, right next to the church of the Santi Quattro
Coronati, one of the city's most fascinating and least-known spots.
Giotto worked in Padua from 1303 to 1305. But roughly half a century
earlier a few anonymous Byzantine masters had decorated this chapel
in Rome with the (false) story of the Donation of Constantine, by
which the emperor Constantine I supposedly transferred authority
over Rome and the western part of the Roman Empire to the pope.
The paintings in Rome are almost a political manifesto, implying that
the emperor ceded power when in reality he never did. But the oratory
of San Silvestro echoes the same scene as the Scrovegni Chapel: Christ,
enthroned, is flanked by the Virgin Mary and John the Baptist, as two
angels hover overhead: one sounds the trumpet of the Last Judgment,
the other rolls up the starry sky to show that the end has come.

Naturally, Giotto's work is on a whole other level, and much more
complex. Below, at the base of the cross on the left, we see the artist's
patron, Enrico Scrovegni, offering Mary the building he commissioned
to atone for the sins of his father, Reginaldo, a usurer of such infamy
that Dante includes him in the long list of sinners in the *Inferno*. Giotto,
too, condemns him to roast amid the fires of hell, and in the lower right
corner we see Reginaldo venturing down a gloomy tunnel that feels a
bit like the burrows of an anthill, headed toward eternal damnation;
behind him, a servant with a sack on his back schleps all of his riches.
In such a setting—chock-full of references to both earthly and eternal
life, with symbols nodding to the scriptures' and prophecies' most poignant and tragic episodes—this realistic little touch of the rich man
trying to carry a bag full of gold with him is deeply pathetic. It is not
hard to imagine that just a few steps farther, as the man crosses the fatal

threshold, a guardian devil will snatch it all away, casting both him and his bag of treasures into the eternal flames.

————————

Another spectacular Last Judgment is depicted in a Byzantine mosaic on the island of Torcello, in the Venetian lagoon. Not only is it spectacular, it is powerfully evocative—moving, even. Today, just a few dozen people live on this island. The low skyline of its few buildings is only interrupted by a tall bell tower and the large cathedral of Santa Maria Assunta. Approaching the island by boat amid a silence broken only by the steady hum of the engine, those two structures stand out above the otherwise the homogenous line of rooftops and low vegetation as the boat floats forward through the stagnant waters, passing marshy tufts of grass as you catch glimpses of the lagoon's sandy bottom here and there. Compared with everything else, the sheer scale of those imposing structures gives you an idea of how important they have been over the past ten-plus centuries since their construction. The cathedral, later rebuilt and renovated several times, dates back to 640, the umpteenth bit of evidence that each and every corner of this country has marked the passage of its remarkable history with some marvel.

The Last Judgment scene covers the entire entrance wall, so in order to see it you have to get at least halfway down the nave and then turn back to face the door. In keeping with the Byzantine tradition, it shows the death of Jesus followed by his descent into hell before the resurrection. The avenging angels, armed with long spears, chase the damned down into the flames of hell, reigned over (just like in Padua) by a monstrous Hades holding a tender young child in his arms. The name Hades refers to both the king of the underworld as well as the place of eternal punishment. Here he represents the Antichrist, whose deceptively innocent appearance tricks human beings into following him. And here, once again, we see an angel rolling up the starry sky, signaling the end of all creation.

Among the many others that dot this extraordinary country, another spectacular Last Judgment is the one painted by Luca Signorelli in the cathedral of Orvieto. It was created about four or five centuries after the more Byzantine version on Torcello. This brings us up to the height of the Renaissance, and two immense angels dominate the panel depicting the resurrection of the flesh. Their trumpets awaken the dead: some have already risen, shreds of flesh hanging from their bones; some are still skeletons; others struggle to emerge from the ground and are shown half buried, half risen. There could be no clearer evocation of the spirit of Revelation—you can hear Dante's *Inferno*, but there is also a hint of Michelangelo at work here. Indeed, just thirty years later he created his own masterful *Last Judgment* for the Sistine Chapel. The apocalyptic feeling grows even stronger in the panel depicting hell itself, shown with hallucinatory realism: amid a mass of palpitating limbs, devils with green buttocks pierce, prod, maim, and blind the damned; up above, flying demons throw down yet more sinners, whose flailing limbs foreshadow those of the poor souls who, terrified by the flames gushing from the Twin Towers in New York on September 11, 2001, leapt out into the void. At center stage the archetypal "prostitute" (a detail that has become even more famous on its own) is carried off to eternal damnation on the back of a horned demon with batlike wings. His face expresses anguish, and perhaps regret that his life could have been better. Above, three unwavering angels, swords in hand, stand guard so that no one escapes punishment.

Michelangelo's immense painting has inspired its own vast literature, to which nothing need be added here. I would just like to mention a few curiosities and some meaningful or funny details—the human touches that encapsulate the spirit and aim of these terrifying scenes; happily for us, in this case they also reveal the artist's irreverent and irrepressible free spirit. Amid the crowd in the lower right corner of the fresco, which covers a total of 1,830 square feet, there is a man with a haggard countenance and donkey ears. A large serpent encircles his chest, its coils descending to his groin, its fangs biting his testicles.

Who is this unfortunate Minos, surely one of the most miserable of all the damned? It is Biagio da Cesena, who served Pope Paul III Farnese as master of ceremonies. He had stopped in to see the work in progress, and had imprudently said he thought it more suitable for a bathhouse than a chapel. Michelangelo took revenge by including this immortal portrait. Vasari gives us some background, in a tone that betrays his amusement:

> Michelagnolo had already carried to completion more than three-fourths of the work, when Pope Paul went to see it. And Messer Biagio da Cesena, the master of ceremonies, a person of great propriety, who was in the chapel with the Pope, being asked what he thought of it, said that it was a very disgraceful thing to have made in so honourable a place all those nude figures showing their nakedness so shamelessly, and that it was a work not for the chapel of a Pope, but for a bagnio or tavern. Michel-agnolo was displeased at this, and, wishing to revenge himself, as soon as Biagio had departed he portrayed him from life, without having him before his eyes at all, in the figure of Minos with a great serpent twisted round the legs, among a heap of Devils in Hell; nor was Messer Biagio's pleading with the Pope and with Michelagnolo to have it removed of any avail, for it was left there in memory of the occasion, and it is still to be seen at the pres-ent day.[4]

Serves him right, you might be saying. According to Vasari, this epi-sode even had a sequel. Upset and offended by his placement (and his threatened testicles), Messer Biagio went to complain to the pope, who asked him where, exactly, the artist had put him. "In hell," Biagio said, to which the pope replied: "If he had painted you in Purgatory, there might be some remedy, but in hell no one can be saved." Apparently even popes like to crack a joke every now and then.

In 1564, the year Michelangelo died, censors decided to clean up the Sistine Chapel's scandalous nudes. Fortunately the artist, who died in February, was no longer around to witness the debacle. The decision enacted one of the principles laid out in the Council of Trent the previous year, and from then on the infamous Counterreformation swept across Italy, stifling scientific research and hindering the arts as well. Daniele da Volterra, one of Michelangelo's collaborators, as well as one of his heirs, was hired for the task. It was a matter of covering all the nude bits with britches, much the way hypocritical tendencies both old and new have required ballerinas' legs to be fully clothed. Hapless Daniele—known to history as *il Braghettone*, "the pantmaker"—cleverly chose to cover the frescoes with tempera paint, so that once the storm passed and the moralizers forgot their cause the figures could simply be stripped back to their original form. He used that reversible technique on all but one fresco, the one about halfway up on the right depicting two martyrs of the New Covenant: St. Blaise and St. Catherine. Michelangelo had painted St. Catherine nude, with pendulous breasts, bent over a breaking wheel, the torture device upon which she was martyred. We know the two figures' original positions thanks to a faithful copy Marcello Venusti completed before the censors' intervention.

This portion could not be easily restored because Daniele had not just painted clothes on the surface, he had actually scratched into the original fresco, primed it with a new coat of plaster, and completely repainted the two saints in different poses. In Michelangelo's version Catherine was, as I said, bent forward; Biagio stood right behind her, also bent forward, in a posture that would easily lead any sexually troubled mind (the kind of mind that often plagues celibate men) to view it as a scene depicting *coitus a tergo vel more ferarum*, or "sexual intercourse in the manner of wild beasts"—basically, the two saints were going at it, doggy style.

Of course these were all petty scruples, considering the work's tragic strength, and Michelangelo would certainly have been furious—he never allowed anyone to question his work. We catch a glimpse of his infamous obstinacy in another anecdote. As he was busily working on the ceiling (grueling, laborious work done roughly twenty-five years before he got to the *Last Judgment*), Pope Julius II Della Rovere, who had commissioned the fresco, stopped in to see how things were going. After having a close look here and there and asking the artist to explain a few parts, the pope expressed some dismay. In particular, he noted that, on the whole, the paintings did not seem "rich enough." Michelangelo's reply—a retort only someone like him could throw in the pope's face—was simply that "the people painted herein were, in reality, quite poor." It seems this remark was met with utter silence.

Such strong reactions prove that Michelangelo was fully aware of both his artistry and his indomitable temperament. He gave his work the weight it deserved, which he felt put him on a par with his patron, or perhaps even made him superior—even when his patron was the pope.

———————

There is another important aspect of the Sistine Chapel worth mentioning. Michelangelo's *Last Judgment* is located behind the altar, not on the facing wall like all the others. Traditionally, Last Judgments were always painted on the wall opposite the altar, because they served as a warning. After facing the altar during the course of the service, the faithful then turned around to leave and were shown the various penalties awaiting those who violated divine law. In the Sistine Chapel the exact opposite happens: the celebrant and the faithful are forced to stare at the *Last Judgment* as they say their prayers. I do not know whether it was the chapel's floor plan that imposed this solution or the artist's iron will. We could probably easily find out by asking an expert. I never have, because I like to imagine (albeit without any historical basis) that Michelangelo chose this configuration so as to make his work a warning addressed not only to the average churchgoer, but to the cardinals, celebrants, and the pope himself.

After all, Rome was very corrupt back then and the Reformation was in full swing. It traumatized Michelangelo, who was a member of the so-called spiritual Franciscans we heard about in chapter 7, and the papacy considered the movement's followers Lutheran sympathizers. That suspicion is almost certainly unfounded, but it is true that this small coterie aimed to encourage a revival of the evangelical spirit as a remedy for the Church's corruption. The group's unofficial leader was Vittoria Colonna, widow of Ferdinando Francesco d'Avalos, Marquis of Pescara, who had withdrawn to the convent of San Silvestro al Quirinale to live an almost cloistered existence. A small court of intellectuals gathered with her: high priests, writers, poets, and artists, including Michelangelo, who gave her a number of his works as presents. There has been speculation that the two were romantically involved, which is both plausible and irrelevant. Whatever the nature of their relationship, what really counted was their intellectual and spiritual bond. In his biography of Michelangelo, the painter and writer Ascanio Condivi reports that, upon Vittoria's death at the age of fifty-six (February 25, 1547), Michelangelo was overcome with emotion and leaned down to kiss her face.[5]

———————

But the question that all of these Last Judgments pose is: why and to what end was it such a popular, widespread subject? Various churches throughout Italy also boast sculpted versions of the Last Judgment, often lining the pulpits so as to impress upon the minds of the faithful, during the sermon, the idea of impending doom. This is obviously not about the quality of the works—which are often very good, when not excellent or downright supreme—but rather about their practical and pedagogical purposes. The punishments sinners are condemned to for all eternity in such scenes are not dissimilar to the equally atrocious ones Christian martyrs suffered in times of persecution, or those inflicted on witches and heretics by the courts of the Holy Inquisition. At the church of Santo Stefano Rotondo in Rome there is a series of sixteenth-century frescoes by Pomarancio depicting scenes of martyrdom. Its repertoire is vast: we see limbs amputated, people being whipped, stoned, crushed, flayed—everything the cruelest part of the human mind has ever devised for doing harm is depicted here. According to legend even the Marquis de Sade, the man whose name is synonymous with an obsession for inflicting pain on others, was troubled by the scenes. The difference lies in how such punishment is received by its victim. The faces of the martyrs glow with ecstasy, despite their suffering; but the faces of the damned, as in Matthew 22:13, show only "darkness . . . weeping and gnashing of teeth."

In other words, Last Judgments were one of the many means through which the Church tried to uphold orthodoxy and enforce obedience. Had the situation necessitated, actual torture and burnings could be arranged, harbingers of the true torments of hell, but the ideological inculcation of this precept was entrusted to these works of art, designed to spread a stern warning.

———————

From time immemorial one of religion's aims has been to contain the self-destructive forces inherent to human communities. As early as the fifth century B.C.E. the Sisyphus fragment, attributed to the Greek Sophist Critias, hypothesized that the gods were invented to restrain human passions and enforce moral behavior. This point has been hotly debated over the centuries, so much so that even present-day "modern thinkers" often complain that the promise of eternal life and the threat of eternal punishment no longer receive due consideration.

There are at least three ways to curb the antisocial tendencies that can develop in some individuals: threaten otherworldly punishment; threaten temporal punishments such as jail, forced labor, and death; or find a way to make most people share a belief in the need for moral behavior. In other words, ensure that civil rights and obligations are

observed out of a deep conviction. This third tactic is the most difficult but, once implemented as broadly as possible, it is also the safest.
Spinoza was one of the first to point out that this was the best solution.
Not even Kant liked the idea that people be forced to behave properly
only out of a fear of punishment. The Enlightenment ideal (or utopia,
if you will) was that good behavior be the result of a freely developed
conviction.

The imposition of any precept by threatening divine punishment
runs the risk of leading to a theocracy, or to a society where there is
no distinction between sin (understood as a divine offense) and the
offense that instead harms humans' ability to coexist—which would
be the worst approach, as attested to even today by the most strictly
observant Islamic theocracies.

A sense of the "sacred" is positive if fostered within each individual's conscience, because it generally embraces rules that people
have developed in order to protect themselves from themselves. But
when anyone tries to spread the sense of the sacred as if it were a social value for absolutely everyone, that constitutes a dangerous over-
reach. That is what happens when religious moral values are imposed
on those who do not participate in that religion—a phenomenon that,
from the eighteenth century onward, most advanced societies have
considered a serious violation of individual rights. In most present-day
civil societies, the legal punishments established for those who commit
crimes are based on certain rules, voted on by parliament or a similar
governing body. Divine punishment, on the other hand, stirs people's
darkest fears with threats of frightening and often unspecified punishments, and hinges upon credulity, which can in turn easily cross over
into superstition and fanaticism. That is a highly emotional, dangerous combination, as we have learned from all religious warfare, both
ancient and modern, regardless of who promotes it.

The idea of the "sacred" turned into faith, and faith elevated in
turn to a precept of truth—or claims of exclusive possession of the
"Truth" with a capital T—is the source of all intolerance, because Truth

does not tolerate contradiction. When the upper echelons of religious hierarchy say that the values they profess are "nonnegotiable" and that they should therefore be imposed on everyone, regardless of their beliefs, they betray the principle of charity—which, in theory, is the very foundation of many religions. Religions like Christianity.

This is one of the most contentious points separating the religious way of life and the secular idea of tolerance. Moreover, the separation between the ethical-religious sphere and the sphere of civil rights and duties is one of the greatest achievements of Western civilization. As the scholar Claudio Magris observed a few years ago, "The sublime evangelical sermon on the mount is greater than any code of conduct, but it is also unfit to be taken as a code of conduct."[6]

All in all, it is a good thing that these Last Judgments no longer scare anyone, and can now be appreciated for what they often are—namely, masterful expressions of human creativity.

11.

THE INVENTION OF
THE GHETTO

This final chapter also begins with the story of an individual, but this one comes straight from literature rather than real life—a man made not of flesh, but of feelings and passions. He first appeared in a fourteenth-century novel by Giovanni Fiorentino, and was later reworked by one of the world's finest poets, perhaps the greatest there ever was, William Shakespeare. In his tragedy *The Merchant of Venice* we meet Shylock the Jew, manager of a pawnshop who lends money at the set interest rate; no other profession is open to him, since city laws forbid Jews to pursue any other activity. But when a gentleman named Bassanio comes in to obtain a loan, citing his friend Antonio (the merchant of the play's title) as guarantor, instead of the usual penalties for noncompliance Shylock stipulates that, in case of nonpayment, he will take a pound of flesh from Antonio's body. Shylock's resentment of Antonio, stemming from the latter's open anti-Semitism, had grown into genuine hatred over time. At one point he tells Antonio: "Thou call'dst me dog before thou hadst a cause; But, since I am a dog, beware my fangs." The plot takes many twists and turns, with various subplots, but the tragedy remains focused on Shylock's hatred, which explodes in the famous soliloquy in act 3, scene 1. In this passage, at once both

invective and confession, Shylock bares his soul to show us the turbulent feelings underlying his cruel request:

> He hath disgraced me, and hindered me half a million; laughed at
> my losses, mocked at my gains, scorned my nation, thwarted my
> bargains, cooled my friends, heated mine enemies; and what's his
> reason? I am a Jew. Hath not a Jew eyes? hath not a Jew hands, or-
> gans, dimensions, senses, affections, passions? fed with the same
> food, hurt with the same weapons, subject to the same diseases,
> healed by the same means, warmed and cooled by the same win-
> ter and summer, as a Christian is? If you prick us, do we not
> bleed? if you tickle us, do we not laugh? if you poison us, do we
> not die? and if you wrong us, shall we not revenge? If we are like
> you in the rest, we will resemble you in that.

These are the words of a deeply offended man spewing out the reasons for his resentment; he demands the previously agreed-upon
amount of Antonio's flesh, and not even double or triple the loaned
sum could replace that which has no economic value—redemption.
Even the Doge cannot refuse to apply the law that the bond be paid
as stipulated. Ultimately things work out differently, and the drama
ends on an almost happy note. But the complex interconnectedness of
the various characters and situations is striking, insofar as the details
paint a historically accurate backdrop, beginning with the vast reach of
the *Serenissima*'s maritime trade.[1] The republic's commercial strength
is precisely what required a guarantee that its laws be respected: as
long as Venice's word remained reliable, businesses could continue to
flourish. Indeed, in act 3, scene 2, Antonio is awaiting the return of
some of his vessels, and Bassanio rattles off a list of where they are
coming from:

> From Tripolis, from Mexico and England,
> From Lisbon, Barbary and India?

And not one vessel 'scape the dreadful touch
Of merchant-marring rocks?

Such was the extent of Venice's sixteenth-century trade network, so the play is set during a time when the city was nearing the peak of its splendor. The Jews had facilitated much of its fortune (both literal and figurative) through their deft handling of money, for which they gained a reputation as usurers, but they actually played an essential role that greatly benefited the republic.

In one way or another, money has always be lent all around the globe, even before the advent of banks. Before there were banks there were moneylenders, who issued loans in exchange for pawned goods or for written IOUs. Borrowers who could provide collateral were granted more favorable interest rates. The invention of credit was one of Italy's greatest fifteenth-century innovations. Checks, bills of lading, bearer notes, and promissory notes were some of the new tools that aided the expansion of businesses by eliminating the risk of having to carry around large amounts of money on often adventurous expeditions. These instruments were the ancestors of today's credit cards.

Excluded from many trades and professions, banned from teaching, forbidden to work in real estate and agriculture, the Jews were left with few opportunities to earn an honest living. Two of the few trades still allowed them were in used clothes (the rag trade) and interest-based moneylending, forbidden by the Christian religion. A small group of Jewish bankers based on the mainland, in Mestre, was allowed to do business in Venice proper, provided that they stayed no longer than a fortnight. But then a series of tumultuous events, including the War of the the League of Cambrai in 1508, brought hostile coalition troops to the edge of the city, and many inhabitants of Mestre, including Jews, took refuge in the lagoon. The Jews were looking for a safe haven, the Serenissima was looking for money, the two came together and what had started out as a small Jewish population began to grow. Their residence permits still had a time limit, and they had to pay for them, but now they could stay much longer than the earlier fourteen-day period.

The League of Cambrai included Pope Julius II Della Rovere, who fought Venice because he wanted to extend his dominions past Ravenna and the Romagnan coast. But just a few months later the pope realized that France, an ally in the League, posed a greater danger than Venice, so he switched sides to join the Serenissima. This lessened the threat to Venice, but not the threat to its Jewish inhabitants.

At the moment of greatest distress, when it seemed the coalition of enemy forces might destroy the city, the Jews were faced with yet another danger. From all the city's pulpits Franciscan preachers claimed that the enemies would be pushed away and danger averted only after Venice cleansed itself of the sins it had accumulated. One of those was the presence of the Jews, murderers of Jesus Christ.

Those words did not fall on deaf ears, and the Serenissima, while maintaining its independence, allied itself with the papacy. These were the circumstances in which a measure that would soon change world history—or at least Jewish history—was drawn up. Several members of the city council began speaking out against the Jews, accusing them of corruption and of illegally building synagogues. One of the most outspoken was the prominent Zaccaria Dolfin, who was concerned about the public treasury. Driven by a violent anti-Semitism, on March 26, 1516, he launched the accusation that Venetian Jews were a foreign group whose presence had brought many evils to the city. The solution he proposed was to concentrate them all in a single neighborhood that could easily be patrolled: "they should all be sent to live in the Ghetto Nuovo, which is like a castle, and [it should be closed] off with a wall and drawbridges."[2] Three days later, on March 29, a decree ordered that:

> The Jews must all live together in the Corte de Case, which are
> in the Ghetto near San Girolamo; and in order to prevent their
> roaming about at night: Let there be built two Gates, on the side
> of the Old Ghetto where there is a little Bridge, and likewise

on the other side of the Bridge, that is one for each of said two places, which Gates shall be closed at midnight by four Christian guards appointed and paid by the Jews at the rate deemed suitable by Our Cabinet.[3]

The end of that March brought about a new institution and a new word: *ghetto*. Ghettoization has since grown depressingly widespread, taking various forms worldwide. The word's etymology remains uncertain, although it was apparently derived from the Venetian term *geto*, indicating a foundry, from the Italian verb *gettare*, to cast or pour melted metal. Although Italians would have pronounced it with a soft *g*, it is believed that the German Jews who were the first to move there pronounced it with a hard *g* (hence the later shift in spelling from *geto* to *ghetto*).

Confining a portion of the population to a fenced-off area and locking them in was odious in and of itself. But that was not enough: all doors and windows facing out of the ghetto had to be walled up, the four gates were locked at midnight and reopened only in the morning, and two boats (paid for by the Jews) patrolled the outer canals at night for extra surveillance.

And yet, in its practical application, this otherwise despicable measure nevertheless had a few advantages (backhanded as they were). It established a neighborhood where Jews were allowed to reside, which granted them official recognition and guaranteed certain rights, if not outright privileges. Within those confines Jews could observe their rites in peace, without fear of attack, and they were sheltered from the murderous calls for violence being launched from all the city's pulpits. It was a tight space, and only grew tighter (still today you can see how the ghetto's buildings are even narrower and taller then most in Venice), but it was a protected space. Their banks and shops were protected from attempts at plunder. Moreover, the Venetians' political pragmatism meant that many restrictions were applied with some elasticity, not least because the banks were essential to merchants' ability to receive loans at reasonable interest rates. As a contemporary chronicler pointed out, it helped local "poor folks, since there are no *monti di pietà* here as there are elsewhere."[4] District attorney Antonio Grimani was quick to add, in no uncertain terms, that not only did the Venetians "need Jews to subsidize the poor," but that "in this war they also helped the city hold onto its money." Indeed, the Jewish population continued to bolster the government's coffers, providing a series of "forced loans" to underwrite the many wars the Serenissima found itself involved in over the centuries.

Even the prolific Marin Sanudo (1466–1536), a politician and detailed chronicler, emphasized the social utility of moneylenders. Various passages in his endless diaries (which totaled fifty-eight volumes!) express his thoughts on the matter: "I would gladly have spoken, not to discuss the children of Israel and their scams, lending money at high interest, but . . . to instead prove that the Jews are as necessary in a town like this as bakers are . . . our elders have always advised us to keep the Jews around, so that we have access to loans." Sanudo maintained that expelling the Jews without establishing *monti di pietà* or other moneylending institutions would be a reckless decision.

But establishing the ghetto was not the only measure taken by the Venetian Republic. Any time they exited their neighborhood, Jews had to wear a yellow badge on their clothes, so they could be clearly recognized. Later on, instead of a yellow badge, they had to wear a yellow cap. Only doctors, who were highly esteemed, were exempt from this rule, and even then only for a set period of time. From Maundy Thursday to Easter Sunday they were to remain locked in the house as a sign of penance for their ancient crime, but also so they would be protected against potential Christian attacks spurred on by the memory of Jesus's Passion. In his book *The Ghetto of Venice* the Jewish historian Riccardo Calimani (to whom I am grateful for many valuable insights) notes that locking "foreigners" into a set area was not a uniquely Venetian practice—in the Egyptian city of Alexandria, Venetians were themselves forbidden to leave their homes during the hours of Muslim prayer and on Fridays.

Rome eyed the establishment of the ghetto with great interest. Gian Pietro Carafa, who ascended to the papacy in 1555 as Paul IV, immediately considered imitating it. Just two months after his election he hastened to set one up in Rome with a bull that became (in)famous, known by its first few words, *Cum nimis absurdum*. What, exactly, did he consider so "absurd"?

> Since it is absurd and improper that Jews—whose own guilt has consigned them to perpetual servitude—under the pretext that Christian piety receives them and tolerates their presence should be ingrates to Christians, so that they attempt to exchange the servitude they owe to Christians for dominion over them; we—to whose notice it has lately come that these Jews, in our dear city and in some other cites, holdings, and territories of the Holy Roman Church, have erupted into insolence: they presume not only to dwell side by side with Christians and near their churches, with no distinct habit to separate them, but even to erect homes in the more noble sections and streets of the cities, holdings, and territories where they dwell, and to buy and possess fixed property, and to have nurses, housemaids, and other hired Christian servants, and to perpetrate many other things in ignominy and contempt of the Christian name . . .[5]

This introduction was followed by a series of provisions: first, the establishment of the ghetto, and there was to be no more than one synagogue in each ghetto; further, Jews were forbidden to own real estate; they were to wear an outward sign of recognition; they were forbidden to employ Christians; they were authorized to conduct limited professions, including, once again, trading in used clothing and moneylending. Pope Pius V (Antonio Ghislieri), one of Paul IV's successors (served 1566–72) known for his anti-Semitism, recommended that all neighboring states establish ghettos, an exhortation readily implemented everywhere, with the sole exceptions of Livorno and Pisa.

In Rome, many of these measures were observed for a long time. To choose just one of the many anecdotes, I will point out that the artist Amedeo Modigliani was born in Livorno in 1884 as the direct result of a mishap his great-grandfather had experienced in Rome. The Modigliani family had settled there long before, perhaps because it offered greater business opportunities. Amedeo's ancestor was a wealthy man—perhaps a banker or, more likely, manager of a pawnshop—and had had the opportunity to lend money to a cardinal, sparing him a great embarrassment. The deal ended well for both of them, so well that Modigliani's reckless ancestor thought he could defy the papal ban on owning property, and used his proceeds to buy a vineyard on the slopes of the Alban Hills. When word got out, the curia ordered the insolent Jew to immediately hand over the land, threatening him with hefty fines. Merely saving a Church higher-up from dishonor was not enough to warrant safe-conduct. Modigliani had to obey, but he was annoyed and deeply offended, so he immediately gathered his family and belongings and left Rome for Livorno. He chose Livorno because Ferdinand I, Grand Duke of Tuscany and major patron of the arts and sciences, was eager to populate his growing port city. An astute leader, he turned the town into a free port of sorts, welcoming any- and everyone who wanted to live there, including religious and political exiles. Indeed, Livorno's Jewish community enjoyed real prosperity, as can be seen in the magnificence of its baroque synagogue, among other sites. When the Modigliani family arrived in 1849, there were about 5,000 Jews in Livorno out of a total population of 70,000.

In comparison, the Jewish community in Venice was always much smaller. According to Riccardo Calimani, toward the end of the sixteenth century the total Jewish population of the Venetian Republic was approximately 3,000 out of an overall population of one and a half million. By the mid-seventeenth century there were almost 5,000, but the 1869 census recorded only 2,415 (within an overall population of 114,000), which then rose to 3,000 just before World War I. The Fascist racial laws and raids during the Nazi occupation had tragic consequences: of the 200 Venetian Jews deported, only seven survived. By the end of the war the community counted 1,000 members, and by 2000 it was only half that.

The Venetian community fluctuated in size, and was divided into three parts or "nations." The largest was the German community, followed by the Levantine (Eastern) and Ponentine (Western) communities. Over time, due especially to intermarriage, the diverse languages and rituals began to fade, but they never entirely disappeared. Even rabbis who initially represented only their own "nation" came to be elected, based on personal merits, to represent the entire community. The community's division into "nations" can still be seen in the many synagogues of the Venetian ghetto: the various "schools" included German, Spanish, Italian, and Levantine synagogues. These places exude rich traditions visible in their architecture, interiors, vestments, and silver ritual objects.

Like any closed community, the ghetto also fostered its own kind of eventful relationships: friendly and even amorous relationships thrived, as did hostilities. Intense alliances and rivalries, jealousies and supportive friendships, and quarrels were all commonplace. And all that was made even more complicated by the community's relationship with the city and Christian Church authorities. The general atmosphere in Venice was certainly more relaxed than in Rome or in the Papal States, but it was widely believed that the city had been founded with the help of God, and that its commercial and military fortunes continued to depend on divine benevolence—which gave the clergy a significant influence over all city-related matters.

The Venetian Republic had always tried to maintain its freedom and independence by avoiding any open allegiance to the papacy, which was prevalent in other areas of the Italian peninsula. But, despite its power, not even Venice could completely ignore the Church's hostility toward the Jews, especially during periods when the local government had to strengthen its political or military alliances with Rome.

In 1542, as the vast complex of rules later known as the Counterreformation was being prepared, Pope Paul III Farnese had reinstated the Inquisition with his infamous bull *Licet ab initio*. Five years later, upon the doge's decree, Church tribunals were established in Venice under the supervision of the papal legate, the patriarchs, and a Franciscan who, although forced to swear obedience to the laws of the Venetian Republic, became the de facto inquisitor (after 1560 the roll was passed on to the Dominicans). In any case, Franciscan preachers were the most vocal in proclaiming their belief that God's favor could only be regained if the city purged itself of all sin, and one of its worst sins was that it had given the Jews too much freedom.

The Church's reaction to the Lutheran Reformation empowered the papal inquisitors to pursue "heretics" as well. Toward the end of the century the philosopher Giordano Bruno, who in 1592 had moved to Venice to tutor a nobleman named Giovanni Mocenigo in memorization techniques, was forced to prove his innocence to the Holy Tribunal at his own expense. The arrangement had not worked out well, so when Bruno announced his intention to leave his offended employer ran to report it to the ecclesiastical tribunal. He accused the philosopher of blasphemy, said he despised religion, did not believe in the Trinity, and instead believed in the eternity of the world and that there are infinite worlds—he also supposedly practiced black magic, denied the virginity of Mary, and so on. That very evening Bruno was arrested and put in jail. Perhaps he thought he could get out of the charges, but at that particular time, with a jubilee year approaching, the case was of great interest to Rome, where he was transferred and retried. On February 17, 1600, he was burned at the stake in Campo de' Fiori.

Conversions presented yet another nagging problem. In Rome forced conversions were common practice, but in Venice the Church could not use the same (often brutal) methods applied in the papal capital, because the government would not have allowed it. Furthermore, Jews were not generally considered heretics, except in a few special cases. For example, a decree by Pope Boniface VIII stated that a Jew who converted to Christianity—that is, was baptized—and then decided to go back to Judaism had to be considered a heretic and treated as such. While the Jews of Rome were under constant pressure to convert and were forced to attend catechumenical sermons supervised by the Swiss guards, in Venice Jews generally were not pushed to the new religion. Indeed, conversions were rare, although some cases caused quite a stir.

The baptism of the son of Asher Meshullam, founder of the ghetto, in the church of the Frari aroused a great interest. A solemn ceremony was held, and the new convert was received with high honors, but that was an exceptional case. In general such conversions were discreet, and there were a few embarrassing cases where conversions had effectively been bought in exchange for a handout. That is precisely what happened to an impoverished young jew who was baptized four times in Venice, Ravenna, and Modena. Brought before the Inquisition, he confessed: "I was baptized because my clothes were in rags and in order to have someplace to go . . . I knew it was wrong and that it went against the principles of the Christian religion, and that it was a sin, but I did it because I had no livelihood."[6] They condemned him to twenty years of forced labor in the galleys.

Converts almost always took the surname of their sponsors, and their new name was taken from the saint whose feast day fell on their conversion. Lorenzo Da Ponte, Mozart's famous librettist, is one curious example of such a transition. His original name was Emanuele Conegliano, son of Jeremiah, a leather merchant and fur trader who had been widowed and wanted to take the hand of a Catholic woman as his second wife. But in order to celebrate the marriage he had to be baptized, and he decided to baptize his children as well, including Emanuele. It was 1763, and Emanuele was fourteen years old. The bishop of Ceneda,

Monsignor Da Ponte, gave the boy his surname and baptized him Lorenzo, offering to underwrite his studies in the seminary, which would
lead to an ecclesiastical career. At the age of twenty-four Lorenzo became an ordained priest, and began teaching at various schools around
the Veneto region. But he was not a natural fit for the priesthood. He
knew many women—in the general as well as the biblical sense of the
term—and was an open follower of Rousseau and the Enlightenment.
He also fathered a son with a Venetian noblewoman, which is likely why
he then fled the country. In 1781, now thirty-two years old, he arrived
in Vienna with a letter of recommendation in his pocket addressed to
Antonio Salieri, Kapellmeister at the imperial court. He was given a job
as librettist (nowadays we would probably call him a scriptwriter), dove
into his work, and met many great musicians, including Mozart, for
whom he wrote three major Italian operas: *The Marriage of Figaro, Don
Giovanni*, and *Così fan tutte*. The rest of his rich life was no less adventurous. He embarked for New York, where he taught literature at what is
now Columbia University, and died at the ripe old age of eighty-nine.

———————

The ghetto's borders were actively enforced through the end of the
eighteenth century, and its abolition met with understandable joy, but
the broader circumstances surrounding the event were quite dramatic.
Napoleon had triumphantly concluded his Italian campaigns of 1796–
97, but there was still some concern about the spread of the Austro-
Hungarian Empire, which he wanted to keep in check. For centuries it
had wanted to take possession of the Venetian territories on land and
sea, and Napoleon satisfied that desire by using Venice as a pawn in the
exchange. In April 1797 in Leoben and again the following October in
Campo Formio, Napoleon signed two treaties with an imperial representative. Article 6 of the final agreement stated:

> The French Republic consents that His Majesty the Emperor
> and King should possess in complete sovereignty and proprietor-

ship the countries hereinafter designated, to wit: Istria, Dalmatia, the former Venetian Islands of the Adriatic, the mouths of the Cattaro, the city of Venice, the lagoons and countries included between the hereditary States of His Majesty the Emperor and King, the Adriatic Sea, and a line which setting out from Tyrol shall follow the stream beyond Gardola, and shall cross the Lake of Garda, to Cise; from there a military line to San Giocomo, offering an equal advantage to the two parties, which shall be marked out by engineering officers appointed by both parties before the exchange of the ratifications of the present treaty.

This officially constituted the end of the Serenissima, sanctioned by the man who had waged wars and celebrated victories in the name of republican virtues and freedom for all peoples. But, as usual, there was a bit of quid pro quo, and the loss of Venice was offset by the birth of the Cisalpine Republic, as provided for in Article 8 of the same treaty:

His Majesty the Emperor, King of Hungary and of Bohemia, recognizes the Cisalpine Republic as an independent power. This republic includes the former Austrian territory of Lombardy and the areas of Bergamo, Brescia, Crema, the fortified city of Mantua and its surroundings, Peschiera [del Garda], and all parts of the formerly Venetian territories to the west and south of the line cited in article 6 above; the border of His Majesty the Emperor's states in Italy will run through Modena, the principality of Massa and Carrara, and the three legations of Bologna, Ferrara, and Romagna.

This was not just the end of Venice—the cold language of diplomacy now confirmed the high price all of Italy would continue to pay for its inability to unite into a secular nation-state. Compared with what we now consider the world's superpowers, the political weight of the late great Serenissima was reduced to zero, and the city, its lagoon, its possessions throughout the Adriatic, and most of the Veneto region were gambled away in a round of international poker.

By May 12, 1797, the government had abdicated, opening city gates to the French troops. As the historian Samuele Romanin writes in *Storia documentata di Venezia*: "[This was a] time of extreme dejection under an illusion of independence . . . a time when everything yearned for something new, but the state rulers, be they the deceived or the deceivers, competed to issue the largest pronouncement, reducing government to a theatrical spectacle." We can certainly say, without fear of contradiction, that several times in the history of Italy this "theatrical spectacle" of various governments and their deluded/deceptive rulers have had their go at things, in equally dramatic moments.

In early June the provisional city government, which included three members of the Jewish community, stated that the gates of the ghetto were to be torn down. On July 9, "Year One of Italian Freedom," the Jews were summoned to be told that, as the ghetto gates fell, so too would "every abhorred separation" be brought to an end. That marked recognition of their full citizenship, which had hitherto been very limited, when not outright denied. The National Guard was brought in to execute the order: "The Provisional Town Council . . . has decreed that the gates of the ghetto are to be razed, removing all separations between Venice's Jewish and Gentile Citizens." Pier Gian Maria de' Ferrari, who commanded the Third Battalion, left this vivid description of the event:

> Inexpressible were the satisfaction and the happiness of all the attending Populace, who with happy cries of "Freedom" never tired of dragging those Keys [of the Ghetto gates] on the ground, blessing the hours and the moment of Regeneration. The echo of those bright "Viva"s was almost a single sound with the pulling down of the four gates, one by one, under the direction of Adjutant Goldoni who distinguished himself with the zeal of a patriot . . . As soon as the gates were brought to earth, People of

both Sexes without distinction wove joyful democratic Dances
in the midst of the Square that remained covered by the National Guard, and it is to be remarked that the Rabbis danced
too, dressed in Mosaic garb. . . .[7]

The "broken and shattered" gates were brought back to the main square
of the Ghetto Nuovo, where they were burned amid jubilant cries of
joy. In those hot July days, no one knew yet that the fate of the republic had already been cast, three months earlier, by the first agreement
signed between France and Austria in Leoben. News that the era of
discrimination had come to an end, and that a new life was about to
begin, was all it took to unleash an irrepressible wave of joy.

The jubilant inhabitants of the ghetto were right to embrace that
hope, since that moment of freedom had yet to arrive elsewhere. One
Venetian citizen known only by his last name, Massa, denounced the
ongoing misery of Jewish communities outside Venice: "Massa, the
president of the Patriotic Society, also spoke that day . . . The Jews
have been banished from Naples . . . In Rome they are insulted and
scorned with impunity . . . The Jews are marked in Rome like Beasts at
the Market . . . Thanks then be given to the immortal Bonaparte who
has broken the bonds of Italian servitude."[8] As he spoke with such
enthusiasm, Massa was likely not yet aware that one of the first actions
of the French occupants would be the imposition of a new tax totaling
870,000 ducats, a quarter of which was to be paid by the Jews.

On October 17 the Treaty of Campo Formio came into effect and
Austrian troops entered the city, replacing the French—no one knew
whether to call this transition an occupation or a liberation. It did not
take much for the tide to turn once again, and by January 1798 the Jews'
equality with all other citizens was again revoked. They were now subject to further limitations under Austrian rule, but the humiliation of
being locked in from nightfall to daybreak was never reinstated.

Venice's former glory fell into decline, predictably, because of political shortsightedness and inadequate leadership. The Serenissima's new rulers failed to see the changing times, nor did they understand the new social challenges they were faced with. Reduced to a tiny oligarchy, the government decided to close in on itself and defend the status quo. One of the major faults historians point to was the city's refusal to work with the nobles on the mainland, creating alliances that could have brought a new energy and closer ties between Venice and its vast hinterland. Instead those ties atrophied, and eventually devolved into open hostilities. In addition, Doge Ludovico Manin turned out to be a poor leader. A contemporary chronicler described him in these terms: "He had thick eyebrows, pale brown eyes, a large aquiline nose, a protruding upper lip, and a weary gait, showing weak inclinations. His facial expressions betrayed his general dismay, which informed and governed every action he took." This unflattering portrait accurately captured his nature, judging by his irresolute actions at a time when maximum energy was required of the city leadership.

His last name, of course, calls to mind the much more honorable Daniele Manin, a patriot who brings the latter part of this story right back to the history of the ghetto. Daniele had Jewish ancestry. His grandfather, Samuele Medina, had converted to Christianity in 1759 along with his wife, Allegra Moravia, whereupon she took the surname of her baptismal godfather, Ludovico Manin. Daniele Manin had been imprisoned by the Austrians for his patriotic activities, and to the great joy of his fellow citizens was released (along with famed linguist Niccolò Tommaseo) during the uprisings of 1848.

Ippolito Nievo sketches a scathing portrait of Ludovico Manin, Venice's last doge, in his great novel *Le confessioni di un italiano* (see Preface, note 2). Nievo depicts his fearful character in this concise, tongue-in-cheek passage: "The Most Serene Doge Ludovico Manin, pacing up and down the room while nervously tugging on his britches, spoke these memorable words: 'Tonight we shall not rest securely, not even in our own beds.'"

A few pages later he provides this dramatic description of the last session of the Grand Council, in which Manin had launched into a furious invective:

> The Doge rose to his feet, pale and trembling, before the sovereign of the Great Council, for whom he was the representative, and to whom he dared propose an unprecedented act of cowardice . . . He stammered a few words about the need to accept those conditions, about how resistance was futile, even impossible, and about General Bonaparte's magnanimity . . . [He] continued to dishonor himself, the Great Council, and the homeland with his stuttering, and not a single man present dared wrest from his shoulders the ducal cape, or smash his cowardly head on the floor, toward which the king's ministers and pope's delegates had all lowered their heads.

Giulio Lorenzetti's book *Venice and Its Lagoon* ends the chapter on the fall of the Serenissima with these inconsolable words: "So ended, without honour or a spark of heroism, between the shrinking cowardice of an enfeebled and corrupt aristocracy and the baseless illusions of a rash and fanatical democracy, the glorious Serenissima, 'ornament of Italy and of the world,' whose antique grandeur should have merited a less ignoble close."[9]

———————

The history of Venice's ghetto is not just about the Jews—rather, it has a lot to do with one of Italy's truest, most dramatic "secrets." Indeed, it might best be called an "enigma"—namely, the underlying reasons that explain why, throughout the peninsula's entire history, not once has a proper treaty proclaimed and guaranteed the rights of individuals. Although such declarations are often laborious, drawn up step by step, and sometimes at the cost of much blood, it is curious that Italy has never really had one. In truth, there have been a few attempts, but they were sporadic, short-lived, and quickly stifled: remember Naples in 1799, and Rome in 1849.

Think what you will of Napoleon, who displayed no shortage of deplorable aspects. Even the cold calculation by which he ceded Venice to Austria understandably raises disapproval. Yet it was Napoleon who brought freedom to the Jews of Venice, and it was thanks to him that the process of national unification was finally able to concretely get under way. The cannon shots that rang out in Marengo (near Alessandria, in Piedmont) in June 1800 sounded the alarm that woke Italy up after centuries of deep slumber.

As a curious aside, we should also note that the Battle of Marengo took a contradictory turn. For a good part of the day it seemed that the Austrians had won; indeed, the feeling was so strong that the Austrian commander, General Michael von Melas, sent a dispatch to Vienna with the news of victory. Then, the unexpected rebound of the French, led by General Louis Desaix, brought in fresh troops that suddenly turned the tide of events, leading to an unexpected victory for Napoleon.

Shifting our focus to the melodramatic world of lyric opera, which is always a good point of reference when speaking of Italian history, that battle also played a part in Giacomo Puccini's *Tosca*. News of Napoleon's supposed defeat at Marengo had even reached Rome, where people immediately launched into a "Te Deum" to sing their thanks. But shortly afterward (the timing is, obviously, compressed for the theater) they learn that the tables have turned (*"Melas è in fuga,"* "Melas is on the run") and Cavaradossi soars into his famous cry of victory: *"Vittoria! Vittoria! L'alba vindice appar / che fa gli empi tremar! / Libertà sorge, crollan tirannidi!"* ("Victory! Victory! / The avenging dawn now rises / to make the wicked tremble! / And liberty returns, / the scourge of tyrants!").

So far the plot contains large doses of realism, as the painter Cavaradossi and his friends are portrayed as a small group of isolated patriots stuck in a lazy and cowardly city. But if you dig back into the actual history, the truth is perhaps even worse: in order for Italy to topple its tyrants and give rise to freedom, foreign aid and intervention was often required. Italy has often trivialized liberty, its leaders have often arbitrarily used it and abused it; major civil liberties, the ones that guarantee individuals' rights, have for long periods—our present day included—been neglected and even denied.

I conclude this book fully aware of having skipped over many stories and places that are just as important as the ones I chose to include. The omission of Turin especially weighs on me, as it is one of the country's most significant cities, for reasons both historical and otherwise. Italy simply has too many cities and people whose stories and histories are worth exploring, and they cannot all fit in one book.

My choice to end with Venice was a conscious one, stemming from the deep melancholy that the sad end of the Serenissima has always inspired in me, ever since I was a schoolboy. *How could this happen*, I wondered back then. How could a well-managed, politically shrewd city-state that was so strong in commerce, trade, and military might have come to such a sudden end? And such a wretched one at that? I have boyhood memories of hiking in the mountains of Trentino, and from time to time I stumbled across the old boundary stones in the woods that bore the emblem of St. Mark's lion. Venice stretched all the way up here, the adults explained, and these woods supplied the lumber for its arsenals and fleet of ships. Over time I became convinced that Venice's end could be considered somehow destined, and that its disappearance could be read as a model for other events in Italy's national history. I do not know if a historian would agree. Such conclusions are strictly personal and subjective, and therefore debatable.

The Serenissima fell due to an unfortunate convergence of superior enemy forces, a weakened and divided ruling class, a government that was unable to rise to the occasion, and the lack of an informed citizenry. The very same factors were at work in the disastrous events that preceded the armistice of September 8, 1943. It is certainly no coincidence that, under a slightly different guise, we find the same factors at work in the way Italy's political leaders have spent months and months dealing (or not dealing) with the terrible fiscal crisis that began in 2008, by turns calling it either insignificant or over and done with. Some have actually dared say the economy has recovered just marvelously. . . .

This indecisiveness does not mean that Italians are incapable of stepping back to see the bigger picture and, at least for a little while, set aside their own self-interest for the sake of broader interests. It does, however, allow us to say that the number of people willing to aim higher is rarely enough to achieve politically useful results.

But on a few rare occasions even a minority has been enough to change the course of history. After the infamous day I just mentioned—September 8, 1943—a minority of young people fought Nazism and Fascism, waging a brief civil war (1943–45), organizing the Resistance as best they could, and restoring the dignity Italy had lost when it allied itself with the criminal regime of the Third Reich. Sure, they were in the minority, but from both a political and moral standpoint that was all it took to redeem the country. It was one of the few positive moments in a century in which more negative moments prevailed.

———————

Even Voltaire, a great admirer of English culture and civilization, had read the history of that island as a struggle against the power of despots. In his *Lettres philosophiques* (*Letters on the English*, 1734), known also as his *Letters Concerning the English Nation,* he views the civil war as a war of the nation's liberation from bondage. Voltaire had been seduced by the philosophy of John Locke, father of modern empiricism, and Isaac Newton's later discoveries—which, although Voltaire could not have foreseen it, inspired the work of yet another genius in the following century, Charles Darwin. Voltaire came to view intellectual freedom as a necessary condition for significant theories and discoveries. The French historian Gustave Lanson's book *Voltaire* (1906) called those letters "the first bomb hurled against the Ancien Régime."

In 1688 the English staged a revolution of their own, the so-called Glorious Revolution; in 1776 the Americans secured their independence; and in 1789 another revolution broke out, in Paris. Voltaire did not live to see it (he died in 1778), but he himself had helped pave the way for it.

I list all of these dates because, while on both sides of the Atlantic the world kept moving faster and faster, in the Italian peninsula—from a sociopolitical standpoint, at least—virtually nothing was happening. It took the uprisings of 1848, the Articles of Association, the Five Days of Milan, and the short-lived attempt at a Roman Republic before the country's slow awakening, begun (perhaps) with the cannon fire that had rung out in Marengo, began to take shape.

Of all Italy's secrets, this is the best-kept and most important one, the secret that encompasses almost all others: Why has the history of the peninsula had so little to do with the history of freedom? Many, myself included, have repeatedly asked this question. No one has the definitive answer, but of all the possible hypotheses the one that seems to me to have the most weight lies, once again, in the famous words with which Benedetto Croce responded when asked whence sprang the character of a people. The character of a people, he said, is its history, its entire history. If Croce is right, that is where we must search for the core of this secret—to learn to recognize it, and, who knows, maybe one day finally correct it. These words are nothing new; we have heard them several times before—once from the mouth of the great revolutionary and writer Ugo Foscolo. In a speech given at the University of Pavia on January 22, 1809, known by the title *Dell'origine e dell'ufficio della letteratura* ("On the Origin and Purpose of Literature"), he declared: "Oh Italians, I urge you to write your stories and histories, because no one more than you has experienced such pitiable calamities, so many mistakes to be avoided, nor has so many virtues worthy of respect." We can only hope that, sooner or later, his exhortation is truly heard.

NOTES

A PREFACE, OF SORTS

1. Virgil, *Aeneid*, trans. A. S. Kline, book VI, verses 851–53. [John Dryden's 1697 rendering (New York: P. F. Collier and Son, 1909; also available at MIT's Internet Classics Archive) is less literal and rather more poetic: "But, Rome, 'tis thine alone, with awful sway, / To rule mankind, and make the world obey, / Disposing peace and war by thy own majestic way; / To tame the proud, the fetter'd slave to free: / These are imperial arts, and worthy thee."—Trans.]

2. The 2003 fraud-related bankruptcy of Italian multinational food and beverage company Parmalat has been compared to the collapse of Enron.—Trans.

3. Translated by Lovett F. Edwards and published as *The Castle of Fratta* (London: Folio Society, 1954).

4. The term *corda pazza* comes from Luigi Pirandello's play *Il beretto a sonagli*, translated by John and Marion Field and published as *Cap and Bells* (New York: Manyland Books, 1974); it also inspired the title of a major book about Sicilian culture, Leonardo Sciascia's *La corda pazza: scrittori e cose della sicilia* (Milan: Adelphi, 1991). It's a reference to Pirandello's idea that every Sicilian has an internal mechanism with three cords (serious, civil, crazy) that can be wound up to produce various kinds of social interaction.—Trans.

5. See Ernst Bloch, *The Principle of Hope*, trans. Neville Plaice, Stephen Plaice, and Paul Knight (Cambridge, MA: MIT Press, 1986).—Trans.

6. See Pietro Zullino, *Guida ai misteri e piaceri di Palermo* (Milan: Sugar Editore, 1973), which also describes how in one respect Parma and Palermo are opposites. Eau de Parme or Acqua di Parma is a refined cologne described as *"Lumineuse avec la fraîcheur de l'orange, de la bergamote, du romarin, et de la verveine."* Acqua di Palermo, on the other hand—also referred to as Acqua Tofana—is a poisonous mixture of arsenic and other chemicals, a colorless, tasteless, lethal liquid. Mozart once confided to his wife Constanze that he suspected he'd been slipped a dose of it. I'll take advantage of this name- and geography-related tangle to mention a couple others of a more linguistic nature. *Palermo* in Arabic becomes *Balarm*, just as the general French term for a meat market, *boucherie*, in Palermitan dialect becomes *Vuccirìa*, the city's main open-air market; to follow this even further, if you'll allow, the town of Nablus in the West Bank and the city of Naples both got their names from the Greek *Neapolis*. That has

little to do with all the rest, but it gives you an idea of how close the ties crisscrossing the Mediterranean really are.

7. Attilio Brilli, *In viaggio con Leopardi* (Bologna: il Mulino, 2000).

8. Giacomo Leopardi, *Zibaldone: A Selection*, trans. Martha King and Daniela Bini (New York: Peter Lang, 1992), p. 189, July 23, 1827. [Note that the term *zibaldone* is the rough equivalent of "hodgepodge," which captures a sense of the text's varied topics.—Trans.]

9. Ibid., p. 193, November 30, 1828.

10. Luca Clerici, ed., *Scrittori italiani di viaggio. 1700–1861* (Milan: Mondadori, 2008).

11. Francesco Petrarch, *Canzoniere*, trans. Mark Musa (Bloomington and Indianapolis: Indiana University Press, 1996), p. 237, poem 146, verses 13–14: *"il bel paese / ch'Appennin parte e 'l mar circonda e l'Alpe . . ."*

1. ITALIANS AS SEEN FROM THE OUTSIDE

1. George Gordon Byron, *Byron: A Self-Portrait—Letters and Diaries 1798 to 1824*, vol. II (London: John Murray, 1950), pp. 693–94.

2. In his memoirs, D'Azeglio famously stated: *"L'Italia è fatta. Restano da fare gli Italiani"*—roughly, "Italy has been created, now we must create Italians." —Trans.

3. Corrado Augias, *I segreti di Londra* (Milan: Mondadori, 2003).—Trans.

4. Lucio Sponza, *Italian Immigrants in Nineteenth Century Britain: Realities and Images* (Leicester, UK: Leicester University Press, 1988).

5. Mario Praz, "Scoperta dell'Italia," in *Bellezza e bizzarria. Saggi scelti*, ed. Andrea Cane (Milan: Mondadori, 2002).

6. Ann Radcliffe, *The Italian, or the Confessional of the Black Penitents* (Philadelphia: Robert Campbell and Co., 1797), chapter 11; note that the Italian translation the author quoted in the original (*"gli occhi semiaperti, sintomo di tradimento, saettanti di tanto in tanto"*) casts the aged monk's eyes as "half open, a symptom of treachery . . ."—Trans.

7. Praz, "Scoperta dell'Italia."

8. Percy Bysshe Shelley, "Letters from Italy," from vol. II of *Essays, Letters from Abroad, Translations, and Fragments*, ed. Mary Shelley (Philadelphia: Lea and Blanchard, 1840), letter III, April 20, 1818. The surrounding passage reads: "The people here, though inoffensive enough, seem both in body and soul a miserable race . . . I do not think that I have seen a gleam of intelligence in the countenance of man since I passed the Alps . . . *" The asterisk leads to an equally revealing note added by his wife, Mary Wollstonecraft Shelley, who edited the volume this letter was published in: "These impressions of Shelley, with regard to the Italians, formed in ignorance, and with precipitation, became altogether altered after a longer stay in Italy. He quickly discovered the extraordinary intelligence and genius of this wonderful people, amidst the ignorance in which they are carefully kept by their rulers, and the vices, fostered by a religious system, which these same rulers have used as their most successful engine."—Trans.

9. Ibid., letter XV, December 22, 1818.—Trans.

10. The American writer Edith Wharton expressed similar sentiments: "I think sometimes that it is almost a pity to enjoy Italy as much as I do, because the acuteness of my sensations makes them rather exhausting; but when I see the stupid Italians I have met here, completely insensitive to their surroundings, and ignorant of the treasures of

art and history among which they have grown up, I begin to think it is better to be an American, and bring to it all a mind and eye unblunted by custom." From a letter dated March 8, 1903, in *The Letters of Edith Wharton* (New York: Scribner, 1988).—Trans.

11. See *A Roman Journal*, ed. and trans. Haakon Chevalier (New York: Orion Press, 1957).—Trans.

12. Thomas Mann, *Doctor Faustus*, trans. H. T. Lowe-Porter (New York: A. A. Knopf, 1948), pp. 173–74. [The author's original cites Ervino Pocar's Italian translation.—Trans.]

13. Italy suffered major losses in this 1917 battle (named after the town where it took place, present-day Kobarid, Slovenia), and morale fell so low that most of the troops willingly surrendered. Marshal Luigi Cadorna was forced to resign after the defeat, not least because he had a reputation for poor diplomacy and had dismissed several hundred of his own generals, colonels, and battalion commanders before the battle even began. Following his replacement by Armando Diaz and Pietro Badoglio, the Italian government established propaganda offices, promising soldiers land and social justice in an attempt to make up for the detrimental effects of Cadorna's draconian rule. Henceforth the term "Caporetto" took on particular resonance in Italy, denoting cowardly rule and humiliating defeat.

14. In adition to his memoirs and several essays on tyranny and other forms of government, Alfieri is best known for his many Greek-influenced tragedies, including *Filippo*, *Antigone*, *Saul*, and *Maria Stuarda*.—Trans.

15. See George Macaulay Trevelyan, *The Life of John Bright* (Boston and New York: Houghton Mifflin, 1913), p. 261.—Trans.

2. ITALIANS AS SEEN FROM THE INSIDE

1. Italo Calvino, *Why Read the Classics?*, trans. Martin McLaughlin (London: Jonathan Cape, 1999), p. 6.

2. Verga's *I Malavoglia* was first translated into English by Mary A. Craig and published as *The House by the Medlar Tree* (New York: Harper & Bros., 1890); it was retranslated and reissued by several publishers over the following century. Although Fogazzaro's novel *Malombra* has not yet appeared in English, Carmine Gallone directed a silent film adaptation released in 1917. Collodi's *Le avventure di Pinocchio* was first translated into English by M. A. Murray and published as *The Story of a Puppet, or The Adventures of Pinocchio* (London: T. Fisher Unwin, 1892); it has also been retranslated, republished, and adapted for stage and screen in countless versions.—Trans.

3. De Amicis's *Cuore* (the title literally means "heart") has been translated into English many times—the edition used here was translated by Isabel F. Hapgood and published as *Cuore (Heart): An Italian Schoolboy's Journal* (New York: Thomas Y. Crowell, 1887); in 1948 a film adaptation was released by renowned directors Vittorio De Sica and Duilio Coletti. The version of D'Annunzio's *Il piacere* quoted here was translated by Georgina Harding and Arthur Symons and published as *The Child of Pleasure* (New York: Modern Library, 1898).—Trans.

4. Edmondo De Amicis, *Pagine sparse* (Milan: Tipografia editrice Lombarda, 1874). The original reads: "*Sì, io piccino, io povero, io che campo di pan nero e vo vestito di cenci, io sconosciuto al mondo e oggetto di compassione per i pochi che mi conoscono, io se voglio, se studio, se fatico, posso costringere un giorno diecimila persone, il fiore dei cittadini della mia città, a star zitti, come fanno adesso, per sentire il mio nome, a sporger il capo per*

vedermi; a mormorare: – Eccolo là; – a dire ai loro fanciulli vestiti di velluto: – Fate come lui!... – Sono capace a star levato la notte, io. Non ho lume? Ma io mi farò dare i mozziconi di candela dal vicino."—Trans.

5. Mimì Mosso, *I tempi del Cuore: vita e lettere di Edmondo De Amicis ed Emilio Treves* (Milan: Mondadori, 1925).

6. De Amicis, *Heart*, pp. 8–9. The original Italian has a slightly different tone, whereby Garrone "is always eating," and Votini is "dressed well, *too* well."—Trans.

7. Ibid., p. 63.—Trans.

8. Ibid., preface.—Trans.

9. Ibid., pp. 160, 301.—Trans.

10. Ibid., p. 206–7.—Trans.

11. Literally "The Resurgence," this term refers to the nineteenth-century period that culminated in Italian unification.

12. Ibid., pp. 62–63.—Trans.

13. Umberto Eco, *Diario minimo* (Milan: Mondadori, 1963). [This essay was not included in the English edition of the book. Gaetano Bresci was the anarchist who assassinated King Umberto I of Italy; Eco draws a parallel between Franti and Bresci, recasting the boy in De Amicis's novel as a figure of resistance combating militaristic, nationalist ideologies.—Trans.]

14. Ibid.

15. No publication details are available, but the original reads: *"Era il tempo in cui più torbida ferveva l'operosità dei distruttori e dei costruttori. Insieme con nuvoli di polvere si propagava una specie di follia edificatoria, con un turbine improvviso . . . Fu allora, dappertutto, come un contagio di volgarità. Nel contrasto incessante degli affari, nella furia quasi feroce degli appetiti e delle passioni, nell'esercizio disordinato ed esclusivo delle attività utili, ogni senso estetico fu smarrito, ogni rispetto del passato fu deposto."*—Trans.

16. Edoardo Scarfoglio, *Il libro di Don Chisciotte* (Naples: Liguori Editore, 1990).

17. *"La giovinezza mia barbara e forte / in braccio de le femmine s'uccide."*—Trans.

18. *"La testa / in dietro a l'improvviso abbandonò. Le chiome / effuse le composero un letto ov'ella, come / per morire, si stese. Un irrigidimento, / quasi un gelo di morte, l'occupò. Lo spavento / m'invase . . . / Ma fu morte / breve. Tornò la vita ne l'onda del piacere. / Chino a lei su la bocca io tutto, come a bere / da un calice, fremendo di conquista, sentivo / le punte del suo petto insorgere, al lascivo / tentar de le mie dita, quali carnosi fiori . . ."*—Trans.

19. *"Quando (al pensier, le vene mi tremano pur di dolcezza) / io mi partii, com'ebro, dalla sua casa amata; / su per le vie che ancóra fervean de l'estreme diurne / opere, de' sonanti carri, de' rauchi gridi, / tutta sentii dal cuore segreto l'anima alzarsi / cupidamente . . . / Agile da le gote capaci il Tritone a que' fochi /dava lo stel de l'acqua, che si spandea qual chioma. / Tremula di baleni, accesa di porpora al sommo, / libera in ciel, la grande casa dei Barberini / parvemi quel palagio ch'eletto avrei agli amori / nostri; e il desio mi finse quivi superbi amori: / fulgidi amori e lussi mirabili ed ozii profondi; / una più larga forza, una più calda vita."*—Trans.

20. Gabriele D'Annunzio, *Lettere a Barbara Leoni* (Florence: Sansoni, 1954).

21. D'Annunzio, *Pleasure*, p. 62.—Trans.

22. D'Annunzio, *Pleasure*, p. 195.—Trans.

23. Ibid., p. 4.—Trans.

24. Ibid., p. 20. I have translated the portions in brackets directly from the original, as they were omitted in the (much tamer, censored) English version.—Trans.

25. Ibid., p. 40.—Trans.

26. Ibid., p. 49.—Trans.

27. Ibid., p. 244.—Trans.

28. *"Loreto impagliato ed il busto d'Alfieri, di Napoleone, / i fiori in cornice (le buone cose di pessimo gusto!) / il caminetto un po' tetro, le scatole senza confetti, / i frutti di marmo protetti dalle campane di vetro, / un qualche raro balocco, gli scrigni fatti di valve, / gli oggetti con mònito, salve, ricordo, le noci di cocco, / Venezia ritratta a musaici, gli acquarelli un po' scialbi, / le stampe, i cofani, gli albi dipinti d'anemoni arcaici."*—Trans.

3. LEOPARDI IN ROME

1. Leopardi referred to it as *"l'odiato sepolcro."*—Trans.

2. The author quotes a verse from Leopardi's posthumously published satirical poem *Paralipomeni della Batracomiomachia* inspired by this region: *"Come chi d'Appennin varcato il dorso / presso Fuligno ..."*—Trans.

3. Alfredo Panzini, *Casa Leopardi* (Florence: Le Monnier, 1948).

4. *"Mio signor padre," "Caro signor padre," "Carissimo papà,"* respectively.—Trans.

5. Leopardi, *Zibaldone*, pp. 75–77.

6. *"Les gens d'esprit, à Rome, ont du brio ... Je ne connais pas, en Europe, de salons préférables à ceux de Rome."* Stendhal, *Promenades dans Rome* (Paris: Seule, 1829).

7. Note also that Belli wrote an entire sonnet consisting almost exclusively of a long list of synonyms for this part of the female anatomy.—Trans.

4. PALERMO, ON THE BORDER BETWEEN TWO WORLDS

1. Giuseppe Tomasi di Lampedusa, *The Leopard*, trans. Archibald Colquhoun (New York: Pantheon, 2007), p. 177.—Trans.

2. "A bandit in the eyes of France, a hero in the eyes of Provence."

3. Guido Piovene, *Viaggio in Italia* (Milan: Baldini & Castoldi, 1993), p. 583. The text began as a series of radio transmissions about the author's voyage around Italy between 1953 and 1956, and was issued as a landmark book in 1957.—Trans.

4. Literally, "act of faith"—the Inquisition's ceremony for pronouncing judgment on the accused and determining an act of penance. Broadly speaking, it refers to the execution of a heretic.

5. Zullino, *Guida*.

6. Morris Kline, *Mathematics in Western Culture* (Oxford and New York: Oxford University Press, 1953), p. 235.

7. Translators have rendered this line in various ways, some hewing more closely to the biblical version than others: Geoffrey L. Bickersteth, "Scorn all that is, for all is vain, vain, vain" (Cambridge, UK: Cambridge University Press, 1923); Jonathan Galassi, "the boundless vanity of it all" (New York: Farrar, Straus and Giroux, 2012); David Gascoyne, "the everlasting emptiness of it all" (Portland, OR: Charles Seluzicki, 1983); Eamon Grennan, "the infinite *all is vanity* of it all" (Princeton, NJ: Princeton University Press, 1997); Paul Lawton, "the vast vanity of everything" (Dublin: University College Dublin Foundation for Italian Studies, 1996); J. M. Morrison, "vanity, that sure-set bourne / Reserved for all, thee, Nature, ever scorn" (London: Gay and Bird, 1900); J. G. Nichols, "this infinity of nothingness" (New York: Routledge, 2003); John Humphreys Whitfield, "the infinite vanity of all that is" (Manchester, UK: Manchester University Press, 1967).—Trans.

8. William Shakespeare, *Hamlet*, act 5, scene 1.—Trans.

9. Pirandello, *Cap and Bells*, p. 23. Original: *"Deve sapere che abbiamo tutti come tre corde d'orologio in testa. La seria, la civile e la pazza."*—Trans.

10. Luigi Pirandello, *Henry IV*, trans. Tom Stoppard (New York: Grove Press, 2004), pp. 48–49. Original: *"E via sì sono pazzo! Ma allora, perdio, inginocchiatevi! Inginocchiatevi! Vi ordino di inginocchiarvi tutti davanti a me—così. E toccate tre volte la terra con la fronte! Giù! Tutti, davanti ai pazzi, si deve stare così."*—Trans.

11. See chapter 1, note 3.—Trans.

12. Andrea Camilleri, "La Sicilia degli stravaganti," in *laRepubblica-Venerdì*, April 28, 2000.

13. Germana Agnetti and Angelo Barbato, *Il barone Pisani e la Real Casa dei Matti* (Palermo: Sellerio, 1987). Original: *"Lo abbandono, nel quale trovai per verità questo luogo, se dai miei occhi non fosse stato veduto, da chiunque uditolo avessi, io non lo avrei giammai creduto. Esso la sembianza di un serraglio di fiere presentava piuttosto che di abitazione di umane creature. In volgere lo sguardo nell'interno dell'angusto edificio, poche cellette scorgevansi oscure sordide malsane: parte ai matti destinate, e parte alle matte. Colà stavansi rinchiusi, ed indistintamente ammucchiati, i maniaci i dementi i furiosi i melanconici. Alcuni di loro sopra poca paglia e sudicia distesi, i più sulla nuda terra. Molti eran del tutto ignudi, vari coperti di cenci, altri in ischifosi stracci avvolti; e tutti a modo di bestie catenati, e di fastidiosi insetti ricolmi, e fame e sete, e freddo, e caldo, e scherni, e strazj, e battiture pativano. Estenuati gl'infelici, e quasi distrutti gli occhi tenean fissi in ogni uomo che improvviso compariva loro innanzi; e compresi di spavento per sospetto di nuovi affanni, in impeti subitamente rompeano di rabbia e di furore. Quindi assicurati dagli atti compassionevoli di chi pietosamente li guardava, dolenti oltre modo pietà chiedevano, le margini dei ferri mostrando, e le lividezze delle percosse di che tutto il corpo avean pieno."*—Trans.

14. From notes written by the chaplain of the fortress prison in San Leo (a town in the Appenine foothills southwest of Rimini) where Cagliostro died. Little is known about the chaplain, but this statement is now a panel in an exhibition detailing the horrifying conditions in the prison.—Trans.

15. Both Eco and La Duca's contributions (the latter's essay is titled "Storia e leggenda dei Beati Paoli") appear in the 1971 edition; see Luigi Natoli, *I beati Paoli* (Palermo: Flaccovio Editore, 1971). Unfortunately none of these texts have yet been translated into English. The sect's name literally means "Blessed Pauls."—Trans.

16. *"Complesso d'inferiorità (sociale),"* see Antonio Gramsci, *Letteratura e vita nazionale* (Rome: Editori Riuniti, 1971).—Trans.

17. Leopoldo Franchetti and Sidney Sonnino, *Condizioni politiche e amministrative della Sicilia* (Rome: Donzelli Editori, 2000).—Trans.

18. First published as *I viceré* (Milan: F. Gundani, 1894); English trans. Archibald Colquhoun (New York: Harcourt, Brace & World, 1962).—Trans.

19. Federico De Roberto, letter to Ferdinando Di Giorgi, July 16, 1891.

20. Salvatore Savoia, *Giuseppe Tomasi di Lampedusa* (Palermo: Flaccovio Editore, 2010).

5. THE DISCOVERY OF THE SOUTH

1. Giovanni Belardelli deals with the same issues in an article titled "Italie e nel 1860 il Sud divenne Africa" ("Italies, and in 1860 the South Became Africa"), *Corriere della Sera*, April 9, 1998.

2. Giuseppe Prezzolini, *Codice della vita italiana*, chapter 4 (Florence: La Voce, 1921).

3. Tullio De Mauro, *Storia linguistica dell'Italia unita* (Bari: Laterza, 1963).

4. Luigi Settembrini, *Ricordanze della mia vita* (Milan: BUR, 1964).

5. The term literally means "Lazaruses"—i.e., men who rise again—but is also related to the term *lazzarone*, literally "big Lazarus," but by extension "scoundrel, rascal, lazybones, blackguard, laggard."—Trans.

6. All quotes from Stendhal in this chapter were taken from his essay "Brigands in Italy" in *Roman Tales*, trans. Susan Ashe (London: HarperCollins, 2012), pp. 262, 253, 258, and 265, respectively.

7. Even the hideout of mafia boss Bernardo Provenzano—captured in 2006 after forty years at large—was discovered with sacred imagery and symbols, along with a Bible he read to pass the days, despite the fact that his formal education had ended with the second grade. He had been issued two life sentences in absentia.

8. Cincinnatus refers to Lucius Quinctius Cincinnatus (519–430 B.C.E.), a Roman aristocrat and statesman who was twice granted supreme powers he relinquished as soon as his work was complete, thereby becoming a paragon of modesty and virtuous civic service. Garibaldi's nickname is a nod to the fact that he had proven his valor in both the Old World and the New World.—Trans.

9. A chapter of my book *I segreti di New York* ("Secrets of New York") (Milan: Mondadori, 2000) is devoted to Meucci.

10. Oscar de Poli, *De Naples à Palerme 1863–1864* (Paris: Dupray de la Maherie, 1865).

11. From the parliamentary report on the government investigation of brigandage, in *La civiltà cattolica*, October–November 1863.

12. Massimo d'Azeglio, *I Savoia e il massacro del Sud* (Rome: Grandmelò, 1996).

13. Giosué Carducci, ed., *Letture del Risorgimento italiano* (Bologna: Zanichelli, 1895).

14. Giustino Fortunato (1848–1932) was a prominent historian and politician; Nello Rosselli (1900–1937) was a leading Socialist and historian.—Trans.

15. The author originally referred to *"camorristi e briganti,"* whereas I have opted to reference organized criminals in a more general way. It is worth noting that although the term *mafia* is often used in English in its more general connotation, in Italian it is actually the name for the crime syndicate unique to Sicily. Other regions have their own criminal organizations: the *Camorra* in Campania, the *'Ndrangheta* in Calabria, and the *Sacra Corona Unita* in Apulia. The very fact that Italians draw distinctions between these factions is indicative of how widespread and varied the phenomenon is.—Trans.

6. PARADISE AND ITS DEVILS

1. Titus Livius, *Livy's History of Rome*, book 25, chapter 13, trans. Rev. Canon Roberts (London: J. M. Dent & Sons, 1905). (Note that the term *corn* likely refers to grain-based provisions in general.—Trans.)

2. Tommaso Campanella, *The City of the Sun: A Poetical Dialogue*, trans. Daniel J. Donno (Berkeley, CA: University of California Press, 1981), pp. 63–65. It first appeared in Latin translation as the appendix to his *Politica*, published in Frankfurt in 1623. A note to the excerpt quoted here clarifies that "more recent and reliable estimates put the population of Naples close to two hundred thousand near the end of the sixteenth century."

3. D. A. F. marquis de Sade, *Voyage d'Italie* (Paris: Fayard, 1995).—Trans.

4. This text has not yet been published in English, but its title literally translates as "The Sea Doesn't Bathe Naples," implying that it doesn't touch the city (literally "get it wet"), nor does it wash away its accumulated grime.—Trans.

5. Benedetto Croce, *Un paradiso abitato da diavoli* (Milan: Adelphi, 2006). First published in *Uomini e cose della vecchia Italia* (Bari: Laterza, 1927).

6. Roberto Saviano, *Gomorrah*, trans. Virginia Jewiss (New York: Farrar, Straus & Giroux, 2007). It is interesting to note that the Italian edition (Milan: Mondadori, 2006) was published and publicized as "a novel." The book's title is a dark play on words between the biblical city of sin and the reigning Neapolitan crime organization. A film version directed by Matteo Garrone was released in 2008. Saviano received death threats following publication of the book, so he was given a heavy security detail and went into hiding soon thereafter.—Trans.

7. From an article in *La Repubblica*, August 1, 1991.

8. John Forster, *The Life of Charles Dickens* (New York: Charles Scribner's Sons, 1907), p. 415.

9. The *partigiani badogliani* were named after Pietro Badoglio, the general who was appointed prime minister of Italy after Mussolini's removal from power in 1943. They were part of the Italian Resistance movement loyal to the so-called Regno del Sud (a term denoting southern Italy during the armistice between September 1943 and June 1944) and the Allies against the Nazi occupation.—Trans.

10. Luigi Comencini riffs on this episode in the finale of his film *Tutti a casa* (*Everybody Go Home*, 1960). The famed comic actor Alberto Sordi plays the role of a junior NCO of the disbanded Royal Italian Army who takes command of a small group of insurgents.

11. Curzio Malaparte, *The Skin*, trans. David Moore (Evanston, IL: Northwestern University Press, 1993). A reissue, with an introduction by Rachel Kushner, is forthcoming from New York Review Books.

12. In keeping with other events discussed in this chapter, it is curious to note that both King Louis XVI and Marie Antoinette were put to death in Paris's Place de la Révolution, later renamed Place de la Concorde—from revolutions to accords, world history wends a winding path.—Trans.

13. Originally *"al di qua' e 'al di là' del Faro."*—Trans.

14. The Italian state is subdivided into regions and provinces, the latter referred to with abbreviations (based on the name of the province's capital city) much like the various states of the USA or the various counties of England.—Trans.

15. Edward C. Banfield, *The Moral Basis of a Backward Society* (Glencoe, IL: The Free Press, 1958).

16. Robert Putnam, *Making Democracy Work: Civic Traditions in Modern Italy* (Princeton, NJ: Princeton University Press, 1993).

17. See Saviano's *Gomorrah* and Garrone's film adaptation, in which Toni Servillo plays Franco, a local crime boss who convinces ingenuous farming families to sign their land over to him, and then recruits illegal immigrants and even young children to bury vast quantities of toxic waste there.—Trans.

18. Umberto Bossi is the former leader of the Lega Nord ("Northern League"), a separatist group that contests the validity of the unified Italian state and wants independence for northern Italy, specifically the area known as Padania (the Po River valley).

19. Mario Pirani, "Due Italie in Europa: una in testa e l'altra in coda," in *La Repubblica*, July 7, 2008.

7. HE LINGERED A LITTLE, THEN LEFT THE WORLD

1. Pope Gregory IX commissioned Brother Thomas of Celano to write *La vita beati Francisci* (*The Life of Saint Francis*) in preparation for Francis's canonization in July 1228, just two years after his death. The text's hagiographic intent is clear, not only in its emphasis on the saint's qualities, but also in the weight it places on the undoubtedly exaggerated charges of guilt leveled against the town of Assisi, compared here to Babylon. The passages quoted herein are from *Francis of Assisi—The Saint: Early Documents*, trans. Regis J. Armstrong et al. (New York: New City Press, 1999), pp. 183–84.

2. Ibid., p. 193.

3. The first paragraph of *The Testament of St. Francis* reads: "The Lord granted me, Brother Francis, to begin to do penance in this way: While I was in sin, it seemed very bitter to me to see lepers. And the Lord Himself led me among them and I had mercy upon them. And when I left them that which seemed bitter to me was changed into sweetness of soul and body; and afterward I lingered a little and left the world."—Trans.

4. Ibid., pp. 201–2.

5. Armstrong et al., *Life*, p. 69.

6. Ibid., p. 218.

7. *The Little Flowers of St. Francis of Assisi*, trad. (London: Chatto & Windus, 1908), pp. 23–24.

8. Medieval historian Chiara Frugoni has written several books on Saint Francis of Assisi, including *Storia di Chiara e Francesco* (Turin: Einaudi, 2011), *Francesco e l'invenzione delle stimmate* (Turin: Einaudi, 2010), and *Vita di un uomo: Francesco d'Assisi* (Turin: Einaudi, 1995, reissued 2001).

9. Giorgio Agamben, *Altissima povertà. Regole monastiche e forma di vita* (Vicenza: Neri Pozza Editore, 2011).

10. "Storia di fra Michele minorita."—Trans.

11. Umberto Eco, *The Name of the Rose*, trans. William Weaver (New York: Harcourt Brace & Company, 1984), p. 239.

12. Frugoni points out that Francis himself never mentioned these holy markings, which were actually found on the body of Elias of Cortona, his vicar. Apparently not even Pope Gregory IX believed in them, since his first papal bull marking the canonization of Francis made no mention of them, but he then changed his mind later on. It is a complex issue that seems unsolvable, as it can be interpreted in so many ways. It could be rationalized as a *pia fraus* ("pious fraud") or a psychosomatic syndrome, but on the mystical level it makes Francis the first to have received such a bloody and high distinction.

13. Alessandro Barbero, "L'invenzione di san Francesco," in *Atlante della letteratura italiana*, volume 1 (Turin: Einaudi, 2010).

14. Benito Mussolini, "Messaggio francescano," in *Arte-Luce-Parola*, February 1926, no. 1, p. 5. Original: *"La nave che porta in Oriente il banditore dell'immortale dottrina, accoglie sulla prora infallibile il destino della stirpe, che ritorna sulla strada dei padri. E i seguaci del santo che, dopo di lui, mossero verso Levante, furono insieme missionari di Cristo e missionari di italianità."* (I have rendered *italianità* as "Italian character"; the literal translation would be "Italian-ness," read with a distinct tone of racial superiority. The East referred to in the passage is Italian East Africa—present-day Ethiopia and Eritrea, as well as parts of Somalia and Djibouti—in addition to Libya.—Trans.)

15. Armstrong et al., *Life*, pp. 113–14. Original: *"Laudato sie, mi' Signore, cum tucte le tue creature, / spetialmente messor lo frate sole, / lo qual è iorno et allumini noi per lui. [...] / Laudato si', mi' Signore, per sora luna e le stelle, / in celu l'ài formate clarite et pretiose et belle. / Laudato si' mi' Signore, per frate vento / et per aere et nubilo et sereno et onne tempo, [...] / Laudato si', mi' Signore, per sor' aqua, / la quale è multo utile et humile et pretiosa et casta. / Laudato si', mi' Signore, per frate focu, / per lo quale ennallumini la nocte, [...] / Laudato si', mi' Signore, per sora nostra matre terra, / la quale ne sustenta et governa, / et produce diversi fructi con coloriti flori et herba. / Laudato si', mi' Signore, per quelli ke perdonano per lo tuo amore, / et sostengo infirmitate et tribulatione. [...] / Laudato si', mi' Signore per sora nostra morte corporale, / da la quale nullu homo vivente pò skappare."*

16. Massimo Cacciari, *Doppio ritratto. San Francesco in Dante e Giotto* (Milan: Adelphi, 2012).

17. Original: *"nacque al mondo un sole."*—Trans.

8. THE GOOD DUCHESS

1. Ferdinand Gregorovius, *Wanderjahre in Italien* (Munich: Beck, 1997). (Originally writen in 1856–57.—Trans.)

2. Lorenzo Molossi, *Vocabolario topografico dei Ducati di Parma, Piacenza e Guastalla* (Parma: Tipografia Ducale, 1832–34), pp. 317–18.—Trans.

3. Franz Herre, *Marie Louise: Napoleon war ihr Schicksal* (Cologne: Kiepenheuer & Witsch, 1996).

4. Ibid.

5. Ibid.

6. François-René de Chateaubriand, *The Memoirs of Chateaubriand*, trans. Robert Baldick (New York: Alfred A. Knopf, 1961), p. 259.

7. François-René de Chateaubriand, *Chateaubriand's Memoirs*, trans. A. S. Kline (digital publication), book XX, chapter 13. (This passage, not included in Baldick's version, is from the online source http://wikilivres.ca/wiki/Chateaubriand%27s_memoirs, consulted June 15, 2013.—Trans.)

8. Chateaubriand, *Memoirs*, trans. Baldick, p. 260.

9. Herre, *Marie Louise*.

10. This is a reference to the aforementioned right-wing, nationalist Lega Nord and its desire to secede from the rest of Italy.—Trans.

11. Stendhal, *The Charterhouse of Parma*, trans. C. K. Scott-Moncrieff (London: Chatto & Windus, 1926), "To the Reader."

12. Ibid.

13. Ibid., chapter 18.

14. Ibid., chapter 28.

9. MILAN, BOTH GOOD AND BAD

1. Magda Poli, *Milano in Piccolo* (Milan: Rizzoli, 2007).

2. Ibid.

3. Ibid.

4. Galileo Galilei, "Recantation (June 22, 1633)," quoted in Giorgio de Santillana, *The Crime of Galileo* (Chicago: University of Chicago Press, 1955), pp. 312–13.

5. On April 9, 1953, the body of twenty-one-year-old Wilma Montesi was discovered

at Torvajanica, a beach not far from Rome. The cause of her death remains a mystery. The war had been over for eight years, and this scandal, known as the Montesi Affair, grew to involve top-level politicians. It is also noteworthy because it was the first time that one side of the case (the names are now of little relevance) used the police corps for political ends.

6. Carlo Galli, *I riluttanti. Le élites italiane di fronte alla responsabilità* (Bari: Laterza, 2012).

10. LAST JUDGMENTS

1. Bible (King James Version), Revelation 8:7–9.

2. Giuseppe Gioachino Belli, "Er giorno der Giudizzio" ("Judgment Day"), sonnet 276, November 25, 1831.

3. "Good night" is used in the colloquial sense, meaning that will be the end.—Trans.

4. Giorgio Vasari, *Lives of the Most Eminent Painters Sculptors & Architects*, trans. Gaston Du C. de Vere, vol. 9 (London: Macmillan, 1915), p. 57.

5. Ascanio Condivi, *The Life of Michelangelo*, trans. Alice Sedgwick Wohl (University Park: Pennsylvania State University Press, 1999), first written in 1553.—Trans.

6. Claudio Magris, "Dove batte il cuore dell'Iran," in *Corriere della Sera*, September 5, 2004.

11. THE INVENTION OF THE GHETTO

1. The term *Serenissima* refers to the Most Serene Republic of Venice, as the city and its territories were officially known. To this day it is a common nickname for the city.—Trans.

2. Patricia H. Labalme and Laura Sanguineti White (eds.),*Venice, Città Excelentissima: Selections from the Renaissance Diaries of Marin Sanudo*, trans. Linda L. Carroll (Baltimore: Johns Hopkins University Press, 2008), p. 338.

3. Riccardo Calimani, *The Ghetto of Venice: A History*, trans. Katherine Silberblatt Wolfthal (New York: M. Evans And Company, 1987), p. 1. (Compare this with the slightly different translation of the same document featured in Labalme and White's book on p. 340: "[A]ll Jews who currently live in the various parishes of this city of ours . . . are obligated and must go immediately to live together in the group of houses that are in the Ghetto, near San Hieronimo, a very spacious locale for them to inhabit . . . two high walls are to be built to close off the other two sides that look onto the canals; all of the banks along which the houses run are also to be walled. Moreover, the guardians are to live in this place day and night alone, without family, in order to guard it well, and they will observe whatever other regulations are established by this Collegio. In addition, the Collegio will assign them two boats, with which they will patrol this place day and night and which will be paid for out of the money of the Jews."—Trans.)

4. The *monti di pietà* (literally, "mounts of piety"—collections of donated money) were pawnbrokers run by the Church. As charitable savings and loan institutions, they were developed to counter the spread of what was considered usurious moneylending.—Trans.

5. Pope Paul IV, *Cum nimis absurdum*, quoted in Kenneth Stow, *Catholic Thought and Papal Jewry Policy* (New York: Jewish Theological Seminary of America, 1977), pp. 294–95.—Trans.

6. Calimani, *Ghetto*, p. 63.

7. Ibid., p. 251.

8. Ibid., p. 253–54.

9. Giulio Lorenzetti, *Venice and Its Lagoon: Historical-Artistic Guide*, trans. John Guthrie (Trieste: Lint, 1975), p. 64.

INDEX OF NAMES AND WORKS